EVERYMAN, I will go with thee,

and be thy guide,

In thy most need to go by thy side

JAMES MATTHEW BARRIE

Son of David Barrie, hand-loom weaver, by his wife Margaret Ogilvy; born at Kirriemuir, Angus (formerly Forfarshire), Scotland, in 1860. Educated at Glasgow Academy, Dumfries Academy and Edinburgh University. On staff of *Nottingham Journal*, 1883–4; moved to London, 1885, as free-lance journalist. Achieved fame as novelist, 1888, and as dramatist by 1900. Creator of Peter Pan. Made a baronet in 1913 and awarded the Order of Merit, 1922. Lord Rector of St Andrews University, 1919, and Chancellor of Edinburgh University from 1930 until his death in London in 1937.

J. M. Barrie's
Plays and Stories

EDITED WITH
AN INTRODUCTION BY
ROGER LANCELYN GREEN

DENT: LONDON
EVERYMAN'S LIBRARY

© Introduction, J. M. Dent & Sons Ltd, 1962
All rights reserved
Made in Great Britain
at the
Aldine Press · Letchworth · Herts
for
J. M. DENT & SONS LTD
Aldine House · Bedford Street · London
First included in Everyman's Library 1962
by arrangement with
Hodder and Stoughton Ltd

This book is sold subject to the
condition that it may not be issued
on loan or otherwise except in its
original soft cover

NO. 1184

ISBN: 0 460 01184 7

INTRODUCTION

THE CAREER of J. M. Barrie has been described as the greatest 'success story' in the history of modern literature: it also presents one of the most interesting and controversial in that of literary criticism.

James Matthew Barrie was born on 9th May 1860 in the little four-roomed cottage in the Tenements, No. 9 Brechin Road, Kirriemuir, Angus, Scotland. He was the ninth child and third and youngest son of David Barrie, hand-loom weaver, by his wife Margaret, daughter of Alexander Ogilvy, stone-mason. The death in a skating accident of the middle son, David, when Jamie was six, brought the mother to the edge of a nervous breakdown, and set a mark on the soul of the youngest son that was to affect his whole life. The story of how Barrie set himself to replace the boy David and bring back the smile to his mother's lips is told in *Margaret Ogilvy*, very beautifully and sincerely, but with a lack of emotional restraint that many readers find hard to forgive.

Besides odd years at small schools in Kirriemuir and Forfar, Barrie was educated mainly at the Academies of Glasgow and Dumfries, in both cases with the aid of his eldest brother, Alexander, who achieved distinction as one of the earliest of Her Majesty's Inspectors of Schools. He matriculated at Edinburgh University in 1878, so as to benefit from the teaching of the great English scholar David Masson, and graduated M.A. in 1882.

From his boyhood Barrie had determined to be an author, and in January 1883 he obtained a post as leader-writer to the *Nottingham Journal*, which he held for eighteen months, and which supplied the background to his amusing informal novel *When a Man's Single* (1888). By the time this ended he was having occasional articles accepted, the earliest on record being one (unsigned) in the *Pall Mall Gazette* on 9th August 1884 and one (signed) in *Home Chimes* on 8th November of the same year. A week later 'An Auld Licht Community', published anonymously in the *St James's Gazette*, prompted its editor, Frederick Greenwood, to demand more 'Scotch things', and seven or eight followed, besides four in *Home Chimes* and several later ones in the *British Weekly*, which Barrie revised and in part rewrote as *Auld Licht Idylls*, published in 1888, making the significant change to 'Thrums', instead of 'Wheens', as his fictional name for Kirriemuir.

He had by this time come to London as a free-lance journalist, and after a short period of anxiety, if not of the actual privation which he was apt to suggest in after years when looking back on it, Barrie was making a comfortable income, though still relatively unknown, as most of his contributions were anonymous. The many hundreds of articles, sketches and short stories published in the ten years after he left Edinburgh remain largely uncollected, though the American 'pirates' reprinted a small number, and Barrie himself revised and authorized several more in *The Greenwood Hat*, printed privately in 1930 and published after his death. From the start there was a distinctive touch about his anonymous journalism which must have given away to discerning readers of the *St James's* the single identity of the elusive author who would appear one day as a retired bridge-builder from Burma, and the next as a mother, a Member of Parliament, a half-engaged young lady, a grandfather, a schoolboy or a cat. 'The Courting of T'nowhead's Bell' from *Auld Licht Idylls* seems to be the only story written expressly for that volume, the rest of which is an ingenious mosaic from various articles and sketches.

The book was hailed as a masterpiece, and Barrie followed it with a similar volume formed largely from previously published sketches, *A Window in Thrums* (1889). The immense popularity of these brilliant pictures of a bygone Kirriemuir, based on his mother's recollections of her girlhood, brought a nemesis upon Barrie in the shape of a host of inferior imitators, the calculating sentimentalists of the 'Kailyard' school, headed by S. R. Crockett and 'Ian Maclaren': Barrie's distinctive originality and selective realism came beneath the sickly shadow of *The Lilac Sunbonnet* and has long lain neglected *Beside the Bonnie Brier Bush*. His stories of Thrums deserve a reassessment in their own right as brilliant, if incomplete, pictures of an utterly vanished way of life. Barrie may have set out, at Greenwood's command and in sheer necessity, to caricature the society of Kirriemuir which he remembered from his own boyhood and recaptured from his mother's vivid reminiscences, but he was soon converted by the sterling worth and the basic nobility of those simple followers of the Old Light. When he could write absolutely as he pleased the cynical note faded from his Auld Licht stories, and is completely lacking in his Thrums novel *The Little Minister* (1891)—a book of singular charm and brilliant characterization, which more than compensate for an ill-constructed and improbable plot.

Barrie continued as the novelist of Thrums in *Sentimental Tommy* (1896), a penetrating study of the boyhood of a literary genius; and in the curiously bitter sequel *Tommy and Grizel* (1900), in which the adult Tommy fails to achieve maturity or sincerity, wrecks Grizel's life and wastes his own. The bitterness perhaps reflects Barrie's own married life, which was beginning to break up; but the continuous and exaggerated pillorying of failings which he may have detected in his own character make the book uncomfortable rather than tragic.

Meanwhile he was conquering new worlds in the theatre, which from the start held for him a fascination equal to that of the literary life. He had written and acted in plays as a boy at Dumfries; a one-act farce was published (though never acted) while he was at Nottingham. In 1891 he assisted his friend H. B. Marriott Watson in an historical play, *Richard Savage*, which was produced for a single matinée performance. Barrie's own first play followed later in the same year, a clever burlesque in one act, *Ibsen's Ghost*, which added to the fame of the comedian J. L. Toole and started Irene Vanbrugh on her long career. On the strength of this, Toole commissioned a full-length farce, and *Walker, London* (1892), ran for over a year and toured for long in Toole's repertoire. *The Professor's Love Story* (1894), an artificial comedy with a Thrums background, was less immediately popular; but a dramatic version of *The Little Minister* (1897) set Barrie among the leading playwrights of the day, besides earning him £80,000 in its first year in England and America.

He consolidated his new reputation in 1901 with *Quality Street*, a more completely successful essay in the artificial comedy of romance and sentiment, but far surpassed all his earlier work with *The Admirable Crichton* (1902). Although not a play of realism in the modern sense, it posed an utterly real and vital problem—both overt in the relative positions of Lord Loam and his butler in Mayfair and on an uninhabited island; and covert in the effect which social custom has on the behaviour of men and women—and at the same time afforded the full satisfaction of a superbly constructed story about real, if slightly exaggerated, characters, the whole instinct with a quiet humour and an undercurrent of satire none the less penetrating for being implied rather than underlined.

Barrie's next triumph was the one for which he is best known: the creation of Peter Pan, the only new character of folk-lore to be invented in modern times. The baby of Kensington Gardens from Barrie's medley of magic and whimsy *The Little White Bird* (1902) became 'the boy who wouldn't grow up' of the play *Peter Pan*, which opened in 1904 and has missed annual revival only at the Christmas of the London blitz in 1940, and the hero of *Peter Pan and Wendy* (1911), the play's story-book form which is in itself one of the classics of childhood.

Resting, as it were, after this major act of creation, Barrie produced another slight but amusing comedy of the artificial, *Alice-sit-by-the-Fire* (1905), and the most purely realistic of his greater plays, *What Every Woman Knows* (1908), besides a number of skilful trifles in one act, of which by far the best and most enduring is *The Twelve Pound Look*, first acted early in 1910.

The complete breakdown of his marriage with a divorce from his wife in 1909 was followed by a long period of merely minor literary activity, and the early years of the First World War produced only a number of short plays and playlets mainly for charitable purposes, an attempt at a revue, which was more or less of a failure, and the sweet narcotic of *A Kiss for Cinderella*—a minor play and typical of its period, but not one to be overlooked.

Then suddenly the deeper inspiration seemed to return to Barrie when a chance remark from his friend A. E. W. Mason caused him to hunt out a scheme for a play, which he had discarded some years before, turning on the idea that if people were given a second chance they would make the same mistakes again. On this occasion the time was ripe, and Barrie had *Dear*

Brutus written and in production within six months. With Gerald du Maurier as Dearth giving one of the most outstanding performances of his career, the play ran for nearly a year, and has had several notable West End revivals, besides innumerable provincial productions. One of the most interesting of the latter took place at Kirriemuir on 9th May 1960 to celebrate the centenary of Barrie's birth, and was performed by local amateurs headed by a leading London actor and actress as Mr and Mrs Dearth: this enabled Margaret, the dream-child, to be taken by a girl of thirteen, and their playing of the scene in Lob's Wood can seldom have been equalled.

Dear Brutus, probably Barrie's greatest play (setting aside the isolated phenomenon of *Peter Pan*), was followed by *Mary Rose* —a strange play which seems to have impressed theatre-goers even more strongly. Its magic owed a great deal to the performance of Fay Compton in the lead, and to the inspired production with Barrie in ultimate control; it had three major productions in its first ten years, and was the most talked about of all Barrie's plays. But its strange magic is hard to recapture from the printed page, and its dependence on fantasy has deterred London managers for nearly a generation.

Meanwhile Barrie turned back to realism, and completed the first act of a murder thriller. Having promised a new one-act play for the opening of the Royal Academy of Dramatic Art's new theatre and failed to write one, he allowed this single act to be performed by an all-star cast on 27th May 1921 as *Shall We Join the Ladies?* The tragic death in a swimming accident of his adopted son, Michael Llewellyn Davies, a few days before the production seemed to dry up his interest in the theatre, and as the play had been so satisfactory as a supremely tantalizing fragment, he decided to leave it as such. He may have felt, also, that no subsequent acts could ever come up to the superb opening—but he did not stop because he could not go on. Every detail had been planned, and was known to one or two intimates: but they were sworn to secrecy, and the solution will never be known with any more certainty than that of *Edwin Drood*. But as it stands *Shall We Join the Ladies?* remains one of the finest one-act plays ever written.

After he ceased to write plays, Barrie developed a new art, that of the orator. He had made an occasional speech in earlier
* 184

years, but with *Courage*, his address as Lord Rector to the students of St Andrews on 3rd May 1922, began a new combina-
tion of his skill both as author and actor which was to make him
one of the most sought-after of all public speakers for the next
dozen years. Most of his speeches, collected posthumously as
M'Connachie and J. M. B. in 1938, still make pleasant reading
even without his calculated brilliance of presentation; but
Courage is perhaps the finest among them as pure literature.

The ten years of literary silence following Michael's death
was broken privately in 1930 when *The Greenwood Hat* was
printed for a number of his friends, and publicly at the end of
1931 when *Farewell, Miss Julie Logan* was offered as the only
fiction supplement ever issued by *The Times*, and printed as a
small book early the following year.

This sudden and unexpected return to the neighbourhood
of Thrums is perhaps the most completely satisfying work of
fiction that Barrie ever wrote, and James Bridie seems even to
have set it higher than most of his plays. It may be described
as the essence of Barrie's work distilled through a lifetime of
increased understanding—and of perfected skill as an artist
with words and feelings. There are echoes out of his earlier
writings (notably in the setting, which owes a little to a series
of sketches called 'Life in a Country Manse', or 'A Clachan in
Winter', which was never collected officially), but the real echo
is from his deeper experience, from the touch of the tragic which
lies even beneath the joyous surface of *Peter Pan*.

For the sheer skill in the creation of atmosphere, of character,
and of the achievement of high dramatic effect by utterly natural
understatement, *Farewell, Miss Julie Logan* must rank with the
great short stories of the world—'that lovely story which, had
its author written nothing else, would surely have given him a
niche among the men of letters', as Patrick Chalmers said of it;
'a poem, in the most skilfully wrought of all his prose,' to quote
Denis Mackail, 'a kind of parable, but he would neither seek
nor press the interpretations'.

It was in truth Barrie's swan-song. But in 1934, captivated
by the skill of a new actress, Elizabeth Bergner, and more or
less 'dared' by her to write a play about the boyhood of David,
King of Israel, in which she could star, he set to work to complete the dramatic frame of his theatrical career with the only

play since *Richard Savage* which had taken a ready-made story as basis. All the skill of a supreme master of dramatic writing went into the making of *The Boy David*, and almost achieved the impossible. But the intractable subject, which he must not bend to his artistic will, resulted in a play of many exquisite scenes and interpretations, but incapable of dramatic solution. A series of misfortunes over the production, and a presentation too lavish for what had become a dramatic study rather than a biblical epic, doomed the play to a grudging acceptance and a short run which terminated a few months before Barrie's death in 1937.

This 'dying fall' does little more than form the correct finale to the amazing success story of the Boy from Kirriemuir—for he was already sharing the common lot by entering at the close of his life into that valley of the shadow of criticism through which it seems that all writers of genius are fated to pass.

On the material side, Sir James Matthew Barrie, Bart, O.M., Chancellor of Edinburgh University, Sometime Rector of St Andrews, and holder of honorary degrees from many universities and the freedoms of many cities, had earned vast sums by his plays, and given generously and almost always in secret from the moment he had anything to give. The gift of all rights in *Peter Pan* to the Hospital for Sick Children in Great Ormond Street in 1929 stands but as a monument to a man utterly unspoilt by the accumulation of great wealth and fame, whose generosity was equalled only by his delicacy and thought for others.

Of the place that he will hold in literature it would be presumptuous to speak as yet, since he is only now beginning to emerge from the shadow of critical disapproval which has been deeper than usual in his case since his genius led him along those paths of sentiment and fantasy and Puckish humour—by a cottage in Thrums, across the Never, Never Land, into Lob's Wood—so contrary to the spirit of the age which immediately succeeded his own.

That he is still violently attacked, and as violently defended, loathed with unreasoning bitterness, and loved with perhaps as unreasoning a devotion, proves that Barrie is neither a forgotten author nor one of small importance. A generation that knew him at second hand, under the ban of epithets like 'whimsy' and 'sentimental', are already rediscovering with surprise and delight that the dramatist of *The Admirable Crichton* and *What Every Woman Knows* and *Dear Brutus* had much more than these dubious lures with which to ensnare his audience—as revivals in the centenary year have shown.

At its deepest the shadow of disapproval has emptied few seats in the annual revivals of *Peter Pan*, though adult taste may have made the story-book of *Peter Pan and Wendy* less well known that it might have been.

His other stories and novels have suffered most over the lean years. But their inaccessibility allows them now to be reconsidered freshly and without preconceived opinions; and from that critical gaze the best of the *Auld Licht Idylls*, *The Little Minister* and *Farewell, Miss Julie Logan* have little to fear.

ROGER LANCELYN GREEN.

1961.

SELECT BIBLIOGRAPHY

BOOKS. *Better Dead* (1887), 1888; *Auld Licht Idylls*, 1888; *When a Man's Single*, 1888; *An Edinburgh Eleven*, 1889; *A Window in Thrums*, 1889; *My Lady Nicotine*, 1890; *The Little Minister*, 1891; *A Tillyloss Scandal, Two of Them* and other American 'pirate' volumes, 1893, etc.; *Margaret Ogilvy*, 1896; *Sentimental Tommy*, 1896; *Tommy and Grizel*, 1900; *The Little White Bird*, 1902; *Peter Pan in Kensington Gardens* (from *The Little White Bird*), 1906; *Peter and Wendy*, 1911; *Courage* (speech), 1922; *The Entrancing Life* (speech), 1930; *Farewell, Miss Julie Logan*, 1931; *The Greenwood Hat* (privately printed 1930), 1937; *M'Connachie and J. M. B.: Speeches*, 1938, *Letters of J. M. Barrie*, 1942; *Allahakbarries Cricket Club* (privately printed 1899), 1950; 'Peter Pan: A Film Scenario' (written 1920), in Green's *Fifty Years of 'Peter Pan'*, 1954.

FULL-LENGTH PLAYS. (Date of performance, followed in brackets by date of first publication.) *Richard Savage* (with H. B. Marriott Watson), 1891 (1891); *Walker, London*, 1892 (1907); *The Professor's Love Story*, 1892 (1942); *Jane Annie* (libretto in collaboration with A. Conan Doyle), 1893 (1893); *The Little Minister*, 1897 (1942); *The Wedding Guest*, 1900 (1900); *Quality Street*, 1902 (1913); *The Admirable Crichton*, 1902 (1914); *Little Mary*, 1903 (1942); *Peter Pan*, 1904 (1928); *Alice-Sit-by-the-Fire*, 1905 (1919); *What Every Woman Knows*, 1908 (1918); *The Adored One*, 1913; *A Kiss for Cinderella*, 1916 (1920); *Dear Brutus*, 1917 (1923); *Mary Rose*, 1920 (1924); *The Boy David*, 1936 (1938).

PRINCIPAL ONE-ACT PLAYS. *Caught Napping* (1883); *Ibsen's Ghost*, 1891; *Pantaloon*, 1905 (1914); *Punch*, 1906; *When Wendy Grew Up*, 1908 (1957); *Old Friends*, 1910 (1928); *The Twelve Pound Look*, 1910 (1914); *A Slice of Life*, 1910; *Rosalind*, 1912 (1914); *The Will*, 1913 (1914); *Half an Hour*, 1913 (1928); *Der Tag*, 1914 (1914); *The New Word*, 1915 (1918); *Shakespeare's Legacy*, 1916 (1916); *Seven Women*, 1917 (1928); *The Old Lady Shows Her Medals*, 1917 (1918); *A Well Remembered Voice*, 1918 (1918); *Barbara's Wedding*, 1927 (1918); *The Truth About the Russian Dancers*, 1920; *Shall We Join the Ladies?*, 1921 (1927); *The Fight for Mr Lapraik* (written 1917), 1947 (radio production) (1947).

COLLECTED EDITIONS. Thistle Edition (New York), 12 vols. (novels and sketches), 1896–1902; Kirriemuir Edition, 10 vols. (novels and sketches), 1913, 1922; Uniform Edition of Novels and Plays, 21 vols. (incomplete), 1918–1938; Peter Pan Edition (New York), 14 vols. (novels and plays; incomplete), 1929; *The Plays of J. M. Barrie* (one volume containing 8 full-length and 12 one-act plays), 1928; *The Plays of J. M. Barrie* (revised edition, containing 14 full-length and 12 one-act plays), 1942.

BIOGRAPHY AND CRITICISM. J. A. Hammerton, *J M. Barrie and his Books*, 1900; H. M. Walbrook, *J. M. Barrie and the Theatre*, 1922; Patrick Braybrooke, *J. M. Barrie: A Study in Fairies and Mortals*, 1924; Thomas Moult, *Barrie*, 1928; Herbert Garland, *A Bibliography of the Writings of Sir James Matthew Barrie, Bart, O.M.*, 1928; J. A. Hammerton, *Barrie: The Story of a Genius*, 1929; F. J. Harvey Darton, *J. M. Barrie*, 1929; John Kennedy,

Thrums and the Barrie Country, 1930; James A. Roy, *James Matthew Barrie: An Appreciation*, 1937; Patrick Chalmers, *The Barrie Inspiration*, 1938; W. A. Darlington, *J. M. Barrie*, 1938; Denis Mackail, *The Story of J. M. B.* (official biography), 1941; George Blake, *Barrie and the Kailyard School*, 1951; Roger Lancelyn Green, *Fifty Years of Peter Pan*, 1954; Cynthia Asquith, *Portrait of Barrie*, 1954; Roger Lancelyn Green, *J. M. Barrie*, 1960.

NOTE

THE three plays included in this volume are printed from the Acting Versions, as representing Barrie's first thoughts when writing them specifically for presentation on the stage. In some cases it was many years after the first production that Barrie prepared the 'Library Version' of a play, and when he came to do so he had the reader so much in mind that frequently he altered what he had first written, and added so much in the way of description and background that the result tended more towards a story in dialogue form than a play. While the resultant closet dramas make delightful reading, and represent the form in which Barrie actually wished his plays to be read (at a time when revivals on the stage were many and frequent), the original Acting Versions are as much his work and as typical of his genius as the more polished (and, it must be admitted, more whimsical) reinterpretations of his later years. The usual Library Versions are readily available for comparison in the Definitive Edition of Barrie's plays, or in the uniform volumes published by Messrs Hodder & Stoughton. But the Acting Versions are known only to those who take part in the plays, and are of such interest that it has seemed worth while using them in the present volume. Even the compressed stage directions have their charm, and help to bring the plays before us as we read more nearly as though we were seeing them on the stage— and a play should surely be judged before all else as 'a piece of theatre'.

R.L.G.

CONTENTS

THE ADMIRABLE CRICHTON

A Fantasy in Four Acts

COPYRIGHT D.50335, 1918, BY J. M. BARRIE
COPYRIGHT A.76997, 1934, BY CHARLES SCRIBNER'S SONS

The copying by manuscript, typescript, photography or any other
means of reproduction, of this play either in whole or in part is an
infringement of the copyright.

All applications for a licence concerning the production of this play by
amateurs must be made to:

SAMUEL FRENCH LIMITED,
26 SOUTHAMPTON STREET,
STRAND, LONDON, W.C.2.

The royalty fee payable for one performance is Five Guineas. No
performance may be given unless the licence has first been obtained.

THE ADMIRABLE CRICHTON

Produced at the Duke of York's Theatre, London, on Tuesday, 4th November 1902. The following is a list of the principal characters and the people who played them:

THE EARL OF LOAM	*Mr Henry Kemble*
HON. ERNEST WOOLLEY . . .	*Mr Gerald Du Maurier*
REV. JOHN TREHERNE . . .	*Mr Clarence Blakiston*
LORD BROCKLEHURST . . .	*Mr Carter Pickford*
A NAVAL OFFICER	*Mr J. C. Buckstone*
CRICHTON	*Mr H. B. Irving*
TOMPSETT	*Mr Compton Coutts*
LADY MARY LASENBY . .	*Miss Irene Vanbrugh*
LADY CATHERINE LASENBY .	*Miss Sybil Carlisle*
LADY AGATHA LASENBY . .	*Miss Muriel Beaumont*
COUNTESS OF BROCKLEHURST .	*Miss Fanny Coleman*
FISHER	*Miss Margaret Fraser*
ELIZA ('TWEENY') . . .	*Miss Pattie Browne*

CHARACTERS
(in the order of their appearance)

CRICHTON
THE HON. ERNEST WOOLLEY
LADY AGATHA LASENBY
LADY CATHERINE LASENBY
LADY MARY LASENBY
THE REV. JOHN TREHERNE
THE EARL OF LOAM
LORD BROCKLEHURST
MRS PERKINS
MONSIEUR FLEURY
MR ROLLESTON
MR TOMPSETT
MISS FISHER
MISS SIMMONS
MADEMOISELLE JEANNE
THOMAS
JOHN
JANE
GLADYS
ELIZA ('TWEENY')
STABLE BOY
A KITCHEN WENCH
A PAGE BOY
A NAVAL OFFICER
THE COUNTESS OF BROCKLEHURST

SYNOPSIS OF SCENES

ACT I
The drawing-room of the Earl of Loam's house in Mayfair.
About 4 p.m. in summer.

ACT II
The island. Two months later. Late evening.

ACT III
The hall of their island home. Two years later. Afternoon.

ACT IV
The same as Act I. A few months later. Early evening.

ACT I

SCENE: *The scene is a drawing-room in the Earl of Loam's house in Mayfair. It is about 4 p.m. in summer.*

The doors are at the back. Double doors L.C. leading to the hall. A single door R.C. to other rooms. Windows in the L. wall. The fireplace in the R. wall. At R.C., and down L.C., are settees. Up L.C., an oval table with a tray and tea-things for about eighteen persons. On the R. of this table, an armchair with rather a tall back. At the L. end of the settee R.C., a small round table, with stools above and below it, and a chair to the L. of it. Chairs above and below the fireplace, and at the windows. A large bookcase up L., and a glass-fronted china-cabinet up C., between the two doors.

The furniture is so adjusted that both settees and almost every chair and stool can be occupied without any character being masked.

The furniture and the décor generally is Edwardian, or very late Victorian with a few well-blended additions of the former period.

As the Curtain rises, Crichton, the butler, ushers in the Hon. Ernest Woolley. Crichton is the beau ideal of a butler in a correct establishment. There has never been quite such a perfect butler. He is also an excellent fellow who has achieved greatness in his calling because he thinks it a truly noble one. When agitated, he rubs his hands together a trifle servilely, but at all other times he is dignity personified. His age is about thirty-five.

Ernest is fresh from Oxford and has the complaisant manner of one who knows pretty well everything. He enjoys his gift of epigrammatic conversation.

Crichton enters up L.C. and stands C. as Ernest enters and comes down C., then to below the armchair L.C., and surveys the tea table. As he speaks, Crichton goes up, closes the doors, and turns to cross R.

ERNEST. I perceive, Crichton, from the teacups, that the *great* function is to take place here.

CRICHTON. [*Whom the matter referred to evidently depresses.*] Yes, sir. [*He is going R., but when Ernest speaks he stops C.*

5

Ernest. The servants' hall coming up to have tea in the drawing-room—no wonder you look happy, Crichton.

Crichton. [*Miserably.*] No, sir.

Ernest. [*Looking at him.*] Do you know, Crichton, I think that with an effort you might look even happier.

[*He sits in the armchair* L.C. *Crichton makes the action with his hands and tries to smile.*]

You don't approve of his lordship's compelling his servants to be his equals—once a month?

Crichton. [*Moving down to* R. *of the chair* L.C.] It is not for me, sir, to disapprove of his lordship's radical views.

Ernest. Certainly not. And it's only once a month that he is affable to you, Crichton.

Crichton. On all other days of the month, sir, his lordship's treatment of us is—everything that could be desired.

Ernest. [*Lifting a cup.*] Teacups! Life, Crichton, is like a cup of tea, the more heartily we drink, the sooner we reach the dregs. Ha, ha!

[*He smiles, pleased with his epigram, and looks at Crichton to see how it has impressed him.*]

Crichton. [*Repeats the action with his hands and smiles servilely.*] Thank you, sir.

Ernest. [*Rather confidentially, putting down the cup and rising.*] Crichton, in case I should be asked to say a few words to the servants, I have strung together a little speech. [*Coming down* C. *a pace, looking about. His hand strays to his pocket—he smiles like one who knows what an uncommon good speech it is.*] I was wondering where I could stand. [*He leans over the back of the high chair* L.C. *like one addressing an audience.*] Yes, here.

[*Crichton looks from him to the chair and evidently feels that the chair is too high, crosses for a hassock* R. *and puts it behind the* L.C. *chair for Ernest to stand on, then he exits majestically* R.C. *Ernest, however, is annoyed, and stares after him. He kicks the hassock* R., *then again tries the position.*

Ernest. [*Addressing an imaginary audience.*] Suppose you were all little fishes at the bottom of the sea. [*He smiles, well pleased.*] And suppose——

[*He is not quite satisfied with his position; evidently feels he is a little short. He looks at his hassock, crosses* R. *and lifts it when—*

[*Enter up* L.C., *Lady Agatha Lasenby, followed by Lady Catherine Lasenby. They are lazy, fashionable girls. Ernest is caught with the hassock and affects jocularity, backing down* R.C.

[*Hiding the hassock behind him.*] And how are my little friends today?

[*They see the hassock and look at each other inquiringly.*

LADY AGATHA. [*Crossing to* L. *and shaking her head at him.*] Don't be silly, Ernest. [*Crossing to* L. *and throwing herself on the settee.*] If you want to know how we are, we are dead. Even to think of entertaining the servants is so exhausting.

ERNEST. [*Moving towards the settee* L.C.] Poor ickle sing! Then why do you do it?

LADY CATHERINE. [*Moving down* L. *of the settee* R.C.] Why? Because Father compels us. You know what Father is when he takes up an idea.

ERNEST. [*Turning to her.*] I have noticed that the stouter he grows, the fuller he is of ideas.

[*Lady Catherine moves down* R.

LADY AGATHA. This is his most horrid one. He holds, Ernest— he read it somewhere—that servants are our brothers and sisters, and have hearts and minds and souls just like ours.

ERNEST. I say, he *is* getting stout!

LADY CATHERINE. [*Turning at* R.] And he insists that it is his solemn duty, as a peer of the realm, to elevate and ennoble our servants, and that the best way of doing this is to treat them as our equals—not every day, you know, but once a month.

LADY AGATHA. Yes, once a month we are compelled to receive them here in the drawing-room and chat with them on equal terms and hand them tea and cake—in order to elevate them.

ERNEST. What a joke!

LADY CATHERINE. Joke! It's awful! I'm sure they loathe it, but Father says it brings the time nearer when man and man 'shall brothers be for all that'.

ERNEST. And this is the day when you have to hand round the tea!

LADY AGATHA. It so exhausts me.

[*Lady Catherine sits on the chair down* R.

Ernest. [*Moving* c. *and looking from one to the other.*] You poor overworked things—— [*He crosses to* l.c.] Rest your weary limbs.

Lady Catherine. But why have you a hassock in your hand?

Lady Agatha. Yes.

Ernest. Why! [*He looks at the hassock and conceives an excuse.*] You see, as the servants are to be the guests, I must be the butler, I was practising. This is a tray—observe——

[*Holding the hassock like a tray, he goes mincingly from* l. *to* r. *in waiter fashion.*

[*Enter Lady Mary Lasenby* r. *She is the eldest and laziest of the girls, haughty and rather indolent in an aristocratic way. As Lady Mary comes down* c., *Ernest, at* r., *turns and faces her with the hassock.*

Tea, my lady?

Lady Mary. [*With insolent hauteur.*] It's only *you*, Ernest—— [*She crosses and sits on the settee* r.] I thought there was some-one here.

[*Lady Agatha shows indignation at the remark.*

Ernest. [*Annoyed, throwing down the hassock, on which Lady Catherine puts her foot.*] So I'm nobody, am I? [*He changes to sarcasm as he sees her reclining.*] Had a very tiring day, also, Mary?

Lady Mary. Dreadfully!

[*Ernest arranges the cushions for her comfort.*

I've been trying on engagement rings all morning.

Ernest. [*Excited.*] Eh—what's that! [*Crossing to Lady Agatha.*] Is it Brocklehurst?

[*Lady Agatha nods—Ernest turns to Lady Mary, crossing to above the* r. *settee.*

You have given your warm young heart to Brocky?

[*Lady Mary doesn't bother to answer. Ernest leans over the settee. Lady Mary turns her head away.*

I don't wish to fatigue you, Mary, by insisting on a verbal answer, but if, without straining yourself, you could signify Yes or No—— Won't you make the effort?

[*Lady Mary lazily holds up her left hand on which is a ring. Ernest takes hold of her hand.*

The ring! [*He tragically puts his hand to his heart.*] Then I am too late. [*He crosses to* c., *and repeats like an operatic villain.*]

' I am too late.' [*He moves down* C., *stops suddenly, and turns to Lady Mary.*] May I ask, Mary, does Brocky know?

[*Lady Catherine and Lady Agatha close their eyes. Lady Mary looks indignant and then closes her eyes also.*

I mean—of course, it was that terrible mother of his that pulled this through—mother does everything for Brocky. Still, in the eyes of the law—you will not be her wife, but his—and therefore I hold that Brocky ought to be informed. Now—— [*He looks at her, sees she has got her eyes closed, then looks at the others, who have also got their eyes closed.*] If you girls are shamming sleep in the expectation that I shall awaken you in the manner beloved of ladies, abandon all such hopes.

[*Lady Catherine and Lady Agatha look up.*

LADY MARY. [*Speaking without looking up.*] You impertinent boy!

ERNEST. I knew that was it, though I didn't know everything, Agatha. [*With a clever air.*] I'm not young enough to know everything.

[*He looks from one to the other to see the effect of his epigram.*
[*A pause, in which they all three look at one another.*

LADY AGATHA. [*The only person who really admires Ernest's brilliancy.*] *Young* enough?

ERNEST. Don't you see? I'm not young enough to know everything.

LADY AGATHA. I'm sure it's frightfully clever, but it's so puzzling.

[*Opening the doors up* L.C., *Crichton ushers in the Rev. John Treherne, an athletic, pleasant-faced clergyman.*

CRICHTON. Mr Treherne.

[*Coming down* C., *Treherne bows to Agatha and crosses* R., *to Lady Catherine. Crichton then crosses to above the tea table up* L. *after closing the doors.*

LADY CATHERINE. Ernest, say it to Mr Treherne.

[*Treherne, after greeting Catherine, turns up to Lady Mary.*

ERNEST. Look here, Treherne, I'm not young enough to know everything.

TREHERNE. [*Having shaken hands with Lady Mary.*] How do you mean, old chap?

ERNEST. [*Tartly.*] I mean what I say.

LADY MARY. Say it again—say it more slowly.

ERNEST. I'm—not—young—enough—to—know—everything.

TREHERNE. [*Standing at* R., *with his back to the fireplace.*] *I* see. What you really mean, my boy, is that you are not *old enough* to know everything.

ERNEST. No, I don't.

TREHERNE. I assure you, that's it.

LADY MARY. Of course it is.

ALL. Yes, Ernest, that's it.

ERNEST. [*To Crichton.*] Crichton!

[*Crichton comes from above the table* L.C. *to the* R. *of Ernest.*
I am not young enough, Crichton, to know everything. Ha, ha!
[*A pause. Crichton repeats the hand-business—then smiles.
Ernest smiles to encourage him.*

CRICHTON. Thank you, sir.

[*He turns and exists* L.C., *closing the doors.*

ERNEST. [*Triumphant.*] Ah, if you had that fellow's head, Treherne, you would find something better to do with it than play cricket. I hear you bowl with your head.

[*He moves a little down* L.C.

TREHERNE. [*Good-humouredly, moving towards* C.] I'm afraid cricket is all I'm good for, Ernest.

LADY CATHERINE. [*Who admires him.*] Indeed, it isn't. You are sure to get on, Mr Treherne.

TREHERNE. [*Crossing down* C.] Thank you, Lady Catherine.

LADY CATHERINE. But it was the Bishop who told me so. He said a *clergyman* with a *leg break* was sure to get on in England.

TREHERNE. I'm jolly glad. [*He moves down* R.C., *towards her.*
[*Enter up* L.C., *Lord Brocklehurst, preceded by Lord Loam.
Lord Loam is pompous and fussy. Lord Brocklehurst is
a starchy, correct young man. Brocklehurst crosses to the
back of the settee* R. *and shakes hands with Lady Mary.*

LORD LOAM. [*Crossing down and shaking hands with Ernest.*] You are here, Ernest. [*He shakes hands with Treherne, who has crossed up to him.*] Feeling fit for the voyage, Treherne?

TREHERNE. Looking forward to it enormously.

[*He turns up above the* R. *settee, and shakes hands with Lord
Brocklehurst.*

LORD LOAM. That's right. [*He crosses to* R.] Now then, Mary, up and doing, up and doing. Time we had the servants in—
[*He rings the bell at the fireplace.*]—they enjoy it so much.

[*Lady Catherine rises, crosses up* C., *is joined by Treherne and they go to the table* L.C. *Lady Agatha rises, throws down the cushion, and goes to* L. *of the table* L.C.

LADY MARY. [*Rises.*] They hate it.

LORD LOAM. Mary, to your duties.

[*Lady Mary crosses up to below the table* L.C. *Lord Brocklehurst comes down* C. *Ernest moves towards him.*

ERNEST. [L. *of Lord Brocklehurst.*] Congratulations, Brocky.

LORD BROCKLEHURST. [*Stiffly.*] Thanks.

ERNEST. Mother's pleased?

LORD BROCKLEHURST. [*With dignity.*] Mother is *very* pleased.

ERNEST. That's good. Do you go on the yacht with us?

LORD BROCKLEHURST. Sorry, can't. And look here, Ernest, I will *not* be called Brocky.

ERNEST. Mother don't like it?

LORD BROCKLEHURST. She does not.

[*He crosses down* L. *below the* L. *settee and sits.*
[*Lady Mary, coming to above the* L. *settee, speaks to Lord Brocklehurst. Ernest crosses down* R. *below the fireplace, and stands on the hassock. Two footmen outside open the doors for Crichton and are seen by the audience. Enter Crichton with a teapot on a tray, he comes below the armchair* L.C. *and puts the teapot on the table and remains below the armchair* L.C.

LORD LOAM. [*Crossing to* C., *genially.*] We are quite ready, Crichton.

[*Crichton is reluctant and distressed.*

LADY MARY. [*Sarcastically.*] How he enjoys it!

LORD LOAM. [*Angry.*] He is the only one who doesn't—pitiful creature!

[*The others are all smiling at this.*

CRICHTON. [*Humbly.*] I can't help being a Conservative, my lord.

LORD LOAM. Be a man, Crichton. You are the same flesh and blood as myself.

CRICHTON. [*Rubbing his hands in pain.*] Oh, my lord.

LORD LOAM. [*Sharply.*] Show them in, and, by the way, they were not all here last time.

CRICHTON. All, my lord, except the merest trifles.

LORD LOAM. It must be everyone. [*Threateningly.*] And

remember this, Crichton—for the time being you are my equal. [*Firmly.*] I shall soon show you whether you are not my equal. Do as you are told.

> [*Crichton bows, goes up* C., *and exits, closing the doors, taking the tray with him.*

And girls——

> [*The girls look at him.*

Remember, no condescension. The first who condescends, recites.

> [*Lady Agatha, Lady Catherine and Lady Mary resent the reference to recitation. They hastily busy themselves with preparations for tea.*

By the way, Brocklehurst, can you do anything?

LORD BROCKLEHURST. How do you mean?

LORD LOAM. Can you do anything—with a penny or a handkerchief, make them disappear, for instance?

> [*Ernest here tries to do a trick with a penny and his handkerchief.*

LORD BROCKLEHURST. Good heavens, no.

LORD LOAM. It's a pity. Everyone in our position ought to be able to do something of that sort. Ernest, I shall probably ask you to say a few words—something bright and sparkling.

ERNEST. But, my dear Uncle, I have prepared nothing.

LORD LOAM. Anything impromptu will do.

> [*He moves up* R.C. *and surveys everything with satisfaction.*

ERNEST. [*Moving towards* C.] Oh—well—if anything strikes me on the spur of the moment——

> [*Craftily gets the hassock into position by giving it little kicks —to behind the chair* L.C. *and stands there for a moment.*

LORD BROCKLEHURST. But what is going to happen? I feel alarmed!

> [*Ernest moves* L. *below the table to above the* L. *settee.*

LORD LOAM. [*Coming down* C.] It is simply this, my dear Brocklehurst—I am a man, as you know, who despises class distinction, and I prove it by having all my servants up here to tea once a month. While they are here we treat them precisely as any other guest would be treated; and as this month's meeting happens to be today, you will have an opportunity of seeing how it delights and elevates them.

> [*He moves a little down* R.C., *rubbing his hands.*
> [*Crichton enters* L.C. *The doors remain open. He stands* C., *and*

announces the servants. Lord Brocklehurst rises, standing down L. Mrs Perkins, the housekeeper, enters and comes down C.

CRICHTON. [*Depressed but respectfully.*] Mrs Perkins.

> [*Lady Mary is preparing tea, the others are looking after the cakes, etc., a busy group, above and to L. of the table.*

LORD LOAM. [*Shaking hands with Mrs Perkins.*] Very delighted, Mrs Perkins. [*He brings her down a little, glaring at Lady Mary.*] Mary!

> [*Lady Mary gives a start.*]

Our friend, Mrs Perkins.

> [*Lady Mary crosses below the table to Mrs Perkins, shakes hands and indicates the settee L.*

LADY MARY. Won't you sit here?

> [*She crosses up C. and turns to the tea table.*

LORD LOAM. Agatha!

> [*Lady Agatha comes forward, shakes hands and points to the settee L., crosses and goes to Lady Mary for a cup of tea. Ernest, who is L., shakes hands with Mrs Perkins and moves to below the armchair L.C., as Mrs Perkins goes to the L. settee and sits at the R. end.*

Lord Brocklehurst, my valued friend, Mrs Perkins.

> [*Lord Brocklehurst bows to Mrs Perkins, who rises, bows and sits again. Lady Catherine crosses down R. of the settee and shakes hands with Mrs Perkins. Lady Catherine hands her cake and then returns to the table L. Lady Agatha hands her tea, over the back of the settee. Lord Loam breaks a little R.C., and turns.*

LORD BROCKLEHURST. [*Moving up C., to L. of Ernest.*] For Heaven's sake, Ernest, don't leave me for a moment, this sort of thing is *utterly* opposed to *all* my principles.

ERNEST. You stick to me, Brocky, and I'll pull you through.

CRICHTON. Monsieur Fleury.

> [*Monsieur Fleury, the French cook, enters.*

ERNEST. The chef.

> [*Lord Brocklehurst throws up his hand in disgust and crosses to the fireplace. Fleury comes down C.*

LORD LOAM. [*Moving to C., and shaking hands with the chef.*] Very charmed to see you, Monsieur Fleury.

FLEURY. Thank you very much. [*He bows to the ladies.*

LORD LOAM. [*Glaring.*] Agatha.
> [*Lady Agatha tosses her head impatiently.*

Recitation!
> [*Lady Agatha gets a cup of tea, crosses and stands by Fleury.
> Lord Loam, unseen by the latter, makes another threaten-
> ing gesture. Lady Agatha holds out her hand, which
> Fleury takes.*

LADY AGATHA. How do you do?
> [*She takes him to the armchair down R.*
> [*Lord Brocklehurst turns up R. of the R. settee as Treherne
> crosses down R. and offers cake to Fleury.*

TREHERNE. And how's the weather using you?
> [*Lady Agatha gives Fleury his cup and returns to L. of Lady
> Mary again. Treherne stands talking to Fleury, down R.*

CRICHTON. Mr Rolleston!
> [*Mr Rolleston enters. He is a valet. Lord Brocklehurst moves
> R.C. above the settee.*

LORD LOAM. [*Shaking hands.*] How do you do, Rolleston?
> [*Rolleston stands uneasily, turns and bows to the ladies. Lord
> Loam indicates the chair above the fireplace. Rolleston
> crosses and stands below it. Treherne crosses up and talks
> to him, offering him some cake.*
> [*After watching Rolleston, calls Ernest, who is just getting a
> cup of tea for Rolleston.*] Ernest!
> [*Ernest, carrying the cup, crosses to him.*

I can't understand how Rolleston manages to wear my clothes.
> [*Ernest takes tea to Rolleston and then returns to below the
> R. settee.*

CRICHTON. Mr Tompsett.
LADY MARY. [*On the announcement of Mr Tompsett.*] Ah, here's
old Tompsett!
> [*Mr Tompsett enters with his hat in his right hand. Lord Loam
> is about to shake it in mistake, when Tompsett puts it in
> the other hand.*

LORD LOAM. How do you do, Tompsett!
> [*Lady Mary hands tea for Tompsett to Lady Agatha.*

LADY CATHERINE. [*Crosses down to the lower end of the settee L.
and indicating the place.*] How are you, Tompsett; come and
sit here.
> [*Tompsett crosses down, touches his forehead to the ladies and*

> *shakes hands with Mrs Perkins, puts his hat and gloves under the settee, sits down and takes tea, etc. Lady Catherine and Lady Agatha return to the table.*

CRICHTON. Miss Fisher!

> [*Miss Fisher enters haughtily. Lord Loam, who has crossed to below the armchair* L.C., *turns and shakes hands.*

LORD LOAM. [L. *of Fisher.*] How do you do, Miss Fisher?

> [*Fisher just notices the ladies, who on the other hand, all notice the way her hair is dressed, and remark audibly upon it.*

ERNEST. [*Coming forward.*] This is a pleasure, Miss Fisher.

> [*He escorts her down* R. *Fleury rises and offers her the chair, and they stand talking to her.*

CRICHTON. Miss Simmons.

> [*Miss Simmons enters. Lord Loam turns from Fisher to* C.

LORD LOAM. [*On her* R., *shaking hands.*] You are always welcome, Miss Simmons. [*He passes her across to his* R.

ERNEST. [*Crossing and shaking hands with Simmons.*] At last we meet. Won't you sit down?

> [*He takes her to the settee. Simmons sits at the* R. *end, Ernest talking to her. Treherne here crosses to the table* L.C. *for tea, and puts his plate on the table.*

CRICHTON. Mademoiselle Jeanne.

> [*Mademoiselle Jeanne enters and comes down* L. *of Lord Loam.*

LORD LOAM. [*Shaking hands.*] Charmed to see you, Mademoiselle Jeanne.

> [*Treherne turns, shakes hands with Jeanne and crosses with Fisher's tea down* R. *Ernest rises, comes forward, shakes hands with Jeanne and takes her to the chair* L. *of the* R. *settee. Lord Loam moves to below the armchair* L.C. *The conversation has now become general. Lady Mary rises and crosses down* R.C. *Lady Catherine follows Lady Mary to* R., *offers cake to Fisher and then to Rolleston and Simmons, during the following dialogue.*

LADY MARY. [*During the above bus.*] Your tea is coming, Jeanne. Your tea is coming, Simmons. Ah—Mr Treherne, this is Fisher, my maid.

LORD LOAM. [*Sharply, taking a pace to* C.] Your what, Mary?

LADY MARY. [*With an effort.*] My friend.

> [*She then goes up to* R., *asking Rolleston and Simmons if they*

*have all they want. Then to Lord Brocklehurst, exchanging
inaudible expostulations, then to Jeanne and finally to the
table* L.C., *followed by Lord Brocklehurst.*

CRICHTON. Thomas!

[*Enter Thomas, a footman. Lord Loam crosses up and shakes
hands with him.*

LORD LOAM. [L. *of Thomas.*] How do you do, Thomas?

[*Thomas gives his hand reluctantly, bows to the ladies and
crosses* R.C.

ERNEST. [*Rising and shaking hands.*] How are you, Thomas?

[*Thomas moves* R.

CRICHTON. John.

[*Enter John, another footman, who also comes down* C.

LORD LOAM. [L. *of John, shaking hands.*] How do you do, John?

[*John breaks* R.C. *to Thomas and Ernest. Lord Loam crosses
down to Tompsett and Mrs Perkins* L., *who both rise,
but he makes them sit again and helps them to another
cup of tea, which Lady Mary makes, and after talking a
little while, moves to the chair* R.C. *Ernest shakes hands
with John and calls Lord Brocklehurst, who is up* L.C.

ERNEST. [*Breaking to* L. *of John.*] Brocklehurst!

[*Lord Brocklehurst crosses down to him.*

This is John. I think you have already met on the doorstep.

[*He slaps Lord Brocklehurst on the back and pushes him
towards John and turns up* R.C., *talking to Jeanne above
her chair.*

[*Lord Brocklehurst, annoyed, shakes hands with John, then
crosses* L., *below the table and down to the window* L.
Thomas joins John R.C., *below the* R. *end of the settee.
Lord Loam, noticing they have nothing, calls out.*

LORD LOAM. Agatha! Catherine!

[*They immediately take them tea and cake. Thomas takes his
cup* R. *to the fireplace. Lady Catherine remains up* R.C.
*between them, and Lady Agatha returns to her place
again. Lady Catherine indicates the* L. *end of the* R.
settee, and John sits, a little reluctantly.

CRICHTON. Jane.

[*Jane enters shyly, stands up* C. *Crichton indicates Lord Loam.
Lady Catherine moves down* R. *to Treherne. Thomas
having moved* **up** *above the* R. *end of the* R. *settee.*

LORD LOAM. [*Holding out his hand.*] Jane!

[*Jane crosses down and gives her hand, then stands there until
Treherne crosses, takes her hand and escorts her to the
chair above the fireplace, round in front of the settee* R.C.
Treherne crosses to the table L.C. *for tea and returns to
Jane. Lady Catherine meanwhile crosses to her with cake.*

CRICHTON. Gladys.

[*Gladys enters, hanging her head shyly. Ernest rises and leaves
Jeanne.*

ERNEST. [*Coming down to* R. *of Gladys and shaking hands. She
curtsies.*] How do you do, Gladys. You know my uncle?

[*Gladys shakes her head and sidles down. Ernest turns and
crosses to above the* L. *end of the settee, engaging John and
Jeanne.*

LORD LOAM. [*Holding out his hand.*] Your hand, Gladys? [*He
looks at Lady Agatha, who is doing nothing.*] Agatha!

[*Lady Agatha starts, crosses to* C., *gives her hand to Gladys,
who is biting her handkerchief and takes it awkwardly, and
indicates the chair below the window down* L. *Gladys
crosses* L. *Lady Agatha gets her some tea. Lord Brocklehurst turns and sees Gladys and crosses up* L. *in horror
and remains well up. Lady Agatha takes the tea down to
Gladys. During this John has risen from the* R. *settee,
crossed to Fleury and then to the* R. *end of the settee* R.
*and is talking to Thomas. Lord Loam crosses and says a
a word or two to Fisher and returns to* L.C. *again.*

CRICHTON. Eliza.

[*Eliza, the 'Tweeny', enters, frightened, with eyes on Crichton
and, backing, falls into Lord Brocklehurst, who is crossing
from up* L. *Turning, she then backs down* C., *stumbles over
the hassock, and stops* C.

LORD LOAM. [*On her* L., *giving her his hand.*] So happy to see
you, Eliza.

[*Eliza turns and takes his hand and bobs. Lord Loam turns and
talks to Mrs Perkins. Eliza looks round frightened, bobs
to Simmons and Fisher, then turns and bobs to the ladies.
Lord Brocklehurst crosses from the table with a plate of
cake for Lady Catherine up* R.C. *Fisher gives her cup to
Fleury, which he puts down. Lord Loam turns and sees
Eliza, still standing* C., *distressed.*

Don't be afraid, Eliza.

[*Lady Catherine crosses below the* R. *settee to Gladys and hands her some cake after having taken the plate from Lord Brocklehurst, and then returns to the tea table* L.C.

FISHER. [*Calling to John.*] John! [*He comes to her.*] I saw you talking to Lord Brocklehurst just now, introduce me.

[*She rises and tidies herself.*

[*Lord Loam turns and gives more tea to Tompsett and Mrs Perkins.*

LORD BROCKLEHURST. That's an uncommon pretty girl. If I must feed one of them, Ernest, that's the one.

[*He moves down,* L. *of the* R. *settee.*

JOHN. [*Advancing and introducing Fisher.*] My lord——

[*But Ernest has followed Lord Brocklehurst, who is about to bow when Ernest catches him by the arm and stops the introduction.*

ERNEST. No, it won't do, you are too pretty, my dear!

[*Fisher is at first offended. Then she smirks. John crosses* R., *to Rolleston.*

Mother wouldn't like it. [*He turns and sees Eliza who is watching them open-mouthed.*] Here's something safer. [*He draws Eliza towards Lord Brocklehurst* R.C. *To Lord Brocklehurst.*] Charming girl, dying to know you, let me introduce you, Eliza, Lord Brocklehurst—Lord Brocklehurst, Eliza.

[*Lord Loam now crosses up* C., *and above the table* L.C. *as Lord Brocklehurst turns, sees Eliza, and after a first horrified look, bows and indicates the* R. *settee. Eliza bobs to him, crosses him to the settee, and sits on the* L. *end. From either side of her Jeanne and Simmons regard her with disdain. Lord Brocklehurst crosses* L.C. *for tea and cake, returning with it to the settee. He bows to Simmons, who is sitting at the* R. *end, and then sits in the centre of the settee, watching Eliza. She takes a very large piece of cake and her cup. During this bus. there has been a little movement generally, the girls inquiring from various servants if they want more tea, Ernest has gone down* R. *to talk to Fisher, and Lady Mary has seated herself in the armchair* L.C. *Much of this occurs simultaneously and only occupies a few moments.*

LORD LOAM. [*Looking round.*] They are not all here, Crichton.
  [*Crichton crosses to the doors up* L.C., *and opens them.*
CRICHTON. [*Calling off, facing* R.] Odds and ends!
  [*He returns to his position up* C., *facing down. The remaining
    introductions are got through more quickly. Lord Loam
    has crossed to* C., *and stands below and to* R. *of Crichton,
    facing* L. *The Stable Boy enters, comes down and touches
    his forehead before taking Lord Loam's hand and shaking
    it. For want of something better, Lord Loam laughs. The
    Stable Boy backs a pace and bumps into Lady Mary's
    chair. She and Lady Agatha give a little cry, and the
    former rises, very annoyed. The Stable Boy backs away
    from her, touching his forehead again to her and Lord
    Loam, who indicates to Lady Mary that she must shake
    hands. She moves to him and does so, then indicating
    the stool* R. *of the* L. *settee. The Stable Boy crosses to it
    and sits. Lady Mary flips her fingers as a sign to Lady
    Agatha to attend to his tea. Lady Agatha rushes Lady
    Catherine up to the table and the three argue quietly but
    excitedly as to which is to give the boy his tea. Lord Loam,
    seeing this, crosses to the table and bends over it, speaking
    threateningly.*
LORD LOAM. Which is to recite?
  [*They all look at him for a moment, then each take a cup of tea
    to the Stable Boy. He takes Lady Mary's and the others
    put theirs down and bring him cake. Lady Mary returns
    to and sits in the armchair* L.C. *as a Kitchen Wench enters,
    clasping her hands behind her as she comes down. Lord
    Loam, down* C., *offers her his hand.*
How do you do, my friend?
  [*The Kitchen Wench brings her right arm up from behind her
    like a semaphore, just touches his hand and puts her arm
    behind her again, at the same time bobbing.*
Catherine!
  [*Lady Catherine looks up from* L. *of the table, sees what he
    means, seizes a plate of biscuits and goes below the table
    to* L. *of the Kitchen Wench and offers her hand. The
    Kitchen Wench bobs, and repeats the arm business. Lady
    Catherine indicates the chair* L. *between the windows, as
    Lady Agatha, above the table, takes a cup to Lady Mary*

*to fill with tea. The Kitchen Wench moves to below and
R. of Lady Mary's chair, and shoots her arm out again
almost in Lady Mary's face. Lady Mary gives a startled
cry, jerking the cup, and looks up at the Kitchen Wench.
The Kitchen Wench goes to below the table, repeats the
arm business to Lady Agatha, bobs and crosses to the
chair between the windows and sinks into it. After an
exchange of despairing glances, Lady Agatha takes the
cup from Lady Mary to the Kitchen Wench. Lady
Catherine moves up R. of the table to above it, and Lady
Agatha then joins her. A Page boy has now entered,
looking at Crichton for guidance, who points out Lord
Loam. The Page Boy comes down and Lord Loam offers
his hand. The Page Boy looks again at Crichton before
shaking hands.*

Why, you're getting quite a big boy.

[*He pats the Page Boy on the head and passes him across to R.
Treherne, who is sitting on the stool above the table L. of the
R. settee, indicates the stool below it, and the Page Boy
sits. At the same time Lady Mary rises and moves to L.
of the tea table and Lord Loam moves a little L.C., below
the armchair. The Page Boy, sitting, sees Eliza and nods to
her. At the same time Lady Catherine crosses above the
table and down to him, with tea and cake. The Page Boy
rises, but she makes him sit again, and take the tea. She
then turns up L. of the R. settee and to L. of Treherne.
The Page Boy puts his cake on the floor, finding things a
bit awkward. He then pours the tea into his saucer as it
is too hot, puts the cup on the floor and drinks. Crichton
has now closed the doors and returned to his place. During
the above, Lord Loam goes up to the table, fussing about.*

Keep it going—keep it going . . .

[*He turns to face R., as Lady Catherine returns from Treherne
with the cake-plate.*

Who is this for?

LADY CATHERINE. The coachman.

LORD LOAM. [*Taking the plate.*] I shall give it to him. [*He goes
down to the L. settee.*] Cake, Tompsett?

TOMPSETT. [*Rising and taking cake.*] Thank you, my lord.

[*During this, Lady Catherine has returned to Treherne above*

*the L. end of the R. settee. Lord Loam turns up to below
the tea table and hands the cake-plate to Lady Agatha,
then moving down to the upstage end of the L. settee.*

LORD LOAM. [*To Tompsett*]. And how are all at home?

[*During the next lines Lady Mary returns below the table to
the L.C. armchair and sits while Lady Agatha goes to
Crichton up L.C. to ask him if he will take tea. He bows.
She returns to the table—bus. with cups.*

TOMPSETT. [*During the above.*] Fairish, my lord, if 'tis the
horses you are inquiring for.

LORD LOAM. No, no—the family. How's the baby?

TOMPSETT. Blooming, your lordship.

LORD LOAM. A very fine boy.

[*Several of the servants hear this, look up, and suppress smiles.*
I remember saying so when I saw him—nice little chap.

TOMPSETT. Beg pardon, my lord, it's a girl.

LORD LOAM. A girl? Aha! ha! ha!—Exactly what I said. I
distinctly remember saying if it's spared it will be a girl.

[*He carries this off, crossing to C. The others suppress laughter.
The Page Boy looks and grins at Eliza. Tompsett and
Mrs Perkins exchange glances and smiles. Lord Loam
turns up R.C., to R. of Crichton.*

Very delighted to see you, Crichton. [*He offers Crichton his
hand, who hesitates before taking it.*] Mary, do you know Mr
Crichton?

[*Crichton comes down to R. of the armchair L.C. Lady Mary
rises and pours him out a cup of tea. Lord Loam crosses
down R. to Fisher and Fleury. The former rises on his
approach and then sits again.*

LADY MARY. Milk and sugar, Crichton?

CRICHTON. I'm ashamed to be seen talking to you, my lady.

LADY MARY. To such a perfect servant as you, all this must
be most distasteful.　　　[*She hands him a cup of tea.*
　　　　　　　　　　　　[*Crichton is too respectful to answer.*
Oh, please do speak or I shall have to recite—you do hate it,
don't you?

CRICHTON. [*Taking the tea.*] It pains me, your ladyship. It
disturbs the etiquette of the servants' hall. After last month's
meeting, the page boy, in a burst of equality, called me
Crichton. He was dismissed.

LADY MARY. [*Sitting in the chair* L.C.] I wonder—I really do— how you can remain with us.

[*Lady Agatha is now talking to Mrs Perkins over the settee.*

CRICHTON. [R. *of Lady Mary.*] I should have felt compelled to give notice, my lady, if master had not had a seat in the Upper House. I cling to that.

[*There is a pause. Lord Loam looks around and coughs. Lady Mary offers Crichton some cake, rising as Lady Agatha busies herself with the Stable Boy and the Kitchen Wench. Lady Catherine offers cake to Eliza and Simmons over the back of the* R. *settee and then returns to Treherne. Lord Loam moves across up* C., *and then to up* L., *beaming around. At the same time, Ernest is moving from one to the other at* R., *eventually reaching Thomas, talking to him on his* R., *over the* R. *settee.*

LADY MARY. Do go on speaking. [*She gives Crichton more milk.*] Tell me, what did Mr Ernest mean by saying he was too young to know everything?

CRICHTON. I have no idea, my lady.

LADY MARY. But you laughed.

CRICHTON. My lady, he is the second son of a peer.

LADY MARY. Very proper sentiments. You are a good soul, Crichton.   [*She sits again.*

[*Lord Loam has come down to the Kitchen Wench and Gladys at* L., *and then to Mrs Perkins, talking to her below the* L. *settee.*

LORD BROCKLEHURST. [*Desperately, to Eliza, with whom he has been trying to make conversation.*] And now tell me—what sort of weather have you been having in the kitchen?

[*The Page Boy is much amused.*

Have you been to the opera? Do you enjoy the Great Wheel?

[*Eliza gurgles.*

For Heaven's sake, woman, be articulate.

[*There is no response to this. Lord Brocklehurst rises, gives a despairing glance at Treherne, and crosses up* C., *wiping his brow, working over to* R. *near Ernest, who joins him with Treherne. At the same time Lady Catherine speaks to Eliza over the back of the settee, seeing she is very hot, and then crosses* L., *opens the windows and returns to Eliza with a fresh cup of tea. Meanwhile, Lord Loam*

*has left Mrs Perkins, and reached the table, standing
above it with Lady Agatha on his left. The Stable Boy
has left his stool and is* L., *talking to the Kitchen Wench.*

CRICHTON. [*Still talking to Lady Mary.*] No, my lady, his
lordship may compel us to be equal upstairs—

> [*Lord Loam is moving across up stage towards* R.

—but there will never be equality in the servants' hall.

> [*Lord Loam checks up* R.C., *and comes down* R. *of Crichton,
> some paces from him.*

LORD LOAM. [*Coming down* C.] What's that? No equality?
Can't you see, Crichton, that our divisions into classes are
artificial; that if we were to return to nature—which is the
aspiration of my life—all would be equal.

> [*Some of the servants who have been quietly conversing, stop,
> and turn to listen.*

CRICHTON. If I may make so bold as to contradict your
lordship.

LORD LOAM. [*With an effort.*] Go on.

CRICHTON. The divisions into classes, my lord, are not artificial.
They are the natural outcome of a civilized society. There
must always be a master and servants in all civilized com-
munities, my lord, for it is natural, and whatever is natural is
right.

LORD LOAM. [*Tartly.*] It is very unnatural for me to stand here
and allow you to talk such nonsense.

> [*Ernest has crossed up* R.C.

CRICHTON. [*Eagerly.*] That is what I have been striving to
point out to your lordship.

> [*Lady Mary takes Crichton's cup, and moves with it below
> and up* L. *of the table. Crichton moves respectfully
> towards Lord Loam, who is pondering, finding himself
> in a quandary. He the crosses below and to the* L. *of
> Crichton, taking out the notes for his speech. Crichton
> quietly places the hassock above and slightly on the* R.
> *of the armchair* L.C., *and Lord Loam turns up and stands
> on it. There is some restlessness among the company, the
> putting down of cups, and unhappy anticipation of the
> coming speech.*

LORD LOAM. [*Holding up his hand for silence—clears his throat—
addresses the company.*] My friends——

[*The Kitchen Wench says,* "'Ear, 'ear!' *but is checked by
Crichton's look of disapproval.*

I am glad to see you all looking so happy. It used to be predicted
by the scoffer, that these meetings would prove distasteful to
you—are they distasteful? I hear you laughing at the question.

[*All are silent. He looks round in surprise. Crichton gives a
short unnatural laugh and the others follow suit.*

No harm in saying now that among us today is one who was
formerly hostile to the movement, but who today has been
conquered. I am sure Lord Brocklehurst—

[*All turn and look at Lord Brocklehurst, the servants at back
rising to get a sight of him.*

—will presently say to me that if the charming lady now by his
side has derived as much pleasure from his company as he has
derived from hers he will be more than satisfied.

[*Lord Brocklehurst, standing above Eliza, shows his teeth—
Eliza trembles.*

For the time being the artificial and unnatural—I say unnatural
—[*he glares at Crichton*]

[*Crichton bows slightly.*

—barriers of society are swept away. Would that they could be
swept away for ever.

[*Ernest moves to above the* L. *end of the* R. *settee.*

PAGE BOY. 'Ear, 'ear!

LORD LOAM. [*Turns to the Page Boy—looks—speaks emphatic-
ally.*] But that is entirely and utterly out of the question. And
now for a few months we are to be separated.

[*The Page Boy turns to Eliza, rubbing his hands—the others
also show delight.*

As you know, my daughters and Mr Ernest and Mr Treherne
are to accompany me on my yacht on a voyage to distant parts
of the earth. In less than forty-eight hours we shall be under
way.

[*Cheers.*

Do not think our life on the yacht is to be one long idle holiday.
My views on the excessive luxury of the day are well known,
and what I preach I am resolved to practise. I have therefore
decided that my daughters, instead of having one maid each,
as at present, shall, on this voyage, have but one maid between
them.

[Jeanne rises and looks at Simmons and Fisher—they also look at each other.

LADY MARY ⎫   ⎧ *[Rises.]* Father!
LADY AGATHA ⎪ *[Almost together.]* ⎨ Father!
LADY CATHERINE ⎬   ⎪ Father! *[She half rises.*
CRICHTON ⎭   ⎩ My lord!

LORD LOAM. My mind is made up.

ERNEST. I cordially agree.

[The girls look daggers at Ernest.

LORD LOAM. And now, my friends, I should like to think that there is something I could give each of you to take away.

[The Page Boy pounces on a large piece of cake.

Not cake. *[He crosses to him.]* Some thought, some noble saying, over which you might ponder in my absence.

[He pats the Page Boy on the head and returns to his place.
[Crichton takes the cake from the Page Boy and places it on the table up L. *and returns to* C.

In this connection I remember a proverb, which has had a great effect on my own life—I first heard it many years ago—I have never forgotten it, it constantly cheers and guides me. That proverb is—that proverb was—the proverb I speak of——

[Lord Loam taps his forehead. All look uncomfortably at one another.

LADY MARY. *[After looking at Lord Loam, half rises.]* Oh dear —I believe he has forgotten it. *[She sits again.*

LORD LOAM. The proverb—that proverb—the proverb to which I refer——

[There is general distress. Crichton gives short applause, looking around at the servants as a sign for them to follow suit, which they do rather half-heartedly. Lord Loam becomes more and more desperate.

I have it now.

[All strain forward, thinking he has remembered, but he cannot recall it.

LADY MARY. *[Rises.]* Crichton!

[She indicates to him to dismiss the servants. Crichton moves down a little and signs, first to Mrs Perkins down L., *and then to Simmons at* R. *All the servants rise. The Page Boy replaces his stool nearer the table, and stands there*

> *as Eliza passes him to up* C. *Then he goes up and stares into Lord Loam's face until Crichton pushes him off. So far as possible the general exeunt is in the same order as the entrances, and is quick and silent. During all this, Lord Loam, with his right arm upraised, is making efforts to remember the proverb. As the last servant leaves, Crichton takes lord Loam's right arm, places it on his own, and, moving with him to* C., *says:*

CRICHTON. Mr Treherne.

> [*Treherne crosses and takes Lord Loam's left arm, and they conduct his Lordship off up* R.C.

LORD LOAM. [*As they turn to go up* R.C.] The proverb—it was— one moment, etc.—— [*Until off.*

LADY MARY. [*Coming down* L.C. *below the table.*] One maid among three grown women! [*She turns to below the* L. *settee.*

> [*Ernest crosses up to the table* L.C., *and eats a biscuit, Lord Brocklehurst is pettish—Ernest is sulky and in the position from which he was to make his speech. The three girls have collapsed. Lady Agatha on the chair above the table. Lady Catherine on the* R. *settee.*

LORD BROCKLEHURST. [*Rising, crossing to* C.] Mary, I think I had better go. That dreadful kitchenmaid!

LADY MARY. [*Crossing to him, on his* L.] I can't blame you, George.

> [*They kiss coldly and Lady Mary crosses below the settee to* R. *Lord Brocklehurst then bows to the others and goes up* C. *He checks there and turns to Lady Mary.*

LORD BROCKLEHURST. Your father's views are shocking to me, and I am glad I am not to be one of the party on the yacht. My respect for myself, Mary—my natural anxiety as to what mother will say—I shall see you, darling, before you sail.

> [*Exit Lord Brocklehurst* L.C.

ERNEST. [*At* C., *looking after him, kicking the hassock to* R.] Selfish brute—only thinking of himself. What about my speech?

LADY MARY. [*Crossing and sitting in the chair* R.C.] One maid among three of us! [*Tragically.*] What's to be done!

ERNEST. Pooh! You must do for yourselves—that's all.

LADY MARY. Do for ourselves—how can we know where our things are kept?

LADY AGATHA. [*Rising.*] Are you aware that dresses button up
the back? [*She comes down* L. *of the tea table.*

LADY CATHERINE. How are we to get into our boots and be
prepared for the carriage?

LADY MARY. Who is to put us to bed, and who is to get us up,
and how shall we ever know it's morning if there is no one
to pull up the blinds?

[*Lady Catherine rises and goes down to the fireplace. Crichton
re-enters up* R.C. *Ernest and the girls turn to him.*

ERNEST. How is his Lordship now?

CRICHTON. [*Closing the door.*] A little easier, sir.

[*He crosses towards the doors up* L.C.

LADY MARY. [*Rising.*] Crichton, send Fisher to me.

[*Crichton bows and exits* L.C., *leaving the doors open.*

ERNEST. [*Coming down* C. *again.*] I have no pity for you girls,
I——

LADY MARY. [*Turning away and throwing herself on the settee*
R.C.] Ernest, go away and don't insult the broken-hearted.

ERNEST. And uncommon glad I am to go. Ta, ta, all of you.
[*He goes up* C., *and turns below the doors.*] He asked me to say
a few words—I came here to say a few words—and I'm not
at all sure that I couldn't bring an action against him.

[*He exits, closes the doors after him.*

LADY MARY. [*Hearing the doors shut, thinks out a plan, rises,
crosses and sits in the armchair* L.C.] My poor sisters, come here.

[*They go to her doubtfully. Lady Catherine on her right. Lady
Agatha stands below the table on her left. She is now quite
the mother to them.*

We must make this draw us closer together. I shall do my best
to help you in every way. Just now I cannot think of myself at
all.

LADY AGATHA. [*Looks at her in surprise.*] But how unlike you,
Mary!

LADY MARY. [*Looking up at her.*] It is my duty to protect my
sisters. [*Giving her a sisterly smile.*

LADY CATHERINE. I never knew her so sweet before, Agatha.
[*She takes her hand.*] What do you propose to do, dearest
Mary?

LADY MARY. I propose, when we are on the yacht, to lend
Fisher to you, when I don't need her myself.

Lady Agatha. [*Rising.*] Fisher?

Lady Mary. Of course, as the eldest, I have decided that it is *my* maid we shall take with us.

Lady Catherine. [*Backing a pace.*] Mary, you toad.
                                    [*She goes down* L., *below the* L. *settee.*

Lady Agatha. [*To above the* R. *end of the* L. *settee.*] Nothing on earth would induce Fisher to lift her hand for either me or Catherine.

Lady Mary. [*Languidly.*] Dear Agatha—[*swinging her foot*] I was afraid of it. That is why I am so sorry for you.

> [*Her sisters turn as if about to speak, but Fisher's entrance stops them. She enters* C. *and closes the doors and crosses to* C. *Lady Mary rises, smiling triumphantly and crosses to the table* L. *of the* R. *settee for a book and paper-knife. Lady Catherine sits down* L.C. *Lady Agatha crosses to behind the settee* L., *near her.*

[*Turning to Fisher.*] Fisher, you heard what his Lordship said?

Fisher. [*At* C.] Yes, my lady?

> [*Lady Catherine and Lady Agatha notice Fisher's manner.*

Lady Mary. [*Coming and sitting on the chair* L. *of the settee* R., *with her back to Fisher, languidly.*] You have given me some satisfaction of late, Fisher, and to mark my approval I have decided you shall be the maid who accompanies us.

Fisher. I thank you, my lady.

Lady Mary. [*Sees Fisher still standing.*] That is all—you may go.

Fisher. If you please, my lady, I wish to give notice.

> [*Lady Catherine and Lady Agatha are delighted—Lady Agatha whispers to Lady Catherine and then goes up to behind the table* L.C.

Lady Mary. [*Starts—then is coldly indignant.*] Oh, certainly—you may go.   [*She lifts her book and reads.*

Lady Catherine. But why, Fisher?

Fisher. [*Turning to Lady Catherine.*] I could not undertake, my lady, to wait upon three. We don't do it. [*In an indignant outburst to Lady Mary.*] Oh, my lady, to think that this affront——

Lady Mary. [*Looking up coldly.*] I thought I told you to go, Fisher.

> [*Fisher stands for a moment irresolute. Then she turns and*

exits L.C., *rather huffily, leaving the doors open. As soon as she has gone, Lady Mary puts down her book—the others gloat over her.*

LADY AGATHA. [*Crossing to above the settee* R.C.] Serves you right.

[*Enter Crichton* C., *closing the doors.*

LADY CATHERINE. [*Rising.*] It will be Simmons after all.

[*She moves up to the armchair* L.C.
[*Lady Agatha up* R., *shows annoyance and comes down* R. *of the settee. Crichton comes to* C.

[*To Crichton.*] Send Simmons to me.

CRICHTON. [*Coming down* C. *a little, after hesitating.*] My lady, might I venture to speak?

LADY CATHERINE. What is it?

CRICHTON. [*To Lady Catherine.*] I happen to know, your ladyship, that Simmons desires to give notice for the same reason as Fisher.

LADY CATHERINE. Oh!   [*She sits* L.C. *in the armchair.*

LADY AGATHA. [*Below the* R. *settee, triumphant.*] Then, Catherine, we take Jeanne.

CRICHTON. And Jeanne also, my lady.

[*There is general gloom, but though Lady Catherine and Lady Agatha give way to their emotions before Crichton, Lady Mary is always cold and haughty.*

LADY AGATHA. Oh! Oh! Oh! [*She sits, infuriated, on the* R. *settee.*] We can't blame them. Could *any* maid, who respected herself, be got to wait upon three?

LADY MARY. I suppose there are such persons, Crichton?

CRICHTON. [*Guardedly.*] I have heard, my lady, that there are such.

LADY MARY. [*A little desperate.*] Crichton, what's to be done? We sail in two days—could one be discovered in the time?

[*Crichton reflects.*

LADY AGATHA. [*To Crichton.*] Surely you can think of someone.

CRICHTON. [*Makes a movement with his hands—heavily.*] There is in this establishment, your ladyship, a young woman——

LADY MARY. [*All the girls look at one another.*] Yes?

CRICHTON. A young woman on whom I have for some time cast an eye.

LADY CATHERINE. [*Rising; eagerly.*] Do you mean as a possible lady's maid?

CRICHTON. I had thought of her, my lady, in—[*coughs*]—another connection.

LADY MARY. Ah!

[*The girls exchange glances.*

CRICHTON. But I believe her to be quite the young person you require. If you could see her, my lady.

LADY MARY. I shall certainly see her. Bring her to me.

[*Exit Crichton up* L.C.

You two needn't wait.

LADY CATHERINE. [*Crossing to* L. *of Lady Mary's chair.*] Needn't we! [*She goes down to the fireplace.*] We see your little game, Mary.

LADY AGATHA. [*Rising and going to the* L. *end of the settee* R.] We shall certainly remain and have our two-thirds of her. Catherine, let us stick together.

[*Moving down* R. *to Lady Catherine.*
[*They take hands and defy Lady Mary, who rises, stamps her foot, then sits, as Crichton enters with Eliza on his* L. *Crichton enters* C., *leaving the doors open, showing in Eliza, who is quaking with self-consciousness. She regards Crichton as a god, and curtsies to him.*

CRICHTON. [L. *of the chair* R.C.] This, my lady, is the young person.

LADY CATHERINE. Oh!

[*All three show that they consider her quite unsuitable. Lady Agatha moves to the* R. *end of the settee.*

LADY MARY. Come here, girl——

[*Eliza, down* C. *below and* L. *of Crichton, does not move.*
Don't be afraid.

[*Crichton brings her forward—she keeps her eyes on him; he crosses her to* R.C. *She bobs, he breaks to* C. *His manner is that of one who knows himself to be her superior but who, nevertheless, has a genuine pride in her.*

CRICHTON. [*Turning at* L.C.] Her appearance, my lady, is homely, and her manners, as you may have observed, deplorable, but she has a heart of gold.

[*This is said openly before Eliza and in the tone of one honestly doing his best for her—she is gratified.*

LADY MARY. What is your position downstairs?
  [*Eliza turns to Lady Mary and mutters nervously, then turns an appealing face to Crichton.*
CRICHTON. [*Kindly.*] Speak up, speak up.
ELIZA. [*Bobs.*] Yes, sir. [*She turns to Lady Mary.*] I'm a tweeny, your ladyship.
LADY CATHERINE. A what?
ELIZA. Er—er—— [*She looks at Crichton again appealingly and fingers her dress nervously.*] A tweeny!
CRICHTON. [*Takes a step forward.*] A tweeny, that is to say, my lady, she is not at present, strictly speaking, anything—a between-maid, she helps the vegetable maid. It is she, my lady, who transfers the dishes from the one end of the kitchen table where they are placed by the cook, to the other end where they enter into the charge of Thomas and John.
LADY MARY. I see. And you and Crichton are—ah—keeping company.
                              [*Crichton draws himself up, hurt.*
ELIZA. [*Aghast.*] A butler don't keep company, my lady.
LADY MARY. [*Impatiently.*] Does he not?
CRICHTON. No, your ladyship, we butlers may—[*he makes a gesture with his arms*]—but we do not keep company.
LADY CATHERINE. [*Sits on the arm of the chair below the fireplace.*] I know what it is—you are engaged?
                              [*Eliza looks longingly at Crichton.*
CRICHTON. Certainly not, my lady. The utmost I can say at present is that I have cast a favourable eye.
                              [*Eliza is in ecstasies.*
LADY MARY. [*Indifferently.*] As you choose. But I'm afraid, Crichton, *she* will not suit *us*.
                              [*Eliza shows her disappointment.*
CRICHTON. [*A little hotly.*] My lady, beneath this simple exterior are concealed a very sweet nature and rare womanly gifts.
LADY AGATHA. Unfortunately that is not what we want.
CRICHTON. And it is she, my lady, who dresses the hair of the ladies' maids for our evening meals.
  [*All show interest. Lady Catherine rises, taking a pace towards Lady Agatha, who turns to her.*
LADY MARY. [*Quickly.*] She dresses Fisher's hair?

Eliza. Yes, my lady, and I does them up when they goes to parties.

Crichton. [*Pained at her language.*] Does!

Eliza. Doos. [*To Lady Mary.*] And it's me what alters your gowns to fit 'em.

Crichton. [*Again pained.*] *What* alters?

Eliza. [*Greatly distressed.*] Which alters.

Lady Agatha. Mary!

Lady Mary. I shall certainly have her.

Lady Catherine. *We* shall certainly have her. Tweeny, we have decided to make a lady's maid of you.

Eliza. [*Delighted.*] Oh, lawks!

Lady Agatha. We are doing this for you so that your position socially may be more nearly akin to that of Crichton.

Eliza. Oh!

Crichton. [*Gravely.*] It will undoubtedly increase the young person's chances.

Lady Mary. Then if I get a good character for you from Mrs Perkins, she will make all arrangements.

[*She resumes her reading.*

Eliza. [*Glorious.*] My lady!

Lady Mary. By the way, I hope you are a good sailor.

Eliza. [*Startled.*] You don't mean, my lady—I'm to go on the ship?

Lady Mary. Certainly.

Eliza. But—— [*To Crichton.*] You ain't going, sir?

Crichton. No.

Eliza. [*Alarmed.*] Then neither ain't I.

Lady Agatha. [*Crosses to* l. *of the chair* r.c.] You must!

Eliza. [*Moves to Crichton.*] Leave him! Not me!

[*Lady Agatha turns up, to above the* l. *end of the settee.*

Lady Mary. Girl, don't be silly. Crichton will be—considered in your wages.

Eliza. I ain't going.

Crichton. I feared this, my lady.

Eliza. Nothink'll budge me.

Lady Mary. [*Angrily.*] Leave the room.

[*Crichton crosses to Lady Mary.*

Put her out!

[*The sharpness of the order displeases Crichton, and he shows*

Eliza out with marked politeness, indicating the doors up
L.C., *and conducting her to them. She exits. He closes the*
doors and then returns to C. *The sisters are gloomy.*

LADY AGATHA. [*Moving* C. *to* R. *of Crichton.*] Crichton——
                                    [*Crichton checks.*
I think you might have shown more displeasure.

CRICHTON. [*Contrite.*] I was touched, your ladyship. I see, my
lady, that to part from her would be a wrench to me, though
I could not well say so in her presence, not yet having decided
how far I shall go with her.

   [*Lady Agatha crosses to below the table* L.C. *Crichton is about*
   to turn up L.C., *when Lord Loam enters in a passion*
   up R.C.

LORD LOAM. [*Coming down* C.] The ingrate! The smug! The
fop!

LADY CATHERINE. [*Down* R.C.] What is it now, Father?

LORD LOAM. That man of mine, Rolleston, refuses to accompany us because you are to have but one maid.

LADY AGATHA. Hurrah! [*She moves round to* L. *of the tea table.*
   [*Lord Loam glares at her. The girls look delightedly at one*
   another.

LADY MARY. [*Rising and crossing his arm.*] Darling Father,
rather than you should lose Rolleston, we will consent to take
all three of them.

LORD LOAM. [*Pushing her off.*] Pooh—nonsense.
                            [*Lady Mary moves away to up* R.C.
[*Crossing to below the armchair* L.C.] Crichton!
                            [*Crichton comes down* C.
Find me a valet who can do without three maids.
                            [*He sits in the armchair.*

CRICHTON. Yes, my lord. [*Troubled.*] In the time—the more
suitable—
   [*Lady Agatha beckons Lady Mary to come round the back to*
   above the table L.C.
the party, my lord, the less willing will he be to come without
the usual perquisites.

LORD LOAM. Anyone will do.
                       [*He rises and goes to the windows down* L.

CRICHTON. [*Shocked.*] My lord!
                 [*Lady Mary hurries across to Lady Agatha up* L.C.

LORD LOAM. [*In an exasperated tone, looking out of the window.*]
The ingrate! The puppy!

LADY AGATHA. [*With sudden idea.*] Mary!
                    [*She whispers to her across the table.*

LADY MARY. I ask a favour of a servant—never!
                    [*She crosses back to the settee.*

LADY AGATHA. [*Crossing c., as Crighton moves below the chair.*]
Crichton, would it not be very distressing to you to let his
Lordship go, attended by a valet who might prove unworthy?
                    [*Crichton turns R., to face her.*
It is only for three months—don't you think that you—you——
[*As Crichton sees what she wants he pulls himself up with noble
offended dignity, and she is appalled.*
I beg your pardon.
[*Crichton bows stiffly and backs a step or two. Lord Loam paces
fretfully up L.*

LADY CATHERINE. [*To Crichton, moving in a pace.*] But think
of the joy to Tweeny.
[*Crichton is moved, but shakes his head. Lady Catherine turns
away down R.*

LADY MARY. [*Above the R. settee.*] Crichton! [*She leans over and
gets her books—moves R., and sits on the settee.*] Do you think
it safe to let the master you love go so far away without you,
while he has these dangerous views about equality?
[*Crichton hesitates, profoundly stirred. Lady Agatha and Lady
Catherine almost beg him with their hands—Lady Mary
is also really eager, but when he looks at her, she coldly
opens the book and begins to read. Crichton turns up c. a
few paces, obviously having an inward struggle. He checks,
and turns down to Lord Loam, who is now chafing at L.
of the table L.C. Lady Agatha quietly slips across to above
the chair L. of the R. settee and watches.*

CRICHTON. My lord!
[*Lord Loam turns, and crosses to below the settee.*
I have found a man.

LORD LOAM. [*Crossing to below the chair L.C.*] Already? Who
is he?
                    [*Crichton presents himself with a gesture.*
Yourself?

LADY CATHERINE. [*Coming in a pace.*] Father, how good of him.

LORD LOAM. [*Pleased, but thinking it a small thing.*] Uncommon good. Thank you, Crichton!

> [*He crosses up* C., R. *of Crichton, who bows.*
> [*Lady Agatha moves above the settee to Lady Mary.*

[*Turning up* C., *to Crichton.*] This helps me nicely out of a hole, and it will annoy Rolleston. Come with me and we shall tell him. [*He turns towards the door up* R.C.] Not that I think you have lowered yourself in any way. Come along.

> [*Exit Lord Loam* R.C. *Crichton is about to follow, when Lady Agatha crosses to* C. *and speaks to him.*

LADY AGATHA. Crichton! [*She holds out her hand.*] Thank you.

CRICHTON. My lady—a valet's hand.

> [*Lady Mary turns her head to look. He won't shake hands—he is suffering from deep genuine emotion. Lady Agatha and Lady Catherine are a little touched. Lady Mary is rather curious.*

LADY AGATHA. [*After a look at Lady Catherine and Lady Mary.*] I had no idea you would feel it so deeply—why did you do it?

> [*Crichton is too respectful to reply.*

LADY MARY. [*Rising.*] Crichton!

> [*Crichton comes down a little* L. *of* C.
> [*Taking a pace to* R.C.] I am curious, I *insist* upon an answer.
> [*Lady Agatha moves to above the chair* R.C. *Lady Catherine comes in a pace towards Lady Mary, below and on her* R.

CRICHTON. My lady, I am the son of a butler and a lady's-maid —perhaps the happiest of all combinations—

> [*The girls laugh to themselves.*

—and to me the most beautiful thing in the world is a haughty aristocratic English house with everyone kept in his place. Though I were equal to your ladyship—where would be the pleasure to me?—it would be more than counterbalanced by the pain of feeling that Thomas and John were equal to *me*.

LADY CATHERINE. But Father says if we were to return to nature——

CRICHTON. If we did, my lady, the first thing we should do would be to elect a head. Circumstances might alter cases— the same person might not be master—the same persons might not be servants. I cannot say as to that, nor indeed should we have the deciding of it. Nature would decide it for us.

Lady Mary. You seem to have thought it all out carefully, Crichton.

> [*She moves a cushion to the* L. *end of the settee and puts her feet up on the* R. *end.*

Crichton. Yes, my lady.   [*He backs a step.*

Lady Catherine. And you have done this for us, Crichton, because you thought that—that Father needed to be kept in his place?

Crighton. I should prefer you to say, my lady, that I have done it—for the house.

Lady Agatha. Thank you, Crichton. [*She crosses above and to* R. *of Lady Mary at the back of the settee.*] Mary——

> [*She wants Lady Mary to be kind, but Lady Mary has begun to read again. Lady Agatha returns to* L. *of the chair* R.C. *Crichton moves up* C.

[*To Crichton.*] If there was any way in which we could show our gratitude——

Crichton. [*Moves down a little.*] If I might venture, my lady, would you kindly show it by becoming more like Lady Mary. [*Looking at her.*] That disdain is what we like from our superiors. Even so do we, the upper servants, disdain the lower servants, while they take it out of the odds and ends.

> [*Exit Crichton up* L.C. *The girls become lazy again.*

Lady Agatha. [*Crossing down* L.] Oh dear, what a tiring day!

> [*She sits on the lower end of the settee, putting her feet up.*

Lady Catherine. [*Crossing* L. *to the same settee.*] I feel dead. Tuck in your feet, you selfish thing.

> [*She sits at the upper end, putting her feet up on the downstage end, to Lady Agatha's discomfort.*
>
> [*Lady Mary is lying reading on the other settee. They are all sleepy. A pause.*

Lady Mary. [*Looking up from her book.*] I wonder what he meant by circumstances might alter cases?

Lady Agatha. [*Yawns.*] But don't talk, Mary—I was nearly asleep.

> [*A pause.*

Lady Mary. [*Sleepily.*] I wonder what he meant by the same person might not be master and the same persons might not be servants?

LADY CATHERINE. Do be quiet, Mary, and leave it to Nature—
he said Nature would decide.

               [*A pause—she turns and snuggles into the pillows.*

LADY MARY. [*Sleepily.*] I wonder——

    [*She tries to read, but her eyes close and the book drops on to
        her lap, and then it and the paper-knife roll on to the
        floor.*

LADY AGATHA. [*Almost asleep.*] What?
All seem to be asleep, as—

THE CURTAIN FALLS

Act II

Scene: *The Island*

Two months have elapsed and the scene is a tropical island on which the travellers have been wrecked. The actual place is a wild spot in a wood which stretches far away on both sides, the trees being bread-fruit, banana, coconut, etc. The ground is a dense tangle of long grass growing about six feet high, bamboo and prickly coarse vegetation, and at the rise of the Curtain this seems to cover the stage and shuts out most of the view at back. Thus, at the opening, the sea is not seen though it is really on the back-cloth. In the stillness of the opening, however, the splash of the waves can be heard, adding melancholy to the scene. The whole effect should be one of desolation and discomfort. The wood around is mysterious, sullen, dangerous.

As far as possible the scene should convey the impression that horrible animals prowl in the woods and that snakes may come out of the grass. In the background on R. a rude hut is in course of erection, but at present only the top of it is seen owing to the denseness of the vegetation in front.

At L.C., low rocks rise to higher ledges leading off L., through the trees and jungle vegetation. At C., there is a bucket, with a board across it to form a seat. Slightly below it, at R.C., a large tripod of stout branches indicates where a fire has been made. An iron pot hangs from the tripod. The grass in the centre acting area had been cut down somewhat, but elsewhere, up stage and on either side, it is very long indeed.

When the Curtain roses, Treherne can be seen now and again on the roof of the hut, building it with logs and rough planks for which he descends from time to time.

Lady Mary, Lady Agatha and Lady Catherine are seated on the lower rocks at L.C. Lady Mary is between the others with Lady Catherine slightly below and on her L., and Lady Agatha perched a little higher and on her R. Ernest is seated on the bucket, writing on a piece of paper. All are dressed eccentrically in such confused garments as people roused from sleep by shipwreck might fling on

*or have flung on them. Thus, one lady has a common sailor's blue
jacket over a skirt. Another wears a jersey and a sailor's red cap.
The third wears a long ulster to cover half a dress underneath.
They wear bath slippers, etc.—all hopelessly bad for a prickly
jungle. They walk as if on needles. The men dress to correspond
and are unshaven. No one has boots.*

*The sun is streaming down, and Treherne seems very hot, but the
others, not working, are cool. During the opening scene, Treherne
is joined occasionally by Crichton about the hut structure. This
hut, it should be noted, has the makings of a window opening
facing down stage, and a rough door opening in the wall facing* L.
*As the scene commences, the sea is heard, and the knocking of
hammers on wood about the hut.*

ERNEST. [*Looking up from his writing and across at the ladies.*]
This is what I have written—listen!

[*Treherne disappears.*

'Wrecked, wrecked, wrecked! On an island in the tropics . . .
[*the sound of the sea dies away*] the Hon. Ernest Woolley, the
Rev. John Treherne, the Ladies Mary, Catherine and Agatha
Lasenby, with two servants. Sole survivers of Lord Loam's
steam yacht *Bluebell*—

[*Lady Catherine and Lady Agatha sob; Lady Mary comforts
them.*

—which encountered a fearful gale in these seas and soon
became a total wreck. The crew behaved gallantly, putting us
all into the first boat. What became of them I cannot tell, but
we, after dreadful sufferings, and insufficiently clad in whatever garments we could lay hold of in the dark——'

LADY MARY. [*Drawing her clothes about her.*] Please don't
describe our garments.

ERNEST. '—succeeded in reaching this island with the loss of
one of our party.

[*The ladies look at one another and then sob.*
Namely, Lord Loam,—

[*The ladies weep louder. Lady Catherine leans her head on
Lady Mary's shoulder and Lady Agatha hers on Lady
Mary's knee.*

—who flung away his life n a gallant attempt to save a
servant who had fallen overboard.'

[*The girls dry their eyes and look up.*

LADY AGATHA. [*Strongly.*] But, Ernest, it was Crichton who jumped into the sea trying to save *Father*.

ERNEST. Well, you know it was rather silly of Uncle to fling away his life trying to get into the boat first;

[*Lady Agatha puts her head down.*

and as this document may be printed in the papers, it struck me—an English peer, you know.

LADY MARY. Ernest, that's very thoughtful of you.

ERNEST. 'By night the cries of wild cats, the hissing of snakes, terrify us extremely—[*he scratches out writing*]—terrify the *ladies* extremely. Against these we have no weapons except one cutlass and a hatchet. A bucket washed ashore is at present our only comfortable seat——'

LADY MARY. And Ernest is sitting on it.

ERNEST. Sh! Oh, do be quiet. It's utterly impossible for me to go on with all these rotten interruptions. It's sickening— that's the word—sickening! 'To add to our horrors, night falls suddenly in these parts, and it is then that savage animals begin to prowl and roar.'

LADY MARY. [*Comforting the other two girls.*] Have you said that vampire bats suck the blood from our toes as we sleep?

[*Treherne mounts the hut again and works at it.*

ERNEST. Hush, that's all.

[*The sea again is heard.*

I end up: 'Rescue us, or we perish—rich reward. Signed, Ernest Woolley, in command of our little party. This is written on a leaf taken out of a book of poems that Crichton found in his pocket.'—Fancy Crichton being a reader of poetry. Now I shall put it into the bottle and fling it into the sea. [*He puts it into the soda-water bottle, knocks in the cork and crosses with it to* R.] The tide is going out—mustn't miss the post. [*He calls.*] Crichton! Crichton!

[*Ernest turns a little to* C. *Lady Agatha rises and gets on to the rock above Lady Mary. Crichton enters* R. *hastily through the grass, thinking it some important matter.*

CRICHTON. [R.C., *looking at the ladies anxiously.*] Anything wrong, sir?

ERNEST. The tide, Crichton, is a postman who calls at our island twice a day for letters. Ha, ha!

CRICHTON. [*After a pause.*] Thank you, sir.

> [*He retires through the grass out of sight* R. *up stage.*

ERNEST. [*Crossing to the rocks* L. *and mounting them.*] Poor Crichton! I sometimes think he is losing his sense of humour. [*He pulls Lady Agatha up.*] Come along, Agatha.

> [*They exit along the rocks up* L. *Treherne disappears behind the hut* R.

LADY CATHERINE. How horribly still it is.

LADY MARY. It is best when it is still.

LADY CATHERINE. [*In a fearful voice.*] Mary, I have heard that they are always still just before they *jump*!

LADY MARY. Don't!

> [*Distant chopping is heard—eight loud chops. Lady Mary and Lady Catherine rise fearfully and move* C. *Lady Catherine goes* R., *screams and runs back to Lady Mary.*

Ah! it is only Crichton knocking down trees.

LADY CATHERINE. [*Taking her hand and pulling her to* R.] Mary, let us go and stand beside him.

LADY MARY. Let a servant see that I am afraid!

LADY CATHERINE. [*Going.*] Don't then, but remember this, dear—— They often drop on one from above. Mr Treherne! Mr Treherne!

> [*Exit Lady Catherine up* R.C. *and off* R. *in the direction of the knocking. Lady Mary looks round, moves* L., *creaking sound makes her start and run quickly to* R.

LADY MARY. Crichton! Crichton!

> [*Crichton forces his way through the* R. *undergrowth at the back, carrying a cutlass.*

CRICHTON. Did you call, my lady?

> [*Treherne is seen cutting grass at the back* R.

LADY MARY. [*Concealing her agitation.*] I? [*She crosses to* L.C.] Why should I? Why should I call?

CRICHTON. My mistake, your ladyship. If you are afraid of being alone, my lady——

LADY MARY. [*Turning.*] Afraid? Certainly not. You may go.

> [*She moves to* R.C. *and sits.*

CRICHTON. I must clear away this grass, at any rate.

> [*Treherne cuts grass at the back from* C. *to* L. *Crichton crosses up* L.C. *and starts cutting down grass. Lady Mary takes off oilskin coat and sou'wester and fans herself,*

> *looking at Crichton. When he has made three cuts she speaks.*

LADY MARY. I wish, Crichton, you could work without looking so hot.

CRICHTON. [*Who is perspiring.*] I wish I could, my lady.
> [*Putting the grass out in heap down* L.C.

LADY MARY. It makes me hot to look at you.

CRICHTON. Strange, for it almost makes me cool to look at your ladyship.   [*He goes up, cutting more grass.*

LADY MARY. Anything I can do for you in that way, Crichton, I shall do with pleasure.
> [*Treherne moves out of sight, up* L.

CRICHTON. Thank you, my lady.

> [*Lady Mary looks round at the loneliness, leans on the bucket and sobs. Crichton stops working, and comes to her down* C.

Don't give way. Things might be worse, my lady.
> [*The sound of the sea dies away.*

LADY MARY. [*In real anguish.*] My poor father!

CRICHTON. If I could have given my life for his——

LADY MARY. You did all a man could do. Indeed, I thank you, Crichton. [*With some real admiration.*] You *are* a man.

CRICHTON. Thank you, my lady. [*He starts working again up* C.

LADY MARY. [*In anguish.*] But it is all so awful, Crichton. Is there any hope of a ship coming?

CRICHTON. [*Stops work—after hesitation—brightly.*] Of course there is, my lady.   [*He resumes work.*

> [*Lady Mary sees that he is saying this simply to comfort her.*

LADY MARY. [*Rises.*] Don't treat me as a child. [*She crosses up* L.C.] I've got to know the worst and face it. Crichton, the truth.

CRICHTON. [*Dropping a pace or two down* R.C.] We were driven far out of our course, your ladyship. I fear some distance from the track of commerce.

LADY MARY. [*Turns away.*] Thank you. I understand.

> [*She is courageous but has a great struggle to control herself; she gives way to tears then pulls herself together.*

CRICHTON. [*Who has been watching her, moving to* C.] You *are* a good plucked 'un, my lady!

LADY MARY. [*Moving down* L.] I shall try to be—— [*She stops and turns to him.*] Crichton, how dare you!

CRICHTON. I beg your ladyship's pardon, but you are! [*Laughingly.*] And until a ship does come up we three men are going to do our best for you ladies.

[*He goes up and cuts the grass* R.C.

LADY MARY. Three men? Mr Ernest does no work.

CRICHTON. [*Cheerily.*] He will, my lady.

LADY MARY. I doubt it.

CRICHTON. No work—no dinner will make a great change in Mr Ernest.

LADY MARY. [*Going up a little* C.] No work—no dinner! When did you invent that rule, Crichton?

CRICHTON. [*Still cheery.*] I didn't invent it, my lady. I seem to see it growing on the island.

LADY MARY. Crichton, your manner strikes me as curious.

[*Crichton stops work.*

CRICHTON. [*Distressed.*] I hope not, your ladyship.

LADY MARY. You are not implying anything so unnatural I presume, as that if I and my sisters don't work there will be no dinner for *us*.

[*Crichton throws down the cutlass* R., *takes another bundle of grass and throws it off* R., *picks up the cutlass and goes up* L., *cutting the remaining grass.*

CRICHTON. [*During the above, after a tiny pause.*] If it is unnatural, my lady, that is the end of it.

LADY MARY. If! [*Crossing to* R.C. *and turning to face up* L.] Now I understand! The perfect servant at home holds that we are all equal now. I see!

CRICHTON. [*Up* L.C.; *hurt.*] My lady! Can you think me so inconsistent?

LADY MARY. That *is* it.

CRICHTON. [*Taking a pace down* C.] My lady, I disbelieved in equality at home because it was against nature, and for that same reason I as utterly disbelieve in it on an island.

[*He goes on cutting grass, moving up* R.

LADY MARY. Thank you, Crichton. I apologize.

[*She moves to the low rocks* L.C.

CRICHTON. [*Working a little down* R.C.] There must always, my lady, be one to command and others to obey.

[*He resumes work.*

LADY MARY. [*Satisfied.*] One to command—others to obey

[*She turns suddenly and goes quickly to Crichton, looking into his face.*] Crichton!

CRICHTON. [*Looking up.*] What is it, my lady?

[*Lady Mary backs, still watching, off up* L.C. *behind the rocks. Crichton drops the cutlass, looks after Lady Mary, then goes up* R. *for sticks, crosses down to* R. *of the fire and puts some more on. Eliza, now generally known as Tweeny, comes on singing from up* L. *behind the rocks and runs down to* L. *of the tripod.*

TWEENY. [*Showing coconuts in her skirt.*] Look what I found!

CRICHTON. Coconuts! Bravo!

TWEENY. They grow on trees!

CRICHTON. Where did you think they grew?

TWEENY. [*Making a gesture.*] I thought as how they grew in rows on top of little sticks.

CRICHTON. [*Pained.*] Oh, Tweeny, Tweeny!

TWEENY. [*Anxiously.*] Have I offended of your feelings again, sir?

CRICHTON. A little.

[*He rises and crosses up* R.C. *for sticks and comes down to the fire again—kneeling there.*

TWEENY. [*In an outburst, throws down the coconuts.*] I'm full o' vulgar words and ways, and though I may keep them in their holes when you are by, as soon as I'm by myself out they come in a rush like beetles when the house is dark.

[*Gestures of distress from Crichton.*
[*Crossing to the rocks* L.C., *putting one foot on them and breaking small twigs which she has picked up.*] I says them gloating like, in my head—'Blooming', I says, and 'All my eye!' and 'Ginger' and 'Nothink' and 'Shut yer mug!' and all the time we was being wrecked I was praying to myself: 'Please the Lord it may be an island as it's natural to be vulgar on!'

CRICHTON. Oh!

[*He flings up his hands—Tweeny becomes patheticc.*
TWEENY. That's the kind I am, sir. [*Sitting.*] You'd better give me up.

CRICHTON. [*Rising and crossing to above her.*] I won't give you up. It is strange indeed that one so common should attract one so fastidious, but so it is. There is something about you, Tweeny. [*A pause.*] There is a *je ne sais quoi* about you.

TWEENY. [*Joyous—rising on her knees and facing him.*] Is there—
is there?—I am glad!

CRICHTON. [*Putting his hands on her shoulders.*] We shall fight
your vulgarity together.

TWEENY. Oh, sir!
[*She rises, singing, picks up coconuts and puts them* L.

CRICHTON. [*Crossing to above the fire.*] Bring me some grass,
Tweeny, some very dry grass.
[*Tweeny gets grass and holds it while he takes out a lens and
focuses the sun's rays on to it.*

TWEENY. What are you going to do?

CRICHTON. Light a fire.

TWEENY. What a funny way to light a fire.

CRICHTON. It may be funny, Tweeny, but it lights it all the
same. Now get your head out of the way, I don't want to light
that.
[*When the grass lights, they both blow, and Tweeny puts it
under the fire.*

ERNEST. [*Heard outside.*] Come along, Agatha, it's all right,
don't be afraid.
[*Tweeny rises, goes up* C. *and looks off. Ernest rushes on* L.
below the rocks, followed by Lady Agatha—both excited.
Danger! Crichton, a tiger-cat!
[*He crosses to* R.C., *followed by Lady Agatha on his* L.

TWEENY. Aha!   [*She moves down* C. *a little.*

CRICHTON. [*Who is standing down* R.C.] Where? [*He gets the
cutlass.*] My God! The ladies!   [*He crosses to the rocks* L.C.

LADY AGATHA. [*Up* R.C.] It is at our heels.

ERNEST. [*Down* R.] Look out, Crichton!

CRICHTON. Quiet!
[*Lady Mary and Lady Catherine enter up* L. *above the rocks,
followed by Treherne. They group up* C. *and* R.C.
[*Speaking over his shoulder.*] Mr Ernest says he was chased by
a tiger-cat.
[*Lady Mary and Lady Catherine run into the hut up* R. *Lady
Agatha and Tweeny retreat to the lower end of the hut.
Ernest comes in to* R.C. *with a big stick and Treherne, who
has gone up* R.C. *for a hatchet, comes to* C. *Crichton waits
at the edge of the rock* L.C. *All are watching towards
down* L.

ERNEST. It will be on us in a moment! Whish!

> [*Bus. with the stick.*
> [*Heavy breathing is heard off down* L.

TREHERNE. [*Who has suddenly seen the grass down* L. *moving.*] The grass is moving—listen!

> [*The breathing is louder. The girls suppress little cries. All are tense. Lord Loam crawls through the long grass down* L., *rises, and staggers, assisted by Crichton, to the bucket, where he sits exhausted.*

LORD LOAM. Oh . . . thank Heaven!

> [*The others regroup. The girls run down to Lord Loam with cries of relief and sympathy. Lady Catherine comes down on his* R. *Lady Agatha runs across, kisses him and settles on his* L. *Lady Mary comes down by Lady Catherine and kneels above and slightly on his* R. *Treherne and Ernest come in to* R.C. *while Crichton stands above and slightly* L. *of the group. Tweeny has come in a little down* R. *During this, the following lines are almost simultaneous:*

LADY MARY. Father!

LORD LOAM. Mary—Agatha! Oh dear, my dears! My dears—oh, dear!

LADY MARY. Darling!

LADY AGATHA. Dear Father!

LADY CATHERINE. Thank Heaven!

> [*As Ernest and Treherne come forward and shake hands, the girls fuss round Lord Loam.*

TREHERNE. Glad to see you, sir.

> [*He shakes hands and moves up* C., L. *of the group.*

ERNEST. [*Shaking hands very profusely.*] Uncle—Uncle! Dear old Uncle . . .

TREHERNE. [*Tactlessly.*] Ernest thought you were a tiger-cat.

LORD LOAM. [*Dropping his hand quickly.*] Oh, did you! I knew you at once. I knew you by the way you ran.

CRICHTON. [*Coming down* L.C., *and touching his cap.*] My lord, I am glad, glad!

ERNEST. [*Down* R.] But you are also idling, Crichton. [*He sits on the ground down* R.] We mustn't waste time—to work, to work.

CRICHTON. [*After looking at him.*] Yes, sir.

> [*He crosses up to the hut and disappears.*

TREHERNE. Ernest, you be a little more civil. Crichton, let me help.

[*He crosses* R., *above the group to the hut and exits up* R., *after Crichton.*

TWEENY. [*Who has come down* R.C.] Oh, sir! Oh, sir!

[*She bobs to Lord Loam and crosses off* R., *through the hut.*

LORD LOAM. [*Seeing the pot.*] Is that—but I suppose I'm dreaming again. [*Timidly.*] It isn't by any chance a pot on top of a fire, is it?

LADY MARY. Indeed it is, dearest. It is our supper.

LORD LOAM. [*Rising.*] I have been dreaming of a pot on top of a fire for two days. [*He goes to it, touches it.*] —It's real! [*Timidly, turning to Mary.*] There's nothing in it, is there?

ERNEST. Sniff, Uncle.

LORD LOAM. [*Awestruck, after sniffing.*] It smells of onions! You don't mean to say there's an onion grove on the island?

LADY MARY. They came from the yacht.

LORD LOAM. From the yacht? Did Crichton——?

LADY CATHERINE. He swam back to her twice before she went to pieces.

LADY AGATHA. And the last time he was nearly drowned.

ERNEST. [*Rising.*] And for what? [*He moves across up* L.C. *and turns.*] Onions! Pooh, onions are all very well in their way, but he wasted a lot of time bringing away a lot of useless truck. [*Coming down a little at* L.C.] Electric batteries, wires and all that rubbish, he loaded up a raft with them, and not a single bottle of Pommery or a tin of sardines, to say nothing of some very expensive neckties hanging in full view in my stateroom!

LADY CATHERINE. [*Coming down to* C. *and attracting the others' attention.*] Father—you have boots!

LADY MARY. So he has.

LORD LOAM. Of course I have.

[*He sits on the bucket again. Lady Catherine on his* L., *and Lady Agatha on his* R., *sit on the grass watching the boots. Lady Mary stands behind.*

ERNEST. [*Signing to her to be quiet.*] You are actually wearing boots, Uncle. It's very unsafe, you know, in this climate.

LORD LOAM. Eh! What!

ERNEST. We have all abandoned them, you observe. The blood —the arteries, you know.

[*Lord Loam lifts his foot—Ernest kneels below and on his left, and tries to take them off.*

Lord Loam. I hadn't a notion.

Ernest. [*Easing the left boot.*] Oh Lord, yes!

Lady Mary. Father, he is trying to get your boots from you.

Lord Loam. [*Pulling both feet away.*] Ernest!

Lady Mary. There is nothing in the world we wouldn't give for boots.

Ernest. [*Rising.*] I only wanted the loan of them.

Lady Agatha. [*Cuddling on to Lord Loam's R., kneeling near Lord Loam.*] If you lend them to anyone, it will be to us, won't it, Father?

Lord Loam. [*Puts his arms around her.*] Certainly, my child.

Ernest. Oh, very well. [*Turning up* C.] I don't want your boots. [*Turning down again.*] You don't think you could spare me *one* boot, Uncle?

Lord Loam. I do not.

Ernest. Quite so. Well, all I can say is I'm sorry for you.

[*He crosses up and lies on the rocks* L.C.

[*Lady Mary crosses down* R.C. *and sits in front of Lord Loam.*

Lady Mary. Father, we thought we should never see you again.

Lord Loam. I was washed ashore, my dear, clinging to a hen-coop. How awful that first night was!

Lady Mary. Poor Father!

Lord Loam. When I awoke, I wept. Then I began to feel—extremely hungry. There was a large turtle on the beach. I remembered from the *Swiss Family Robinson* that if you turn a turtle over, he is helpless. My dears, I crawled towards him, I flung myself upon him—— [*He pauses and rubs his leg.*] The nasty spiteful brute!

Lady Mary. You didn't turn him over?

Lord Loam. [*Vindictively.*] Mary, the senseless thing wouldn't wait—I found that none of them would wait.

Lady Catherine. We should have been as badly off if Crichton hadn't——

Lady Mary. [*Quickly.*] Don't praise Crichton!

Lord Loam. And then those beastly monkeys! I always understood that if you flung stones at them they would retaliate by flinging coconuts at you. Would you believe it, I flung a

hundred stones and not one monkey had sufficient intelligence
to grasp my meaning. How I longed for Crichton!

LADY MARY. For us also, Father?

LORD LOAM. For you also. I tried for hours to make a fire. The
authors say that when wrecked on an island you can obtain a
light by rubbing two pieces of stick together! [*Fiercely.*] The
liars!

LADY MARY. And all the time you thought there was no one on
the island but yourself.

LORD LOAM. I thought so until this morning.

> [*The girls are interested.*

I was searching the pools for little fishes, which I caught in
my hat, [*dramatically*] when I suddenly saw before me—on
the sand——

LADY CATHERINE. What?

LORD LOAM. A hairpin.

> [*The girls' hands go to their heads instinctively.*

LADY MARY. A hairpin! It must be one of ours. Give it to me,
Father.

LADY AGATHA. No, it's mine!

LORD LOAM. I didn't keep it.

> [*Disappointed, they draw away from him, kneeling up.*

LADY MARY. Didn't keep it—found a hairpin on an island and
didn't keep it.

> [*They draw away from him, a little farther.*

LORD LOAM. My dears!

> [*They move away still more. By this time Treherne is again
> visible, about the hut.*

LADY AGATHA. Oh, Father, we have returned to nature more
than you bargained for.

> [*Ernest rises and strolls up* C., *looking towards the hut,
> pensively.*

LADY MARY. [*Rises slowly.*] For shame, Agatha. [*She moves to*
L. *of Lord Loam and puts her arms around him.*] Don't mind
her, Father. [*Anxiously looks at the hut.*] Dear, there is something I want you to do at once.

> [*Lord Loam looks up.*

I mean—to assert your position as chief person on the island.

> [*Lady Catherine rises.*

LORD LOAM. But who would presume to question it?

C 184

LADY CATHERINE. [*Crossing down* R.] She means Ernest.

> [*She turns, standing* R. *of, and below, the fire.*

LADY MARY. [*Puzzled and not addressing anybody.*] Do I?

> [*She looks at the hut again.*

LADY AGATHA. [*To Lady Catherine.*] It's cruel to say anything against Ernest.

LORD LOAM. If anyone presumes to challenge my position I shall make short work of him.

> [*Ernest, who has not heard all this, strolls back to down* L.C.

LADY AGATHA. [*Rises.*] Here comes Ernest—now see if you can say these horrid things to his face.

LORD LOAM. [*Confidentially.*] I shall teach him his place at once.

LADY MARY. [*Anxiously.*] But how?

LORD LOAM. [*Chuckling.*] I have just thought of an extremely amusing way of doing it.

> [*Lady Mary crosses to* R. *behind Lord Loam and joins Lady Catherine, watching Ernest.*

Ernest——

ERNEST. [*Loftily, down* L.C.] Excuse me, Uncle, I'm thinking —I'm planning out the building of this hut.

LORD LOAM. I also have been thinking, Ernest.

ERNEST. That don't matter.

> [*With a gesture to indicate his preoccupation.*

LORD LOAM. Eh?

ERNEST. Silence, if you please.   [*He ponders.*

LORD LOAM. I have been thinking that I ought to give you my boots.

ERNEST. [*Turning sharply.*] What!

LADY MARY. Father!

LORD LOAM. [*Genially.*] Take them, my boy.

> [*He holds out his feet—Ernest eagerly pulls off boots and puts them on. The girls cannot understand.*

I dare say you want to know why I give them to you, Ernest?

ERNEST. Not at all. The great thing is I've got 'em, I've got 'em.

> [*He stamps up* C., *triumphantly.*

LORD LOAM. [*Rising and moving up* R.C. *and back to Ernest. Bus. of thorn in his foot.*] My reason is that as head of this little party— [*He gives the girls a knowing look.*]—you, Ernest, shall be our hunter, you shall clear the forests of those savage

beasts that make them so dangerous. [*Pleasantly.*] And now
you know, my dear nephew, why I have given you my boots.
                                       [*He moves away up* R.C.

ERNEST. This is my answer.
 [*He kicks off the boots, flings them to Lord Loam, crosses to* L.
 and puts on his pumps again.
 [*Lady Agatha creeps round, snatches the boots and crosses up*
 C. *and off behind the hut.*

LADY MARY. Father, assert yourself.

LORD LOAM. I shall now assert myself. [*He crosses above the
bucket to* C., *but does not know what to do.*] Call Crichton.

LADY MARY. [*Going to his* R.] Oh, Father!

LADY CATHERINE. [*Moves up* R., *calling.*] Crichton!
                                       [*He moves down* R. *again.*
 [*Crichton enters from behind the hut up* R., *and crosses to below
 and* R. *of the fire.*

ERNEST. [*Standing* L.C.] Crichton, look here——

LORD LOAM. Silence! Crichton, I want your advice as to what I
ought to do with Mr Ernest. He has defied me.

ERNEST. [*Moves towards Lord Loam.*] Pooh!

CRICHTON. May I speak openly, my lord?

LADY MARY. [*Boldly and significantly at* R. *of Lord Loam.*] That
is what we desire.

CRICHTON. Then I may say, your lordship, that I have been
considering Mr Ernest's case at odd moments for the last two
days.

ERNEST. My case?

CRICHTON. Since we landed on the island, my lord, it seems
to me that Mr Ernest's epigrams have been particularly
brilliant.

ERNEST. [*Gratified.*] Thank you, Crichton.

CRICHTON. But I find—I seem to find it growing wild, my lord,
in the woods, that sayings which might be justly admired in
England are not much use on an island. I would therefore
most respectfully propose that henceforth every time Mr
Ernest favours us with one of his epigrams his head should
be immersed in a bucket of cold spring water.

LORD LOAM. Serve him right.

ERNEST. [*Crosses up to* L. *of Lord Loam.*] I should like to see you
try to do it, Uncle.

CRICHTON. My feeling, my lord, is that at the next offence, I should conduct him to a retired spot, where I shall proceed to carry out the undertaking in as respectful a manner as is consistent with a thorough immersion.

> [*His manner, though quiet, is firm—he evidently means what he says.*

LADY MARY. Father, you must not permit this. Ernest is your nephew.

LORD LOAM. [*Seeing the point.*] After all, he is my nephew, Crichton, and as I am sure he now sees that I am a strong man——

ERNEST. [*Stepping a pace nearer to Lord Loam.*] A strong man! You! You mean a stout man, Uncle. You are one of mind to two of matter. Ha, ha!

> [*Lord Loam turns to Lady Mary. Ernest smiles on seeing he has said a good thing, then starts as he observes that Crichton is quietly pulling up his sleeves. Ernest is alarmed and backs to L. Lord Loam makes no movement. Crichton walks towards Ernest. Ernest addresses Crichton with feeble firmness.*

Sit down, sir.

CRICHTON. [*In the tone of one not to be trifled with.*] Is it to be before the ladies, Mr Ernest, or in the privacy of the wood?

> [*He fixes Ernest with his eye.*
> [*Ernest is cowed.*

Come! [*He crosses up* C., *and turns.*] Come!

ERNEST. [*Affecting bravado.*] Oh, all right! [*He moves* C.] I don't care!

CRICHTON. [*As Ernest reaches the bucket.*] Bring that bucket.

> [*He crosses up* C. *and off* R. *behind the hut, followed by Ernest, who takes the bucket. Treherne has come down to Lady Catherine* R.

LORD LOAM. [*Following them up* C., *then turning back to* C.] I'm sorry for him, but I had to be firm.

LADY MARY. [*Distressed.*] Oh, Father, it wasn't you who was firm. Crichton did it himself.

LORD LOAM. Bless me—so he did.

LADY MARY. [*Crosses up to him* C.] Father, be strong.

LORD LOAM. You can't mean that my faithful Crichton——

LADY MARY. [*Crossing below and to* L. *of Lord Loam.*] Yes, I do.

TREHERNE. [*Coming up to* R.C.] Lady Mary, I stake my word that Crichton is incapable of acting dishonourably.

LADY MARY. [*Puzzled, yet with conviction—crossing up* L. *of the tripod, resting one hand on it.*] I know that—I know it as well as you. Don't you see that that is what makes him so dangerous?

TREHERNE. By Jove—I—I believe I catch your meaning.

LADY CATHERINE. [*Going up* R. *and looking off.*] He is coming back.

LORD LOAM. [*Struck with the idea.*] Then let us all go into the hut.

  [*Lady Mary hands him his sou'wester which he took off and put by the bucket.*

Just to show him at once that it is our hut.

  [*He crosses up* C. *and towards* R., *followed by Lady Mary and Lady Catherine. Lady Catherine enters the hut and stands at the window, Lord Loam and Lady Mary remain at the door, Treherne gets on the roof.*

LADY MARY. Father, I implore you, assert yourself now and for ever.

LORD LOAM. I will.

LADY MARY. And please don't ask him how you are to do it.

LORD LOAM. Mary!

  [*Crichton enters from up* R., *at* C., *and crosses to* L. *of the tripod, kneeling at it.*

Have you carried out my instructions, Crichton?

CRICHTON. [*Putting sticks on the fire.*] Yes, my lord.

  [*Enter Ernest with the bucket from up* R., *at* C., *leaves it by the hut, crosses up and sits on the rocks* L. *Lady Agatha follows him on and sits beside him, below him, and helps to dry his head with palm leaves, etc.*

LADY AGATHA. It's infamous!

LORD LOAM. *My* orders, Agatha!

LADY MARY. [*Encouraging him.*] Father!

LORD LOAM. Before I give you further orders, Crichton——

CRICHTON. Yes, my lord.

        [*He rises, moves* L., *picking up twigs for the fire.*

LORD LOAM. [*Delighted—to the others.*] Pooh! It's all right.

LADY MARY. No.

LORD LOAM. [*Crossing to* L.C., *followed by Lady Mary, on his* R.]

Well, well! This question of leadership—what do you think now?

CRICHTON. My lord, I feel it is a matter with which I have nothing to do.   [*He moves down* L. *for more wood.*

LORD LOAM. Excellent! Mary! That settles it, I think.

LADY MARY. It seems to, but——

CRICHTON. [*Below the rocks* L., *picking up twigs.*] It will settle itself naturally, my lord, without any interference from us.

   [*The others exchange disturbed glances, turning to each other, very concerned.*

LADY MARY. Father!

LORD LOAM. [*Crosses down* L.C.] It settled itself long ago, Crichton, when I was born a peer, and you, for instance, were born a servant.

CRICHTON. Yes, your lordship, that was how it all came about quite naturally in England. We had nothing to do with it there and we shall have as little to do with it here.

   [*He crosses Lord Loam to* R. *of the fire, after breaking a twig on his knee.*

TREHERNE. [*Relieved, on the roof.*] That's all right.

                              [*Crichton is about to kneel.*

LADY MARY. One moment. [*She crosses to the tripod and puts her hand on it.*] In short, Crichton, his lordship will continue to be our natural head.

CRICHTON. I daresay, my lady; I daresay.   [*Kneeling.*

LADY CATHERINE. [*Through the window.*] But you must *know.*

CRICHTON. [*Turning to face her.*] Asking your pardon, my lady, one can't be sure—on an island.

   [*Lady Mary moves to Lord Loam, encouraging him to speak.*

LORD LOAM. Crichton, I don't like this.

CRICHTON. [R.C., *rising.*] The more I think of it, your lordship, the more uneasy I become. When I heard, my lord, that you had left that hairpin behind——   [*He shakes his head.*

   [*Lady Catherine has come out of the hut. Lady Agatha is standing on the lower edge of the rock, above and to* R. *of Ernest.*

LORD LOAM. One hairpin among so many would only have caused dissension.

CRICHTON. Not so, my lord. From one hairpin we could have made a needle—with that needle we could out of the skins have

sewn trousers of which your lordship is very much in need.
[*He kneels again.*] Indeed, we are all of us in need of them.

ALL. All!

> [*Lady Catherine moves to* R. *of Lady Mary at* L.C.; *Lady
> Agatha jumps down and comes on Lady Mary's* L., *who
> puts protecting arms around them.*

CRICHTON. On an island, my lady.

LADY AGATHA. Father!

> [*Treherne jumps off the roof and stands down* R.

CRICHTON. [*In agony.*] My lady! If nature does not think them
necessary you may be quite sure she will not ask you to wear
them. But among all this undergrowth——

LADY MARY. [*Coming down* L. *and turning to face the others.*]
Now you see this man in his true colours.

LORD LOAM. Crichton, you will either this moment say 'Down
with nature' or——

CRICHTON. [*Scandalized.*] My lord!

LORD LOAM. [*Loftily.*] Then this is my last word to you—take
a month's notice.

> [*The sound of the sea is heard again. Lord Loam motions his
> daughters, who, in silence, file into the hut, Lady Catherine
> first, Lady Agatha second, Lady Mary third. Lady Mary
> goes to the window. Lord Loam follows and stands at the
> door. Ernest is now sitting on a high rock* L.

CRICHTON. [*In great distress—crosses up to* L.C.] Your lordship,
the disgrace——   [*He turns to face* R.

> [*The sea effect continues until the end of the Act.*

LORD LOAM. [*As if to bar his entrance to the hut.*] Not another
word—you may go.

LADY MARY. [*Through the window.*] And don't come to me,
Crichton, for a character.

ERNEST. Aren't you all forgetting that this is an island?

> [*They are all taken aback. Lord Loam, at a loss, turns to Mary
> for aid.*

LADY MARY. [*Coming out of the hut to* C.] It makes only this
difference—that you may go at once, Crichton, to some other
part of the island.

> [*Crichton moves back to down* R. *in silence, drops the twigs, then
> turns and takes off his hat. The scene has become slowly
> darker, the sunset tints fading.*

CRICHTON. My lady, let me work for you.

LORD LOAM. Go!

CRICHTON. [*Moving up* R.C.] You need me, you need me sorely, my lord.

> [*They all look at Crichton, then at Lady Mary.*

I—I can't desert you—I won't!

LADY MARY. [*Moving down* L.C.] Then, Father, there is but one alternative, *we* must leave him.

> [*Crichton comes slowly down to* L. *of the tripod.*

TREHERNE. [*Moving in a little* R.C.] It seems a pity.

LADY CATHERINE. [*Through the window—to Treherne.*] *You* will work for us.

TREHERNE. Most willingly. But I must warn you all that so far Crichton has done nine-tenths of the scoring. I have only managed to help him by keeping my end up.

LADY MARY. [*A pace nearer* C.] The question is—*are we to leave this man?*

LORD LOAM. [*Crossing to the rocks* L.] Come, my dears.

> [*Lady Catherine and Lady Agatha, with the boots under her arm, follow, to the rocks.*

CRICHTON. [*Turning to face them.*] My lord!

LORD LOAM. Mr Treherne—Ernest—get our things.

> [*They hesitate.*

ERNEST. [*Coming down to a lower ledge of rock.*] We—haven't any, Uncle. They all belong to Crichton.

TREHERNE. [*Above and* R. *of the tripod.*] Everything we have he brought from the wreck—he went back to it before it sank. He risked his life.

CRICHTON. Take them, my lord, anything you would care for is yours.

> [*Lord Loam is about to speak.*

LADY MARY. [*Sharply, stops her father.*] Nothing.

ERNEST. Rot! If I could have your socks, Crichton——

> [*Coming down* L. *a little.*

LADY MARY. Nothing! Father, we are ready.

> [*Lord Loam moves up the rocks, followed by the girls.*

CRICHTON. [*Moving to* C.] My lord, I implore you—I am not desirous of being head. You have a try at it, my lord.

LORD LOAM. A try at it!

CRICHTON. It may be that you will prove the best man——

LORD LOAM. Maybe! Come, my children!

> [*They exit* L., *up the rocks.*

TREHERNE. [*Going after the others, but turning up* L.C.] Crichton, I'm sorry, but, of course, I must go with them.

> [*The moonlight is now rising.*

CRICHTON. Certainly, sir! One moment. [*He turns a little down* R.C. *and calls.*] Tweeny!

> [*Tweeny enters down* R., *and he takes her hand.*

Will you be so kind as to take her to the others?

TREHERNE. Assuredly.

TWEENY. But what do it all mean?

CRICHTON. Does, Tweeny; does. [*He kindly passes her over towards Treherne.*] We shall meet again soon, Tweeny. Good night.

> [*Treherne helps her up the rocks and she exits.*

TREHERNE. [*Turning on the lower ledge of rock.*] Good night. I dare say they are not far away.

CRICHTON. They went westwards, sir, and the wind is blowing in that direction.

TREHERNE. Why, what does that matter?

CRICHTON. It may mean, sir, that Nature is already taking the matter into her own hands. They are all hungry, sir. The wind is blowing westward and—[*he lifts the lid*]—and that pot is full of Nature, full of Nature, Mr Treherne. Good night, sir.

> [*The scene has become very dark, but soon the moonlight is brighter, casting a pool of light around the fire and the hut.*

TREHERNE. Good night.

> [*He exits* L. *Crichton stirs the pot again and puts twigs on the fire. The growl of a beast is heard off* L. *Crichton picks up the cutlass and looks cautiously in that direction, moving across* L. *to the long grass. Then he backs carefully to* C., *and lays the cutlass down. Moving to the fire, he takes out his pipe, and fills it with tobacco from various pockets, and lights it from the fire. The leaves rustle. He stirs the pot, replaces the lid, and sits above the fire smoking patiently. Presently Ernest and Lady Agatha re-enter* L., *down the rocks, followed by Lord Loam and then Tweeny. A moment later Treherne follows with Lady Catherine. They all move, a trifle shamefaced, across above the fire and sit in a group around it. Crichton has not moved. He*

is gazing out front, and smoking. The last to arrive is Lady Mary, who seats herself on the lowest ledge of the rocks L.C., *and hides her face in her hands, and cries. Only then does Crichton turn his head to look at her as—*

THE CURTAIN FALLS

Act III

Scene: *The hall of their island home, two years later*

The walls and roof are of stout logs. Across the joists supporting the roof are implements such as spades, etc., all home made. From hooks hang cured hams, etc. Heads of tiger-cats and other animals ornament the walls, and on the wooden floor are several skins.

The back wall, as to the R. *section, is somewhat angled and contains a long low window and a small but higher one at about* C.

The L. *section of the back wall shows a deep recess which is the kitchen. In the centre of this is the fireplace, a section of an old boat serving as a chimney.* R. *of the fire, a small table, stool and a drying rack.* L. *of the fire, a small sink and another stool. Folding screens at either side enable this apartment to be shut off from the rest. The* R. *screen has a serving-hatch at about shoulder height.*

To L. *of the kitchen is an opening which leads on to a passage to other rooms. There are other doors down* R. *and down* L. *respectively.*

R.C., *a wooden settee, home made.* C., *an armchair which may be home made or salvaged from the wreck. At* L.C., *a rough wooden table to seat six persons. Above, below and at either side are roughly made stools, their seats square or triangular but revealing their source of manufacture.*

There is a dresser at L., *a small table at* R., *a low bench or chest below the window up* R.C., *another stool or so, and below the small window up* C., *a contraption like the spokes of a steering-wheel without the rim, set in a frame. This is the lever which will set off the beacon lights.*

The general effect is romantic but quite barbaric.

The time is late afternoon, or early evening, but there is plenty of sunshine streaming into the room.

When the Curtain rises, Tweeny is seated on the settee at R.C., *singing, and plucking the feathers of an armadillo bird and dropping them on to a cloth spread on the floor. She is dressed in*

59

*her maid's dress, carefully mended, though with many patches.
Outside, an unseen person whistles as if to draw her attention.
She turns her head and then resumes her work and singing. The
whistler now appears at the long window. It is Lord Loam,
wearing clothes of leather. He looks into the room cautiously and
then whistles to Tweeny in the manner of an English policeman
whistling to a cook. There is no response.*

LORD LOAM. Tweeny!

TWEENY. [*Without looking round.*] Get away with you!

> [*Lord Loam climbs in through the window opening. He is
> carrying a home-made concertina. He is now the handy
> man about the house, but happy and in gay spirits. He
> dances down to* C., *and then up* L.C., *playing his concer-
> tina and singing.*

LORD LOAM. I'm a chicketty chicketty chick chick! Chicketty
chicketty chee! [*Dancing down* L.C. *and up.*] I'm a chicketty
chicketty chick chick—chicketty, chicketty chee . . .

> [*He stops as a buzzing is heard and a hand-printed card appears
> in the passage opening up* L., *with the word 'SILENCE'
> on it. Lord Loam is cowed, and turns to Tweeny, who
> laughs.*

I thought the Gov. was out!

> [*He crosses quickly to* L., *and puts the concertina on the stool
> below the dresser, and returns to* C. *During this, Tweeny
> rises and puts the bird on the seat* R.C., *crosses to the table,
> opens the drawer, takes out a table napkin and begins to
> set the table. Lord Loam, seeing this, goes* R.C. *and takes
> up the task of plucking the bird.*

TWEENY. [*During the above.*] Well, you see he ain't. If he was to
catch you here idling . . .

LORD LOAM. [*Hastily commencing to pluck the bird—cautiously.*]
What is he doing now?

TWEENY. [*Spreading a cloth on the table.*] I think he's working
out that plan for the hot and cold.

> [*She gets two knives, forks, spoons and goblets, and sets them
> at the top end of the table, evidently for one person.*

LORD LOAM. [*Enthusiastic.*] And he'll manage it too! The man
who could build a blacksmith's forge without tools——

TWEENY. He made the tools.

> [*She is now finishing the business at the table.*

LORD LOAM. Out of half a dozen rusty nails. The saw-mill, Tweeny, the speaking tube—the electric lighting—and look at the use he has made of the bits of the yacht that were washed ashore [*pointing to boat and settee* R.], and all in two years. He's a master I'm proud to pluck for.

[*He hums happily that he's a chicketty chick. Tweeny crosses to him and looks at him in wonder.*

TWEENY. Daddy, you're of little use, but you're a bright cheerful creature for to have about the house.

[*Lord Loam hums on, beaming at her. A slight pause.* [*Getting a stool from* R. *of the table and sitting* R. *of Lord Loam. Curiously.*] Do you ever think—of old times now?

[*Lord Loam pulls his hand across his eyes in a dazed way.* We was all a bit different then.

LORD LOAM. [*Heavily.*] Circumstances alter cases.

[*He resumes the plucking contentedly.*

TWEENY. But, Daddy, if the chance was to come of getting back?

LORD LOAM. [*Contentedly.*] I have given up bothering about it.

TWEENY. You bothered that day, long ago, when we saw a ship passing the island. How we all ran like crazy folk into the water, Daddy, and screamed and held out our arms!

[*They both hold out their arms to an imaginary ship, a little agitated.*

But it sailed away and we never seen another.

LORD LOAM. If we had had that electrical contrivance we have now, we could have attracted that ship's notice. [*Looking at the apparatus above the door* R.] A touch on that lever, Tweeny—

[*He points to it. She rises, crosses round to* R.C., *and gazes at it in wonder.*

—and in a few moments bonfires would be blazing all round the shore.

TWEENY. [*Almost touching the apparatus, then backing away.*] It's the most wonderful thing he has done.

[*She sits on the* L. *end of the seat* R.

LORD LOAM. And then—England—home!

[*He is picturing it in his mind.*

TWEENY. [*Also seeing visions.*] London of a Saturday night!

LORD LOAM. [*Feeling himself in the Upper House—puts bird*

down—rises.] My lords, in rising once more to address this
historic chamber—I feel that——

TWEENY. There was a little ham and beef shop in the Old Kent
Road—as I used to go to——

[*Lord Loam shakes off these visions.*

LORD LOAM. [*Crossing to* R. *of the chair* C. *Ingratiatingly.*]
Tweeny, do you think I could have an egg to my tea?

[*Ernest enters at the window* R.C., *also in leather, carrying two
pails suspended by a pole on his shoulder after the rustic
fashion—one is the bucket, the other a large tree bark
covered with skins.*

ERNEST. [*Standing on the window-ledge.*] What is that about an
egg? Why should you have an egg?

LORD LOAM. [*With hauteur.*] That's my affair. [*He crosses above
the table to* L. *and down.*] I—I—— [*Over his shoulder at the
door* L.] The Gov. has never put *my* head in a bucket.

[*He exits conceitedly* L. *Ernest comes down into the room and
puts the buckets down up* C. *Tweeny rises, crosses* L. *and
puts the lamp on the lower* L. *end of the table. She then
moves the stool* L.C. *back to the* R. *edge of the table.*

ERNEST. [*During the above bus.*] Nor mine for nearly three
months. It was only last week, Tweeny, that he said to me,
'Ernest, the water cure has worked marvels in you, and I
question whether I shall require to dip you any more.' [*Com-
placently.*] Now you know, that sort of thing encourages a
fellow.

[*He moves below the chair* C. *to* R.C. *Tweeny crosses above the
table to* L. *of the chair.*

TWEENY. I will say, Erny, I never seen a young chap more
improved.

ERNEST. [*Turning, at* R.C., *gratified.*] Thank you, Tweeny—
that's very precious to me.

TWEENY. Oh, go on.

[*She crosses up to kitchen and works the bellows, poking the fire.
During the following scene she moves a stool that is* L. *of
the hearth down stage, makes three slices of toast, puts
them in a toast-rack, crosses to the sink and gets a large
and a small shell and starts wiping them with a dish-cloth.
This business takes her from the time she goes up until
Ernest comes and speaks to her later. Treherne enters*

down L. *carrying a small box. He sees Ernest and crosses
sideways, trying to hide it—crosses to* R.]

ERNEST. [*To below the chair* C.] What have you got there, John?

TREHERNE. [*Coming to Ernest above and to* L. *of the chair.*] Don't
tell anybody. It is a little present for the Gov.—a set of razors.
One for each day in the week.

> [*He opens the box and takes one out.*

ERNEST. Shells! He'll like that. He likes sets of things.

TREHERNE. Have *you* noticed that?

ERNEST. Rather.

TREHERNE. [*Down level with Ernest.*] He's becoming a bit
magnificent in his ideas.

ERNEST. John, it sometimes gives me the creeps.

TREHERNE. [*After a glance up* L., *over his shoulder.*] What do
you think of that brilliant robe he got the girls to make for
him?

ERNEST. [*Leaning on Treherne's* R. *shoulder, confidentially.*] I
think he looks too regal in it.

TREHERNE. Yes, but I sometimes fancy that that's why he's so
fond of wearing it. [*He closes the box and crosses* R.] Well, I
must take these down to the grindstone and put an edge on
them.

> [*He exits, reappearing outside the long window a moment later.*

ERNEST. [*Going up to the window.*] I say, John, I want a word
with you.

TREHERNE. [*Stops,* R. *of Ernest.*] Well?

ERNEST. [*In some confusion.*] Dash it all—[*he sits on the window-
sill*]—you know you're a parson.

TREHERNE. [*Leaning over the sill.*] One of the best things the
Gov. has done is to insist that none of you forget it.

ERNEST. [*Looking up at Treherne.*] Then—would you—John?

TREHERNE. What?

ERNEST. Officiate at a marriage ceremony, John?

TREHERNE. [*Straightening up, surprised.*] Now that's really odd.
[*He climbs back into the room and sits on the window-sill,* R. *of
Ernest.*

ERNEST. Seems to me it's very natural. And if it's natural, John,
it's right.

TREHERNE. I mean, that same question has been put to me today
already.

Ernest. [*Eagerly.*] By one of the women?

Treherne. Oh no! They all put it to me long ago! This time it was by the Gov. himself.

Ernest. By Jove. [*Admiringly.*] I say, John, what an observant beggar he is!

Treherne. Ah! You fancy he was thinking of you?

Ernest. I do not hesitate to affirm, John, that he has seen the lovelight in my eyes. You answered——?

Treherne. I said yes, I thought it would be my duty to officiate if called upon.

Ernest. You're a brick.

Treherne. But I wonder whether he was thinking of you?

Ernest. Make your mind easy about that.

Treherne. Well, well. Agatha is a very fine girl.

Ernest. Agatha? What made you think it was Agatha?

Treherne. Man alive, you told me all about it soon after we were wrecked.

Ernest. Pooh! [*He rises and crosses to* c.] Agatha's all very well, John, but I'm flying at bigger game.

Treherne. [*Following him down on his* R.] Ernest, which is it?

Ernest. [*Down* L. *of and below the* c. *chair.*] Tweeny, of course.

Treherne. Tweeny! [*After a glance up to the kitchen. Reprovingly.*] Ernest, I hope her cooking has nothing to do with this.

Ernest. Her cooking has very little to do with it, although her light pastry, eh, John?

> [*They both show their appreciation of it.*

Treherne. But does she return your affection?

Ernest. Yes, John, I believe I may say so—I am unworthy of her, but I think I have touched her heart.

Treherne. Some people seem to have all the luck. As you know, Catherine won't look at me.

Ernest. I'm sorry, John.

Treherne. It's my deserts, I'm a second-rater——

> [*He offers his hand, which Ernest grasps.*

Well, my heartiest good wishes, Ernest.

> [*He crosses to the door* R.

Ernest. [*To* R. *of the chair* c.] How's the little black pig today?

Treherne. [*Turning at the door.*] He's begun to eat again.

> [*He exits* R. *and is seen disappearing beyond the window.*

Ernest. [*Turning a little up* c.] Are you very busy, Tweeny?

TWEENY. [*In the kitchen,* L. *end, cleaning shells.*] There's always work to do, but if you want me, Ernest——

ERNEST. [*Turning to face her.*] There's something I should like to say to you if you don't mind listening.

TWEENY. [*Good-naturedly.*] Willingly.

[*She comes down with her work and sits on a stool,* R. *of the table* L.C.

ERNEST. [*Coming slowly down on her* R., *above her.*] What an ass I used to be, Tweeny.

TWEENY. [*Cleaning the shell briskly.*] Oh, let bygones be bygones.

ERNEST. [*Fingering the chair* C., *uncertainly.*] I'm no great shakes even now.

TWEENY. We all like you, Ernest—you're so willing, and it was you as made that seat.

ERNEST. [*Glancing at the seat* R.] It might have been better made.

TWEENY. The Gov. says everyone has a gift, and that yours is for carpentering.

ERNEST. [*Coming down level with her.*] I don't say it's a bad seat, but I could make a better. Tweeny, I should like to make some more chairs—and a table—and a tablecloth—and some knives and forks. I have an idea for a sideboard.

[*Tweeny puts the shells and the cloth on the floor, and bends down to tie up a thong of her boot.*

TWEENY. [*Bus.*] I like to hear you. But we're pretty full now—[*pulling at the thong*]—have you thought where we could put them?

ERNEST. Yes. There's that sunny little glade near Porcupine stream.

TWEENY. [*Looking up at him.*] You would put them *there*?

ERNEST. It's a homely spot.

TWEENY. [*She lifts her leg and continues tying her thong.*] But in the open!

ERNEST. I would build a little house round them, Tweeny—and when it was built, I would go with my hat in my hand to a girl I know, and I would say to her—[*he kneels on her* L.]—'I was an ass when you knew me first, and I'm no great shakes even now, but I love you truly, Tweeny, won't you come to my little house?'

TWEENY. [*Rising.*] Oh, Ernest, I wasn't understanding. It's good of you—but I must say—no!

ERNEST. I feared it would be no.   [*He rises.*

TWEENY. I'm that sorry.   [*She turns to him.*

ERNEST. [*Bravely.*] Thank you, Tweeny—it can't be helped.
                    [*He turns and goes up* R.C.

TWEENY. No!   [*She goes down* L. *and covers up the parrot.*

ERNEST. [*Turning and crossing back to above the table* L.C.] Tweeny,
we shall be disappointing the Gov.

TWEENY. [*Turning.*] What's that?

ERNEST. He wanted us to marry.

TWEENY. [*Half dazed.*] You and me, the Gov.!
    [*She turns to the dresser and buries her face in her hands with
        grief.*
    [*Ernest sighs heavily and leans on the table* L.C. *Someone is
        heard outside, drawing near, singing a gay tune.*
    [*She starts up fiercely.*] That's her, that's the thing what
stole his heart from me! [*She crosses up* C., *to* L. *of the small
window.*
    [*The whistler, who proves to be Lady Mary, appears at the
        window. She is dressed in picturesque boy's garments of
        thin leather, feather leaves, etc., etc., and carries bow
        and arrows, and has a slain buck on her shoulder and a
        couple of ducks.*

LADY MARY. [*Holding up the buck.*] Victory!
    [*Tweeny turns away sourly, comes down to* R. *of the chair and
        picks up the bird and the cloth. Lady Mary throws down
        the buck outside, and jumps in through the window, and
        throws down her hat on the seat* R.

TWEENY. [*Turning up* C.] Drat you, Polly—why don't you wipe
your feet?

LADY MARY. [R.C., *good-naturedly.*] Come, Tweeny, be nice to
me. [*Giving her a hug.*] It's a splendid buck.
    [*Tweeny shakes her off, goes up into the kitchen, with the bird.
        Lady Mary throws the ducks on the small table* R. *and
        takes the bow and quiver off her shoulder.*

ERNEST. [*Coming down* R. *of the table* L.C.] Where did you get
it?   [*He sits on the* L. *side of the table, lower end.*

LADY MARY. [*Moving across above the seat* R., *to* C.] I sighted
a herd near Penguin's Creek, but had to creep round Silver
Lake to get windward of them. [*She hangs the bow and quiver
up on a hook between the windows, standing on a stool.*] However,

they spotted me and then the fun began. [*She jumps down, crosses R. for ducks, crosses again and sits on a stool facing Ernest, pulling it out from the table.*] There was nothing for it but to try and run them down, so I singled out a fat buck and away we went down the shore of the lake, up the valley of rolling stones; he doubled into Brawling River and took to the water, but I swam after him—the river is only half a mile broad there, but it runs strong. He went spinning down the rapids—down I went in pursuit—he clambered ashore, I clambered ashore— away we tore helter-skelter up the hill and down again. I lost him in the marshes, got on his track again near Bread Fruit Wood, and brought him down with an arrow in Fire-fly Grove.

> [*Tweeny has gradually come down and stands between Ernest and Mary—half sitting on the table* L.C.

TWEENY. Ain't you tired?

LADY MARY. Tired? [*She rises.*] It was gorgeous.

> [*She crosses* R., *whistling, picks up the ducks and hangs them on the first hook. Ernest rises and crosses up to the window* R.C.

TWEENY. [*Moving to* C.] I can't abide a woman whistling.

LADY MARY. [*Jumps down.*] Can't you? I like it. [*She whistles.*

TWEENY. Drop it, Polly, I tell you!

LADY MARY. [*Crossing to Tweeny.*] I won't. I'm as good as you are.

> [*They face each other defiantly. Lady Mary goes towards Tweeny, whistling.*

TWEENY. Now, Polly, what do yer want to be so aggravating for? Drop it, I tell yer.

ERNEST. [*Turning.*] I say! I say! Is this necessary? Think how it would pain *him*.

> [*Lady Mary looks at the door* L.C.

LADY MARY. [*Contritely.*] Tweeny, I beg your pardon. If my whistling annoys you, I shall try to cure myself of it.

> [*Ernest returns to the kitchen and sits on the stool* R. *of the hearth. To Lady Mary's surprise Tweeny bursts into tears, crosses and sits on the stool* R. *of the table* L.C.

[*Crossing and sitting on the* L. *arm of the chair* C.] Why, how can that hurt you, Tweeny dear?

TWEENY. Because I can't make you lose your temper!

LADY MARY. Indeed, I often do—would that I were nicer to everybody.

TWEENY. There yer go again. What makes yer want to be so nice, Polly?

LADY MARY. [*Fervently.*] Only thankfulness, Tweeny. [*She throws herself back in the armchair.*] It's such fun to be alive.

> [*A wild cry is heard outside, then Lady Catherine runs to the window and stands with one foot on the ledge, holding in her right hand a rod, and in her left hand some fish. She is in boy's clothes.*

LADY CATHERINE. We've got some ripping fish for the Gov.'s dinner. Are we in time? We ran all the way.

TWEENY. [*Rising and crossing up* R.C.] You'll please to cook them yourself, Kitty, and look sharp about it.

> [*She puts the stool up* C. *back in the kitchen, also picks up the two shells and cloth, and works the bellows.*

LADY CATHERINE. Rather.   [*She jumps into the room.*

> [*At the same moment another wild cry is heard and Lady Agatha enters by the door down* R. *and running to* C. *shows her fish to Lady Mary. Lady Catherine takes her rod and Lady Agatha's and puts them above the dresser* L.

LADY AGATHA. [*Calling.*] Has the Gov. decided who is to wait on him today?

LADY CATHERINE. [*Crossing to the sink in the kitchen with the fish and starting to clean them.*] It's my turn.

LADY AGATHA. [*Going up to below the* R. *side of the kitchen.*] I don't see that.

> [*Tweeny puts down the bellows and turns.*

TWEENY. [*Bitterly—between them.*] It's to be neither of you, Aggy, he wants Polly again.

> [*Lady Mary, with a joyous laugh, rises, and crosses up to above the seat* R.C.

LADY AGATHA. [*Coming to her.*] Polly, you toad——

> [*Lady Mary laughs all the more, and flips her fingers in Lady Agatha's face. Lady Agatha crosses and throws herself full length on the couch.*

TWEENY. [*Coming down towards Mary* C.] How dare you look so happy?

LADY MARY. Tweeny. [*Trying to embrace her, but Tweeny throws her off.*] If there was anything I could do to make you happy also.

TWEENY. Me? [*Recklessly.*] Oh, I'm so happy—— [*She comes down to R. of the table L.C.*] I've just had a proposal, I tell you.
                    [*Lady Mary comes down a little, anxiously.*

LADY AGATHA. [*Jumping up.*] A proposal?

LADY CATHERINE. [*Coming down to C., with the fish, points at Crichton's direction.*] Not—not——
                                                    [*Ernest rises.*

ERNEST. [*Coming to the R. corner of the kitchen.*] You needn't be alarmed, it's only me.
          [*The sisters turn to look up at him. Tweeny faces down stage.*

LADY MARY. Was it you, Ernest?
          [*She crosses to the passage up L. and looks off, then moving to L.C.*

LADY AGATHA. [*Moving up R.C.*] Ernest, you dear—I got such a shock.
          [*She crosses back to the window, jumps up on the sill and picks flowers for the table.*

LADY CATHERINE. It was only Ernest. [*Showing him the fish.*] They are beautifully fresh—come and help me to cook them.
                    [*She returns to the sink, singing.*

ERNEST. [*Looking round and seeing that not one of the four women is taking any notice of him.*] I think you might all be a little sorry for a chap. [*He crosses to L. of Lady Agatha.*] I'm particularly disappointed in you, Aggy. Seeing that I was half engaged to you. I think you might have the good feeling to be a little more hurt.

LADY AGATHA. Oh bother!   [*Picking flowers.*

ERNEST. [*Coming C. and looking round once more—then crossing down to the door L. and turning.*] I shall now go and lie down for a bit.
          [*He exits L. Tweeny moves to R. of the lower end of the table.*

LADY MARY. [*Coming to L. of Tweeny, appealingly.*] Tweeny, as the Gov. has chosen me to wait on him, may I have the loan of—[*she picks up Tweeny's skirt*]—it again?

TWEENY. [*Vindictively—dragging her skirt away.*] No, you mayn't.   [*Backing up stage.*

LADY AGATHA. [*Jumps down from the window-sill, crosses and nudges Tweeny.*] Don't you give it to her.

[*She crosses to the dresser for a vessel, then up to the sink for water, crosses to* L. *of the table again and puts the flowers on it during the following lines.*

TWEENY. [*Backing to* C.] It's mine.

LADY MARY. [*Following Tweeny up.*] You know quite well that he prefers to be waited on in a skirt.

TWEENY. I don't care. [*She replaces the stool by the table* L.C.] Get one for yourself.   [*She turns* R., *but Lady Mary follows.*

LADY MARY. [*Puts her hand on Tweeny's shoulder and turns her round.*] It is the only one on the island.

TWEENY. [*Throwing her off.*] And it's mine.

[*She backs up* C., *and Lady Mary follows. Lady Catherine comes down* C. *Lady Agatha crosses round below the table to* L.C.

LADY MARY. [*Getting in front of her up* C., *threateningly.*] Tweeny, give me that skirt directly!

LADY CATHERINE. Don't!

[*Lady Catherine and Lady Agatha egg Tweeny on, with signs and gestures, behind Lady Mary's back.*

TWEENY. I shan't.

[*Lady Mary advances on Tweeny pugnaciously; their tongues are between their teeth after the manner of women about to struggle—Lady Agatha is backing Tweeny.*

LADY MARY. I shall make you.

TWEENY. Like to see you try.

[*Buzzer and sign.*

They have become loud and speak simultaneously with 'Oh's' and 'Ah's'—suddenly the buzzing is heard and a card appears with the inscription: 'DOGS DELIGHT TO BARK AND BITE.' *All stop, startled. Lady Mary crosses to the dresser for the wreath of green leaves and then down* L. *to the glass, puts it on, Lady Catherine crosses to the sink again, puts the fish down and then to above the table with the toast on a shell and puts it in toast-rack. Lady Agatha crosses to* L. *of the table, gets the menu from the dresser and puts it on the* R. *side of the table. Lady Mary crosses below the table to up* R.C. *Tweeny crosses up to the bellows, then comes down a few steps and looks at Lady Catherine and Lady Agatha. They nod that they are ready. Lady Catherine crosses up and clothes the* R. *door. Lady Agatha*

closes the L. *door. Tweeny also retires into the kitchen.
Lady Mary crosses to see that the table is right—throws
a flower away and puts the one she is wearing in its place
—sounds tom-tom and replaces it, unloops the punkah
and stands like a servant* R. *of the entrance up* L.

NOTE.—*A serving-hole is in the kitchen door for sending dishes
through.*

Crichton enters up L. *from the passage with a book in his hand,
crosses down* L.C., *looks at the table, moves to the chair,
Lady Mary placing it for him. She goes to* R. *of the table
and gets the menu, crosses round to* L. *of him, and hands
it to him. He reads it.*

CRICHTON. Clear, please.

[*Lady Mary crosses up to the hatch, knocks, and Tweeny opens
it. Lady Mary speaks to her, then Lady Catherine hands
soup to Tweeny and she hands it to Lady Mary. Crichton
puts a buttonhole in his coat. Lady Mary crosses to* L. *of
Crichton and puts the soup in front of him, and then goes
up and works the punkah. Crichton takes a spoonful or
two, puts the spoon down and takes a little salt, and then
continues. When he puts his spoon down again, Lady Mary
crosses to* L. *of him and removes his plate. He speaks
without turning round.*

An excellent soup, Polly, but still a trifle too rich.

LADY MARY. Thank you.

[*Lady Mary takes the soup-plate up, and hands it to Tweeny,
who gives her the fish, giving it a finishing touch with a
little parsley. After putting it before Crichton, Lady
Mary returns and works the punkah. Crichton nibbles
the toast.*

CRICHTON. [*While eating.*] Polly, you are a very smart girl.

LADY MARY. [*Bridling in servant manner.*] La!

CRICHTON. And I'm not the first you've heard it from, I'll
swear.

LADY MARY. [*Wriggling shoulders like a servant.*] Oh, Gov.!

CRICHTON. Got any followers on the island, Polly?

LADY MARY. [*Tilting her nose.*] Certainly not.

CRICHTON. I thought perhaps that John or Ernest——

LADY MARY. [*Wriggling conceitedly.*] I don't say that it's for
want of asking——

[*She crosses to down* L. *for a bottle and then up, above the table to* R. *of Crichton.*

CRICHTON. [*During the above bus.—eating.*] I'm very sure it isn't, Polly. [*A silence, in which he goes on eating.*] You may clear.

[*Lady Mary crosses to* L. *of his chair.*

LADY MARY. Thank *you.*

[*She takes the fish plate away. Crichton drinks, meanwhile. Lady Mary gets meat from Tweeny and a dish of vegetables, and crosses* L. *of Crichton, putting meat in front of him. She takes one of the spoons off the table and putting it in the vegetable-dish, holds it for him to help himself, then puts the dish on the dresser, and returns to the punkah.*

CRICHTON. [*Eating.*] Did you lose any arrows today?

LADY MARY. Only one—in Firefly Grove.

CRICHTON. You were as far as that? How did you get across the Black Gorge?

LADY MARY. [*Stops working the punkah.*] I went across on the rope.

CRICHTON. Hand over hand?

LADY MARY. I wasn't in the least dizzy.

[*She works the punkah.*

CRICHTON. [*Moves.*] Ah! You brave girl! [*He sits back agitated over the peril she has been in.*] But you mustn't do that again!

LADY MARY. [*Pouting, coming down* C. *a little.*] It is such fun, Gov.

CRICHTON. I forbid it.

LADY MARY. [*Rebelling.*] I shall!

[*She stops working the punkah and throws the cord aside.*

CRICHTON. [*Turns on her reprovingly.*] Polly! Polly! Polly!

[*He signs to her sternly to step forward—she holds back petulantly—he signs again, and she comes forward sulkily like a naughty child.*

Remember you must do as I say.

LADY MARY. [*In a passion.*] I shan't!

CRICHTON. [*Smiling at her fury.*] We shall see. Frown at me, Polly—there—you do it at once. Clench your little fists, stamp your feet, bite your ribbons——

[*Lady Mary has begun to do all these things before he speaks, so that she seems to be doing his bidding. She is helpless, begins to cry—he is immediately kind.*

You child of Nature—was it cruel of me to wish to save you from harm? Are you angry with me because I couldn't——

LADY MARY. [*Drying her eyes.*] I'm an ungracious wretch. Oh, Gov., I don't try half enough to please you—I'm even wearing —when I know you prefer—[*indicating skirt in kitchen behind her*]—it.

CRICHTON. I admit I *do* prefer *it.* Perhaps I am a little old-fashioned in these matters.

[*Lady Mary sobs.*

Ah, don't, Polly—that's nothing. I know very well that quite as many noble hearts beat in dual garments as in the dwelling-places of the great.

LADY MARY. If I could only please you, Gov.!

CRICHTON. Please me. [*He rises.*] You do please me, child, very much! Very much indeed. [*He sits again.*] No more, thank you.

[*Lady Mary crosses to* L. *of him, above the table, takes the plate and the vegetable-dish off the dresser, gives them through the aperture to Tweeny, crosses to* L., *gets the cruet tray, puts cruets, toast-rack, menu card on it and returns it to the dresser. She then gets a tray and scoop, and scoops the crumbs* L. *of the table. She then crosses to* R., *waits a moment like a servant as Crichton's arm is in the way. He looks up and sees what she means, moves his arm and lets her finish. She then returns the tray to the dresser, gets fruit and a shell, and puts them in front of him. Having done this, she crosses* R. *of the table, pours out wine, then* R. *and turns on the switch of the table-lamp. She then crosses to* L. *of the table again, moves the lamp up towards Crichton and stands, as if washing her hands.*

Polly, there is only one thing about you that I don't quite like.

[*Lady Mary looks up.*

That—action of the hands.

LADY MARY. What do I do?

CRICHTON. So—as if you were—[*he makes a movement*]— washing them. I have noticed that the others tend to do it also.

LADY MARY. [*Archly.*] Oh, Gov.—have you forgotten?

CRICHTON. Forgotten! What?

LADY MARY. That once on a time a certain other person did that!

CRICHTON. [*Surprised.*] You mean myself?   [*Lady Mary nods.* How strange!

LADY MARY. You haven't for a very long time. Perhaps it is natural to servants.   [*She turns towards the dresser.*

CRICHTON. That must be it. [*He rises.*] Polly!

[*Lady Mary turns. He sighs heavily.*

LADY MARY. [*She takes off the wreath, and placing it on the dresser, crosses to below the table.*] You sighed, Gov.

CRICHTON. Did I! [*He crosses up to* C.] I was thinking.

[*Lady Mary crosses to below the chair* R.C. *Crichton then crosses to top of the table at the* R. *edge.*

I have always tried to do the right thing on this island. Above all, Polly, I want to do the right thing by you.

LADY MARY. How we all trust you! That is your reward, Gov.

CRICHTON. [*Moving towards her.*] Oh, Polly, I want a greater reward—— [*Taking her hand—much moved.*] Am I playing the game? Bill Crichton would like always to play the game. If we were in England——! [*He turns* L. *and goes to the table.*

LADY MARY. [*Coming up* C., *above and on his* R.] We know now that we shall never see England again.

CRICHTON. [R. *of the table, facing front.*] I am thinking, Polly, of two people whom neither of us has seen for a long time— Lady Mary Lasenby, and one Crichton, a butler.

LADY MARY. That cold, haughty, indolent girl! Gov., look around you and forget them both.

CRICHTON. [*Moves to* C.] I had nigh forgotten them, Polly. [*He sinks into the chair.*] He has had a chance—that butler—he's had a chance in these years of becoming a man, and he has tried to take it. There have been many failures, but there has been some success, and with it all I have let the past drop away, and turned my back on it. There's something so grand to me in feeling myself a man. That butler seems a far-away figure to me now, and not myself—I hail him, but we scarce know each other—if I am to bring him back it can only be done by force—for in my soul he is now abhorrent to me. [*Speaking more slowly.*] But if I thought it best for you—if I thought it best for you, I'd drag him back—I swear as an honest man I would bring him back to you with all his obsequious ways and deferential airs, and let you see the man you call your Gov. melt for ever into him who was your servant.

LADY MARY. [*Down to* L. *of Crichton.*] You hurt me. You say these things, but you say them—like a king.

CRICHTON. [*Rising.*] A king! A king! I sometimes feel——[*He checks himself.*] I say it harshly, it is hard to say, and all the time there is another voice within me crying——

LADY MARY. If it is the voice of Nature——

CRICHTON. I know it is the voice of Nature.

LADY MARY. Then if you want to say it—very much, Gov.—please say it to Polly Lasenby.

CRICHTON. Polly, some people hold that the soul but leaves one human tenement for another, and so lives on through the ages. In some past existence I may have been a king—who knows? It has all come to me so naturally, not as if I had had to work it out, but as if I remembered. [*He quotes.*]

'Or ever the knightly years were gone
    With the old world to the grave
I was a *king* in Babylon,
    And you were a Christian slave.'

It may have been—you hear me, it may have been.

LADY MARY. [*Who is as one fascinated; backing a pace.*] It may have been.

CRICHTON. I am lord over all—they are but hewers of wood and drawers of water for me—these shores are mine—why should I hesitate? I have no longer any doubt. I do believe *I am* doing the right thing. Polly, dear Polly. [*Crossing to her.*] Dear Polly, I have grown to love you—will you let John Treherne make us man and wife? [*He quotes again.*]

'I was a king in Babylon,
    And you were a Christian slave.'

LADY MARY. [*Bewitched.*] You are the most wonderful man I have ever known, and I am not afraid.

[*Crichton takes her hand and kisses it with emotion—and reverently. There is a pause. He crosses and sits in the chair* R.C. *and motions her to sit on the ground in front of him. She does so.*

I want you to tell me—any woman likes to know—when was the first time you thought me nicer than the others?

CRICHTON. I think, a year ago. We were chasing goats on the Big Slope and you outdistanced us all, you were the first of our party to run a goat down—I was very proud of you that day.

LADY MARY. Gov.! I only did it to please you. Everything I have done has been out of the desire to please you. [*Suddenly.*] The others will be so jealous. [*Anxious.*] If I thought that in taking a wife from among us you were imperilling your dignity——

CRICHTON. Have no fear of that, dear. I have thought it all out. The wife, Polly, always takes the same position as the husband.

LADY MARY. [*Delighted.*] Oh! [*Suddenly.*] I am so unworthy. It was sufficient to me that I should be allowed to wait on you at that table.

CRICHTON. You shall wait on me no longer. At whatever table I sit, Polly, you shall sit there also. [*He holds out a hand.*] Come, let us try what it will be like.

LADY MARY. At your feet?

CRICHTON. No, by my side.

> [*He conducts her to the table and motions her to sit in his chair at the top end. He sits below her and on her left, and they look delightedly at each other, stretching out and touching hands. Lady Agatha has opened the serving-hatch to pass a cup of coffee and is annoyed at what she sees. She taps for Lady Mary to come for the coffee. Lady Mary does not hear. Lady Agatha taps again, and then signs to the others behind the hatch, and the three heads appear, watching indignantly. Then Lady Catherine opens the screen and comes in, switching on the 'chandelier'. This has no effect on the pair at the table. Tweeny hands the tray to Lady Agatha, who brings it down to L. of Crichton.*

[*Not startled, but like one displeased with bad manners.*] Help your mistress first.

> [*The three women are speechless, but Crichton does not notice this. He addresses Lady Catherine vaguely as Lady Agatha serves Lady Mary.*

Are you a good girl, Kitty?

> [*For a moment Lady Catherine cannot find her tongue. Then:*

LADY CATHERINE. I try to be, Gov.

CRICHTON. That's right.

[*Lady Catherine is now* L.C., *above and* R. *of the table, with Tweeny on her* R., *and Lady Agatha has moved above them to stand* R. *of Tweeny. Ernest enters quickly down* L., *but on seeing Crichton, pauses and stands there meekly. Crichton rises and speaks graciously to them all.*

CRICHTON. Sit down! Sit down!

[*He crosses up* C. *as Lady Agatha sits on the seat* R., *Tweeny up* R.C. *by the window, Lady Catherine on a stool* R. *of the table, and Ernest on the stool below the dresser, which he pulls out, first transferring the concertina to the table.*

[*Turning down above and to* R. *of the table.*] Ernest!

[*Ernest rises and stands—Crichton speaks firmly but goodnaturedly.*

You are becoming a little slovenly in your dress, Ernest—I don't like it.

ERNEST. [*Respectfully.*] Thank *you.*   [*He sits.*

[*Crichton resumes his walk up to the kitchen again. Enter at the door* L. *Lord Loam and Treherne* R. *They look in surprise at the situation.*

LORD LOAM. [*Crossing to the top of the table.*] Why—what——?

[*Ernest signs for silence.*

CRICHTON. [*Going up* C.] Daddy, I want you.

[*He crosses and looks into the fire again.*

LORD LOAM. [*Alarmed, crossing up* R.C. *to Tweeny and whispering to her.*] Is it because I forgot to clean out the dam?

[*Crichton crosses down to above the table and pours out some wine in the goblet.*

CRICHTON. [*Holding up the goblet.*] Daddy, a glass of wine with you.

[*Lord Loam moves* C. *in amazement and takes the goblet.*

LORD LOAM. [*Takes goblet.*] Your health, Gov.

[*He is about to drink.*

CRICHTON. [*Holds up goblet.*] And hers!

[*He moves a little up* C.

[*Lord Loam looks to Tweeny. He drinks, all look surprised and the girls disappointed.*

Daddy, this lady has done me the honour to promise to be my wife.

LORD LOAM. [*Astounded.*] Polly?

CRICHTON. [*Puts the goblet down—moves towards Lord Loam.*]

I ought first to have asked your consent—I deeply regret——
But Nature—may I hope I have your approval?

LORD LOAM. *May* you, Gov.! [*Delighted.*] *Rather!* Polly!

> [*He crosses to behind and to her L., and embraces her.*
> [*Tweeny buries her face in her hands and cries quietly.*

TREHERNE. [*Crossing up to R. of Lady Mary.*] We all congratulate
you, Gov., most heartily.

> [*He shakes hands with Lady Mary, who rises and crosses to the
> chair R.C.*

ERNEST. [*Crossing to shake hands with Lady Mary.*] Long life
to you both, sir.

> [*He crosses to the window, sitting on the sill, L. of Tweeny.*
> [*Lord Loam sits on the chair Lady Mary vacates.*

LADY AGATHA. Dear Polly.

> [*Giving her cheek over the back of the chair and then returns
> to the seat R.*
> [*Lady Agatha and Lady Catherine affect to be delighted, Lady
> Catherine crosses, also gives her cheek to Lady Mary and
> crosses back to L. Crichton comes down to above Lady
> Mary's chair C.*

TREHERNE. [*Up L.C.*] When will it be, Gov.?

CRICHTON. [*Questioning Lady Mary, crossing to her.*] As soon
as the bridal skirt can be prepared. [*He comes down R. of the
chair with his back to the audience.*] My friends, I thank you
for your good wishes. I thank you all. [*He crosses up C., L. of
the chair and turns.*] And now perhaps you would like me to
leave you to yourselves. Be joyous. Let there be song and dance
tonight, Daddy, I shall not complain of the noise tonight.
Polly, I shall take my coffee in the parlour—you understand!
[*He crosses to the passage up L.*] And remember, all of you, this
lady is to be treated with as much deference as if she were
already my wife——

> [*Exit Crichton up L. Lady Mary rises, to R. of her chair Lady
> Agatha and Lady Catherine immediately rush at Lady
> Mary and pinch her. She backs up R.C., Lady Agatha
> on her R., Lady Catherine on her L. Lord Loam moves
> up C.*

LADY MARY. [*Rises, backs up C.*] Oh, oh! Father, they are
pinching me.

LORD LOAM. [*Pulling Lady Catherine away.*] Catherine, Agatha, never presume to pinch your sister again. On the other hand she may pinch you henceforth as much as ever she chooses.

[He comes down R. *of the table.*

[Treherne moves L. *of the table. Lady Agatha and Lady Catherine retire up stage. Lady Mary crosses in front of them to the table to get coffee, which she holds ostentatiously before her sisters and exits* L. *up stage, by the passage. Lord Loam moves to the chair* C. *and is drinking his wine. Tweeny has slowly come down* R.C., *and sat on the seat* R. *Ernest comes down to above the table* L.C.

LADY CATHERINE. *[Coming down* L. *of Tweeny.]* Poor Tweeny, it's a shame.

LADY AGATHA. *[Coming down* R. *of Tweeny, and bending over her.]* After he had almost promised *you.*

TWEENY. No, he never did. He was always honourable as could be. 'Twas me as was too vulgar. *[She rises.]* I tell you I'll crack your heads together if you say a word against that man. Out of the way there.

[Tweeny waves Lady Catherine aside and goes to the kitchen. Treherne goes up and comforts her.

ERNEST. *[Coming to behind Lord Loam, draining Crichton's goblet.]* You'll get a lot of tit-bits out of this, Daddy.

LORD LOAM. That's what I was thinking.

ERNEST. *[Turning up to the kitchen.]* I dare say *I* shall have to clean out the dam now.

LORD LOAM. I dare say. *[He jumps up and crosses to the table for the concertina, singing:]* I'm a chicketty chicketty chick chick . . .

[He picks up the concertina and hops across to R., *continuing to sing.*

[Treherne comes down C. *Lady Agatha takes the back and Treherne the front of the armchair and they place it close to the window up* C.

TREHERNE. That's the proper spirit! *[To down* R.C.*]* Kitty!

[He takes hold of her and during the next lines they dance to the music from C. *to* L. *and then to* R. *and back towards the* L. *door, just as Crichton enters.*

ERNEST. *[Wanting to join.]* Tweeny?

TWEENY. *[Sitting on the stool by the fire.]* Not I.

ERNEST. *[Crossing to Lady Agatha.]* Aggy——

[*They dance with the other couple from* R. *to* L. *and back to* R. *as Crichton enters with Lady Mary. At Crichton's appearance Lord Loam stops dead in his playing.*

NOTE.—*Crichton has the feathered mantle on for this entrance —they turn away.*

CRICHTON. No, no, I am delighted to see you all so happy. Go on, go on.

TREHERNE. [R.] They don't like to before you, Gov.

CRICHTON. It is my wish.   [*He moves to below the chair up* C.

[*Treherne crosses to the table. Ernest, at* L., *takes the bottom of the table, Treherne the top, and they place it well* L. *Ernest puts the stool* L. *back against the wall. Treherne puts the stools* L.C. *under the table. Lady Catherine moves the chair at the head of the table to* L., *and stands for Crichton to sit in it. Lady Mary asks Tweeny to join in and she consents. From the time Crichton says* 'It is my wish' *until all are in their places, Lord Loam gives one long chord on his concertina and is sitting on the seat* R. *down stage. All (except Crichton and Lord Loam) go into a dance, of a country type. When the dancing is at its height the boom of a gun is heard, and all stop suddenly as if turned to stone. Ernest runs to the window and stands on the sill looking out.*

TREHERNE. [L.C.] It was a ship's gun. [*He turns to Crichton.*] Gov.!

[*All look to Crichton for confirmation.*

CRICHTON. Yes!

[*He goes up to the small window up* C. *and looks out. Ernest jumps out of the long window followed by Treherne and Tweeny. Lady Agatha holds out her hand to Lady Catherine and they exit* R. *Crichton looks at Lady Mary, who is* C., *then at Lord Loam. Lord Loam is sitting weakly.*

LADY MARY. [*Turning to look out of the window, then crossing to* L. *of her father.*] Father, you heard?

LORD LOAM. [*Placidly.*] Yes, my child.

LADY MARY. [*Alarmed at his unnatural calm.*] But it was a gun, Father!

LORD LOAM. Yes—a gun—I have often heard it. It's only a dream, you know—why don't we go on dancing?

LADY MARY. [*Comes down* C. *facing him—takes the concertina from him.*] Don't you see, they have all rushed down to the beach? Come!

            [*Crichton moves to the long window up* R.C.

LORD LOAM. Rushed down to the beach—yes, always that—I often dream it.

LADY MARY. Come, Father, come!

LORD LOAM. Only a dream, my poor girl.

            [*Crichton comes down* C.

CRICHTON. [C.] We can see the lights within a mile from the shore—a great ship.

LORD LOAM. [*Quietly.*] A ship—always a ship.

LADY MARY. [*Comes behind him, she puts her hand on his shoulder and looks into his face.*] Father, this is no dream.

LORD LOAM. [*Rising and turning to Lady Mary.*] It's a dream, isn't it? There's no ship?   [*He turns to Crichton.*

CRICHTON. [*Down* C., *kindly.*] You are awake, Daddy; there is a ship.

LORD LOAM. [*Crossing and clutching Crichton.*] You are not—deceiving me?

CRICHTON. It is the truth.

LORD LOAM. True—a ship—[*turning away* R.]—a ship—at last!

    [*He staggers out of the room* R. *and goes after the others. Lady Mary gives way, and moves up* R.C.

CRICHTON. [C.] There is a small boat between it and the island—they must have sent it ashore for water.

            [*Mary looks out of the window.*

LADY MARY. [*Huskily.*] Coming in?

CRICHTON. [*Moving up to slightly* R. *of* C.] No—that gun must have been a signal to recall it. It is going back. They can't hear our cries.

LADY MARY. Going away! [*She crosses down* R.C., *to below the seat.*] So near—so near—I think I'm glad.

CRICHTON. [*Affecting cheerfulness—crossing above and* L. *of her.*] Have no fear. I shall bring them back.

LADY MARY. [*Turning to face Crichton.*] What are you going to do?

CRICHTON. [*Taking a step towards her.*] Fire the beacons.

            [*He turns a pace up* C.

LADY MARY. [*Moving up on his* R.] Stop!

[*Crichton turns to her, at* C. *Lady Mary moves a pace towards him.*

Don't you see what it means?

CRICHTON. [*Bravely firm.*] It means—it means that our life on the island has come to a natural end.

[*He takes a pace towards the switch.*

LADY MARY. [*Stopping him—looking around.*] Let the ship go!

CRICHTON. [*Looking at Lady Mary for a moment.*] The old man —you saw what it means to him——

LADY MARY. But I was afraid!

CRICHTON. [*Adoringly, kissing her hand.*] Ah, dear Polly!

[*He turns again towards the switch.*

LADY MARY. [*Catches his arm.*] No!

[*Very kindly but firmly he loosens her hold of him.*

CRICHTON. Bill Crichton has got to play the game.

[*He goes up and turns the lever. She turns up* R., *below the long window and looks out. There is a pause. Then the light of the beacons begins to be seen, the sky is slowly suffused with the glow of it. Then another gun is heard and faint distant cheering and shouts. This is all slowly done, and during that time Crichton and Lady Mary stand, very still, staring out of the window to* R. *He is behind and several paces from her. Presently the sky is very bright from the beacon. Lady Mary turns, without looking at Crichton, crosses slowly down* L. *and sits in the chair set* R. *of the table against the* L. *wall. Crichton then goes up into the kitchen and stares down into the fire. Ernest runs on excitedly outside the window, jumps over the ledge calling 'Polly!'—he sees Lady Mary and goes down to her.*

ERNEST. Polly! The boat has turned back! We're rescued!
[*Above and on her* R.] I tell you—rescued!

LADY MARY. Is it anything to make so great a to-do about?

ERNEST. [*Down a pace.*] Eh?

LADY MARY. [*Rising, and turning to him.*] Have we not been happy here?

ERNEST. [*Crosses and takes spears from the wall.*] Happy—Lord, yes!

LADY MARY. [*Imploringly.*] Ernest, we must never forget all that the Gov. has done for us.

ERNEST. [*Stoutly.*] Forget it! The man who could forget it would be a selfish wretch and a—— [*A sudden thought.*] But I say—this makes a difference.

LADY MARY. [*Quickly, her hand on his left arm.*] No, it doesn't.

ERNEST. [*Thinking of it.*] A mighty difference!

LADY MARY. [*Turning up to the passage up L.*] Oh—you——

[*She exits. Ernest stares after her, then turns towards the windows. In the meantime the light has grown brighter— the cheering is now nearer—Tweeny enters R. excitedly.*

TWEENY. [*Crosses to R. of Ernest at C.*] Ernest, they've landed— they're English sailors—we're saved!

[*She runs down L., and exits.*

ERNEST. [*Staring out of the windows.*] Saved! Saved!

[*He turns quickly and exits down L. Crichton has not moved from the fireplace in the kitchen. Now he turns to face down R. as Lady Agatha rushes on, crosses to the L. door, calls Lady Mary, runs up to the door at the back, calls again, leans on the chair L.C. and cries. Lady Catherine rushes in up R.C. at the window and cries for joy— Treherne following, comforts her. Lord Loam enters R., followed by an Officer, and crosses a little L. of C. Crichton quietly comes down and stands up by the window up C. Two sailors stand outside the windows with lanterns and look in curiously.*

LORD LOAM. [*To the Officer C.*] And here, sir, in our little home itself, let me thank you in the name of us all, again and again and again.

OFFICER. Very proud, my lord! It is indeed an honour to have been able to assist so distinguished a gentleman as Lord Loam.

LORD LOAM. A glorious, glorious day! Let me show you our other rooms. [*He crosses to down L.*] Come, my pets—— [*A pause : then turning at the door down L.*] Come, Crichton.

[*Lady Agatha, Lady Catherine, Treherne and the Officer exit L. down stage. The Sailors go from the window off R. Crichton moves slowly down stage R. of C. Lady Mary comes in softly L. up stage, and stretches out her arms.*

LADY MARY. [*Crosses down a little L. of Crichton.*] Dear Gov.! I shall never give you up.

[*Crichton slowly lets the cloak drop off him to the ground, staring out front.*

Gov.!
      [*She is vanquished—she withdraws slowly backwards to* L.
      *up stage and stands gazing at him. He continues looking
      straight before him, fighting himself. At first he is a strong
      erect figure, but gradually he gets into the humbler bearing
      of a servant, his hands meet and rub together as they had
      done in Act I.*
CRICHTON. [*Beginning to turn slowly towards her.*] My lady!
                              [*He is the butler again.*

CURTAIN

ACT IV

SCENE: *The same as Act I. Early summer evening*
The furniture remains the same, but there are one or two additions.
A large glass case is set L., *between the windows, which is filled*
with curios from the island, including the bucket, suitably labelled.
Other curios, also labelled, are in the china cabinet up C. *There are*
stuffed birds, animals' heads, weapons and other trophies, with
notices showing who destroyed the former or used the latter.
On the R. *settee, towards the* L. *end, sits Lord Loam. He is searching*
the pages of a new book with much gilt on the covers. At his right
side is the concertina. Lady Agatha sits on the stool below the
table L. *of the settee, and Lady Catherine on the stool above it.*
They are in afternoon dress and have newspapers. Ernest is sitting
L. *of the table, near them, looking very complacent. The manner*
of all of them is that of people apprehensive of the door opening
and Crichton walking in.
When the Curtain has risen, and the above state of mind has been
registered, Lady Agatha, after a glance towards the doors up
L.C., *turns to face down stage again and reads from her paper.*

LADY AGATHA. [*Looks towards door* L.—*reading aloud facing the*
audience.] 'In conclusion, we must heartily congratulate the
Hon. Ernest Woolley. This book of his regarding the adventures of himself and his brave companions on a desert isle,
stirs the heart like a trumpet.'
　　[*She puts down her paper and looks round to see what effect*
　　　it has on the others.

ERNEST. [*Looks round at the door* L., *then takes the paper from*
beneath his waistcoat.] Here is another. 　　　[*He gives it to her.*

LADY CATHERINE. [*Reading from her newspaper.*] 'From the first
to the last of Mr Woolley's engrossing pages it is evident that
he was an ideal man to be wrecked with, and a true hero.'
[*Reprovingly.*] Ernest!

ERNEST. That's how it strikes them, you know. [*Looking round*
as before.] Here's another one.

　　　[*He gives her another paper from beneath his waistcoat.*

85

LADY AGATHA. [*Reading from her second newspaper.*] 'There is not much reference to the two servants who were wrecked with the family, but Mr Woolley pays them a kindly tribute in a footnote.' [*She looks at Ernest, then looks at the door.*

LORD LOAM. Excellent, excellent. At the same time, I must say, Ernest, that the whole book is about yourself.

ERNEST. [*High-handed.*] As the author . . .

LORD LOAM. Certainly, certainly. Still you know, as a peer, of the realm—[*with dignity*]—I think, Ernest, you might have given *me* one of the adventures.

ERNEST. I say it was you who taught us how to get a light by rubbing two pieces of stick together.

LORD LOAM. [*Beaming—eagerly.*] Do you—do you? I call that handsome. What page?   [*He searches eagerly in the book.*

[*Enter Crichton quietly up at* L.C., *carrying three evening newspapers. Lady Agatha throws her paper under the table and crosses to* R., *looking up. Lady Catherine throws her paper under the table and crosses to behind the settee* R. *Lord Loam hides his book. Ernest conceals another paper he is just drawing out from beneath his waistcoat. Crichton puts the evening papers on the table* R.C.

[*At last, as if someone had spoken.*] Quite so—quite so.

[*Exit Crichton up* L.C. *There is a sigh of relief and each advances to the table rapidly and picks up a newspaper.*

LADY CATHERINE. Father, the evening papers!

[*All look for the book reviews, and read. Ernest smiles to himself over what he reads, then evidently reads something unpleasant, and dashes the paper to the ground.*

LADY AGATHA. [*Again seated below the table* R.C.] Father, see page eighty-one!

[*Lord Loam tries to find the page. Lady Agatha reads.*

'It was a tiger-cat', says Mr Woolley, 'of the largest size. Death stared Lord Loam in the face, but he never flinched.'

LORD LOAM. [*Searching frantically.*] Page . . . eighty . . . one . . .

LADY AGATHA. 'With presence of mind only equalled by his courage, he fixed an arrow in his bow——'

LORD LOAM. Thank you, Ernest; thank you, my boy.

LADY AGATHA. 'Unfortunately he missed——'

LORD LOAM. Eh?

LADY AGATHA. 'But by good luck I heard his cries——'

LORD LOAM. My cries!

LADY AGATHA. 'And rushing forward with drawn knife I stabbed the monster to the heart.'

[*A pause. Ernest folds his arms. Lord Loam throws his book on the floor. Enter Crichton quietly up R.C., crosses to the cabinet up L. and opens it. They all hide their papers.*

LORD LOAM. Anything in the papers, Catherine?

LADY CATHERINE. No, Father; nothing—nothing at all.

[*Crichton, up L., takes the bucket from the cabinet and puts it on the floor and closes the cabinet.*

ERNEST. The papers! The papers are guides that tell us what we ought to do and then we don't do it. Ha! Ha!

[*Crichton is crossing, up stage, from L. to R., not looking at them, and carrying the bucket in his L. hand as Ernest looks round for approval and sees the bucket. He rises fearfully and follows Crichton to the door up R.C., quite resigned to get a dipping, when the door closes in his face. He staggers back to C., realizing his mistake.*

LORD LOAM. [*Looking across C., at Ernest.*] I told him to take it away.

ERNEST. [*Standing C.*] I thought—— [*He wipes his brow with a handkerchief.*] I shall go and dress.

[*He exits up L.C. with a swagger. The others are uncomfortable.*

LADY CATHERINE. [*Nervously—crosses to behind the settee R. of Lord Loam.*] Father, it's awful having Crichton here! It's like living on tiptoe.

LORD LOAM. While he is here we are sitting on a volcano.

LADY AGATHA. But he is too splendid to divulge anything unless —unless people got suspicious and questioned him. Crichton's one failing is that he simply can't tell a fib.

LADY CATHERINE. [*Moving down R. of the settee.*] Suppose Lady Brocklehurst were to get at him and pump him! She's the most terrifying old creature in England.

LADY AGATHA. [*Rising and going down L.C.*] Don't suppose anything so awful.   [*She moves up towards the table L.C.*

LORD LOAM. [*Tragically.*] My dear, that is the volcano to which I was referring.

[*Lady Agatha turns sharply. Lady Catherine comes in a pace R.C., and both stare at Lord Loam.*

It's all Mary's fault. She said to me yesterday that she would break her engagement with Brocklehurst unless I told him about—you know what.   [*He looks at the door up* R.C.

LADY AGATHA. [*Moving to* R. *of the armchair* L.C.] Is she mad?

LORD LOAM. She calls it common honesty.

[*Lady Agatha turns away impatiently down* L. *and sits on the*
    L. *settee.*

LADY CATHERINE. [*Facing him.*] Father, have you told him?
    [*She sits in the chair down* R.

LORD LOAM. She thinks I have, but—I couldn't. She's sure to find out tonight.

[*He puts his hand unconsciously on the concertina—it squeaks—*
    they all jump up.

LADY AGATHA. Oh!

LADY CATHERINE. It's like a bird of ill omen.

LORD LOAM. I must have it taken away; it's done that twice.

[*Lady Agatha goes up above the table* L.C., *fanning herself.*
    Lady Catherine and Lord Loam sit again. Enter Lady
    Mary up L.C., *in evening dress. She enters swaggering in*
    manly fashion—then sees that she has done so and adopts
    an anxiously ladylike manner.

LADY MARY. [C.] Agatha!

[*She looks around—signs that she wants to be left alone with*
    Lord Loam and moves down L.C.

LADY AGATHA. [*Crossing to up* C.] All right, but we know what it's about. [*She looks at Lady Catherine.*] Come along, Kit.

[*Lady Catherine moves up* C., *turning here and looking at Lady*
    Mary anxiously. Then both girls exit up L.C. *Lady Mary*
    crosses and sits R.C. *on the chair below the table* R.C.,
    crosses the right leg like a boy. She notices this and hur-
    riedly uncrosses it—Lord Loam has not looked up.

LADY MARY. [*With her back half turned to Lord Loam.*] Father!
    [*He doesn't look up.*] Father! [*She whistles sharply to attract*
    him—he starts—so does she—she is in despair.] How horrid of
    me.

LORD LOAM. If you could try to remember.

LADY MARY. I do, but—— [*Sadly.*] There are so many things to remember.

LORD LOAM. [*Sympathetically.*] There are! [*Nervously.*] Do you know, Mary, I constantly find myself secreting hairpins.

LADY MARY. I find it so difficult to go up steps one at a time.

LORD LOAM. [*Staring out front.*] I was dining with half a dozen Cabinet Ministers last Thursday, Mary, and I couldn't help wondering all the time how many of them he would have set to cleaning the dam.

LADY MARY. I use so many of his phrases. And my appetite is so scandalous. Father—

[*Lord Loam looks at her.*
I usually have a chop before we sit down to dinner.

[*Lord Loam nods sympathetically.*

LORD LOAM. As for my clothes—[*wriggling at his collar*—my dear, you can't think how irksome collars are to me nowadays.

LADY MARY. They can't be half such an annoyance, Father, as—— [*Holding up her skirt.*

LORD LOAM. Quite so—quite so. You have dressed early, Mary.

LADY MARY. [*Turns to him.*] That reminds me—I had a note from Brocklehurst saying that he would come a few minutes before his mother as—as he wanted to have a talk with me.

[*Lord Loam rises and moves away* R. *to the fireplace.*
He didn't say what about, but of course we know.

LORD LOAM. [*Turning and crossing to* C.] I—ah——

[*He passes her, nervously.*

LADY MARY. [*Finding it difficult to say—stretches out her hands and catches his arm.*] It was good of you to tell him, Father. Oh, it is horrible to me—[*covering her face*]—it seemed so *natural* at the time. [*She turns down* R.C.

LORD LOAM. [*Petulantly—coming behind Lady Mary and hitting the table.*] Never again made use of that word in this house, Mary. [*He sits on the chair* L. *of the table.*

LADY MARY. [*Turning at* R.C.] Father. Brocklehurst has been so loyal to me for these two years that I should despise myself were I to keep my—my extraordinary lapse from him. Had Brocklehurst been only a little less good—then you need not have told him—my—strange little secret.

LORD LOAM. Polly—I mean Mary—it was all Crichton's fault, he——

LADY MARY. [*Crossing him to* C.] No Father, no—not a word against him. [*She turns at* C.] I haven't the pluck to go on with it—I can't even understand how it ever was—[*moving above the chair* R.C.]—Father, do you not hear the surf? Do you see the curve of the beach?

* D 184

LORD LOAM. [*Staring out front.*] I have begun to forget. But
they were happy days—there was something magical about
them.

LADY MARY. It was glamour. Father, I have lived Arabian
nights. I have sat out a dance with the evening star. [*She sits
on the stool above the table* R.C.] But it was all in a past existence,
in the days of Babylon, and I am myself again. But he has been
chivalrous always. If the slothful, indolent creature I used to
be has improved in any way I owe it all to him. I am slipping
back in many ways, but I am determined not to slip back
altogether—in memory of *him* and *his* island. [*She rises.*] That
is why I insisted on your telling Brocklehurst. [*Crossing down*
L.C.] He can break our engagement if he chooses.

LORD LOAM. But, my dear——

    [*Enter Crichton up* L.C. *and stands below and* R. *of the doors.*

CRICHTON. Lord Brocklehurst.

    [*Lord Brocklehurst enters, crosses* C. *and shakes hands with
    Lord Loam. He then crosses and shakes hands with Lady
    Mary at* L.C. *Crichton, during this, exits up* L.C., *closing
    the doors.*

LADY MARY. Father, dear, oughtn't you to be dressing?

LORD LOAM. [R. *of Lord Brocklehurst.*] The fact is—before I
go—I want to say——

LORD BROCKLEHURST. [*Turning to Lord Loam.*] Loam, if you
don't mind, I wish very specially to have a word with Mary
before dinner.

LORD LOAM. But——

LADY MARY. Yes, Father.

    [*Lord Loam crosses up* R., *and exits, uneasily. Lord Brockle-
    hurst moves to* R. *of* C., *watching him off. He is grave
    and awkward. Lady Mary, strained and nervous, turns
    to below the table* L.C. *Lord Brocklehurst picks up a paper
    nervously.*

I am ready, George.

LORD BROCKLEHURST. [*Putting down the paper.*] It is a painful
matter—I wish I could have spared you this, Mary.

    [*He is agitated.*

LADY MARY. Please go on.   [*She sits on the stool* L.C.

LORD BROCKLEHURST. [*Moving to* C.] In common fairness, of
course, this should be remembered—that two years had elapsed.

You and I had no reason to believe that we should ever meet again.

LADY MARY. [*Gazing down towards* L.C.] I was so lost to the world, George.

LORD BROCKLEHURST. [*Firmly.*] At the same time the thing is utterly and absolutely inexcusable.

LADY MARY. [*Drawing herself up.*] Oh!

LORD BROCKLEHURST. And so I have already said to Mother.

LADY MARY. [*Freezing.*] You have told *her*!

LORD BROCKLEHURST. [*Moving a pace towards her.*] Certainly, Mary, certainly, I tell Mother everything.

LADY MARY. And what *did* she say?

LORD BROCKLEHURST. [*Looking down* R.C.] To tell the truth, Mother pooh-poohed the whole affair.

LADY MARY. [*Amazed—rising.*] Lady Brocklehurst pooh-poohed the whole affair?

LORD BROCKLEHURST. She said, 'Mary and I will have a good laugh over this.'

LADY MARY. [*Furious.*] George! [*Crossing him to* R.C. *and turning.*] Your mother is a hateful, depraved old woman!

LORD BROCKLEHURST. [*Much shocked.*] Mary!

LADY MARY. Laugh indeed! [*She sits on the stool* R.C.] When it will always be such a pain to me.

LORD BROCKLEHURST. [*Crosses to her* L.] If only you would let me bear all the pain, Mary.

LADY MARY. [*Astounded.*] George, I think you are the noblest man—— [*She gives him her left hand, which he takes.*

LORD BROCKLEHURST. [*Caressing her hand and looking away.*] She was a pretty little thing.

[*Lady Mary looks up in astonishment. He releases her hand.* Ah, not beautiful like you.

[*Lady Mary stares. He drops down a pace or two* L.C., *and turns.*

I assure you it was the merest flirtation—there *were* a few letters, but we have got them back. It was all owing to the boat being so late at Calais . . . you see, she had such large, helpless eyes. [*He moves to down* L.C.

[*After a slight pause.*

LADY MARY. [*Controlling her feelings.*] George, when you lunched with Father today at the club——

LORD BROCKLEHURST. [*Moving up* R. *of the armchair* L.C.] I didn't. He wired me that he couldn't come.

LADY MARY. But he wrote you?

LORD BROCKLEHURST. No.

LADY MARY. You haven't seen him since?

LORD BROCKLEHURST. No.

LADY MARY. Then—— [*She rises delighted as she realizes he knows nothing—then suddenly becoming terrible—turns to him.*] George, who and what is this woman?

LORD BROCKLEHURST. [*Coming towards her* C.—*ashamed.*] She was—she is—— Oh, the shame of it! A lady's maid.

LADY MARY. [R.C.] A what?

LORD BROCKLEHURST. [*Looking away* L.] A lady's maid.

> [*Lady Mary waves her handkerchief delightedly, unseen by him—moving down* R.C. *a little.*

I first met her at this house when you were entertaining the servants, so you see it was largely your father's fault.

LADY MARY. A lady's maid. . . .

LORD BROCKLEHURST. Her name was Fisher.

LADY MARY. My maid!

LORD BROCKLEHURST. [*Taking a pace towards her.*] Can you forgive me, Mary?

LADY MARY. [*Moving to him.*] Oh, George, George!

LORD BROCKLEHURST. Mother urged me not to tell you anything about it, but——

LADY MARY. I am so glad you told me.

LORD BROCKLEHURST. You see, there was nothing wrong in it.

LADY MARY. [*Sitting below the table* R.C.] No, indeed.

> [*She is thinking of her own affair.*

LORD BROCKLEHURST. [*Coming near her.*] And she behaved awfully well. She quite saw that it was because the boat was late. I suppose the glamour to a girl in service of a man in high position——

LADY MARY. [*Staring out front.*] Glamour—yes, yes, *that* was it!

LORD BROCKLEHURST. Mother says that a girl in such circumstances is to be excused if she loses her head.

LADY MARY. George, I am so sorry if I said anything against your mother. I am sure she is the dearest old thing.

LORD BROCKLEHURST. *Moving to* C., *and turning there.*] Of course for women of *our* class she has a very different standard.

LADY MARY. [*Feebly.*] Of course. [*She looks away.*

LORD BROCKLEHURST. [*Moving down a little* L.C.] You see, knowing how good a woman she is herself, she was naturally anxious that I should marry someone like her. That is what has always made her watch your conduct so jealously, Mary.

LADY MARY. I know. [*Rising.*] I—I think, George, that before your mother comes I should like to say a word to Father.

LORD BROCKLEHURST. [*Nervously.*] About—this?

LADY MARY. Oh no—I shan't tell him of this. About something else.

LORD BROCKLEHURST. [*Coming to* C.] And you do forgive me, Mary?

LADY MARY. [*Moving towards him.*] Yes—yes—— [*Taking his hand.*] I—I am sure the boat was *very* late, George.

LORD BROCKLEHURST. It really was.
[*Putting an arm round Lady Mary's waist.*

LADY MARY. I am even relieved to know that you are not quite perfect, dear. [*She crosses him to* C., *and then turns.*] George, when we are married we shall try to be not an entirely frivolous couple, won't we? We must try to be of some little use, dear.

LORD BROCKLEHURST. *Noblesse oblige.*

LADY MARY. Yes, yes, I am determined not to be a shirker, George.
[*Lord Brocklehurst looks at her. She turns away as if she feels she is not quite playing the game.*

Except just this once. [*She crosses above the chair* R.C., *and turns—holding out her hand.*] George!
[*Lord Brocklehurst crosses to her and kisses her. She disengages, moves up to the door up* R.C., *and turns there.*

I am so glad she was only a lady's maid.
[*She exits up* R.C., *leaving him happy and relieved. He moves down* R.C. *Enter Crichton* L.C.

CRICHTON. The Countess of Brocklehurst.
[*Lady Brocklehurst enters. She is a very formidable old lady who has also a sense of humour. Crichton switches on some lights and exits up* R.C.

LADY BROCKLEHURST. [*Looking around, seeing no one.* L.C.] Alone, George?

LORD BROCKLEHURST. [*Crosses to* R. *of Lady Brocklehurst.*] Mother, I told her all. She has behaved magnificently.

LADY BROCKLEHURST. Silly boy! [*She turns up to the glass case* L.] So these are the wonders they brought back with them. [*She takes up one.*] Gone away to dry her eyes, I suppose?

LORD BROCKLEHURST. [*Proudly.*] She didn't cry, Mother.

LADY BROCKLEHURST. No? [*She reflects.*] You're quite right—I wouldn't have cried. Cold, icy. Yes, that was it.

> [*At the cabinet, looking at a curio. She brings the curio across to above the table* L.C.

LORD BROCKLEHURST. [*Moving towards her.*] I assure you, Mother, that wasn't it at all. She forgave me at once.

LADY BROCKLEHURST. [*Sharply.*] Oh!

> [*She puts down the curio.*

LORD BROCKLEHURST. She was awfully nice about the boat being late—she even said she was relieved to find that I wasn't quite perfect.

LADY BROCKLEHURST. [*Sharply.*] She said that?

LORD BROCKLEHURST. She really did.   [*He crosses down* L.C.

LADY BROCKLEHURST. I mean I wouldn't. [*She moves thoughtfully to* C.] Now if *I* had said that, what would have made me say it? [*She reflects—her suspicions growing.*] George, is Mary all we think her?

LORD BROCKLEHURST. [*Looking at her.*] If she wasn't, Mother, you would know it!

LADY BROCKLEHURST. Hold your tongue. We don't really know what happened on that island.

LORD BROCKLEHURST. [*Taking a pace or two to* C.] You were reading the book all the morning.

LADY BROCKLEHURST. How can I be sure that the book is true!

LORD BROCKLEHURST. They all talk of it as true.

LADY BROCKLEHURST. How do I know that they are not lying?

LORD BROCKLEHURST. Why should they?

LADY BROCKLEHURST. Why shouldn't they? [*She crosses to* R., *below the settee.*] If I had been wrecked on an island—— [*She reflects.*] I think it highly probable that *I* should have lied when I came back. [*She turns to him.*] Weren't their servants with them?

LORD BROCKLEHURST. Crichton, the butler.

> [*Lady Brocklehurst crosses to* R. *to the fireplace, pauses, rings the bell and moves to the table* R.

Why, Mother, you are not going to——

LADY BROCKLEHURST. Yes, I am—— [R. *of the table, facing him, speaking very pointedly.*] George, watch whether Crichton begins any of his answers to my questions with 'The fact is', because that is always the beginning of a lie.

[*She sits on the settee* R.

[*Lord Brocklehurst crosses* R. *and stands with his back to the fireplace. Enter Crichton up* L.C. *He looks to see who rang —sees Lady Brocklehurst.*

It was I who rang.

[*Crichton crosses to* L. *of the table* R.

So you were one of the castaways, Crichton?

CRICHTON. Yes, my lady.

LADY BROCKLEHURST. Delightful book Mr Woolley has written about your adventures. [*She speaks sharply.*] Don't you think so?

CRICHTON. I have not read it, my lady.

LADY BROCKLEHURST. Odd they should not have presented *you* with a copy.

LORD BROCKLEHURST. [*Coming to* R. *of Lady Brocklehurst.*] The book was only published today, Mother.

LADY BROCKLEHURST. [*Waving him away.*] Sh! [*To Crichton.*] I think you were not the only servant wrecked?

CRICHTON. There was a young woman, my lady.

LADY BROCKLEHURST. I want to see her.

[*Crichton bows, but remains.*

Fetch her up.

[*Exit Crichton up* R.C.

LORD BROCKLEHURST. This is scandalous!

LADY BROCKLEHURST. I am a mother——

[*Enter Lady Catherine and Lady Agatha in evening dress up* L.C. *They are terrified at the sight of Lady Brocklehurst, but move down* C.

[*Shaking hands.*] How d'you do, Agatha?

[*Lady Agatha moves away to* L.C.

LADY CATHERINE. [L. *of the table.*] How do you do, Lady Brocklehurst?

[*She shakes hands and turns to* R. *of Lady Agatha. They stand together, nervously.*

LADY BROCKLEHURST. [*Regarding them.*] You didn't dress like this on the island, I expect. By the way, how *did* you dress?

[*Lady Agatha and Lady Catherine clutch each other.*

LADY AGATHA. [*Anxiously.*] Not—not so well, of course, but quite the same idea.

[*Enter Crichton.*

CRICHTON. Mr Treherne.

[*Enter Treherne. Crichton withdraws. Lady Catherine, relieved, turns up to meet Treherne, who is in clerical dress. She intimates that Lady Brocklehurst is there. He crosses and shakes hands with Lady Brocklehurst, above the table.*

LADY BROCKLEHURST. How d'you do, Mr Treherne? There is not so much of you in the book as I had hoped.

TREHERNE. [*Modestly.*] There wasn't very much of me on the island, Lady Brocklehurst.

[*The girls, hovering at* L.C., *are on needles.*

Only that I did my best; it was rather a poor best.

LADY BROCKLEHURST. I thought that cricket educated Englishmen for everything.

TREHERNE. I used to think so too.

[*He crosses down* L. *of the settee to* R., *and shakes hands with Lord Brocklehurst.*

LORD BROCKLEHURST. [*To Treherne.*] I hear you've got a living. Congratulations.

TREHERNE. Thanks.

LORD BROCKLEHURST. Is it a good one?

TREHERNE. So-so! They are rather weak in bowling, but it's a good bit of turf.

[*He crosses up* R. *and meets Ernest, who enters up* R.C.

ERNEST. [*Crosses* C. *and shakes hands with Lady Brocklehurst across the back of the settee.*] How do you do, Lady Brocklehurst?

[*Lady Catherine joins Treherne up* R.C.

LADY BROCKLEHURST. Our brilliant author. It is as engrossing, Mr Wooolley, as if it were a work of fiction.

ERNEST. [*Doubtful of her.*] Thanks awfully. The fact is——

[*He stops, puzzled because Lord Brocklehurst and Lady Brocklehurst exchange significant glances, and withdraws a little towards* C. *Lady Catherine takes Treherne by the arm and brings him down to above the settee. Ernest moves down* L. *of the chair* R.C.

LADY CATHERINE. Lady Brocklehurst, Mr Treherne and I—we
are engaged.

LADY AGATHA. [*Moving* C., *to Ernest.*] And Ernest and I——

LADY BROCKLEHURST. I see, my dears—thought it was wise to
keep the island in the family.

> [*Lady Agatha and Ernest move down to* L.C. *All are perturbed.
> Lady Catherine and Treherne break a little* R. *as enter
> Lord Loam and Lady Mary up* L.C., *happy and gay. They
> come down.*

LORD LOAM. [*Crossing to behind the settee* R., *and looking down
at Lady Brocklehurst.*] Aha! Ha! ha!—younger than any of
them, Emily.

LADY BROCKLEHURST. Flatterer! [*To Lady Mary, who runs to
her and sits on her* L.] You seem in high spirits, Mary.

LADY MARY. I am.

LADY BROCKLEHURST. After——?

> [*With a significant glance at Lord Brocklehurst.*

LADY MARY. I—I mean I—the fact is——

> [*She stops, seeing Lord Brocklehurst is startled.*

LORD LOAM. [*Gaily.*] She hears wedding bells, Emily.

LADY BROCKLEHURST. [*Coolly.*] Do you, Mary? Can't say I do,
but I'm hard of hearing.

LADY MARY. [*Rising haughtily.*] If you don't, Lady Brocklehurst,
I'm sure I don't.

> [*She moves to below the chair* L. *of the settee and turns up.*

LORD LOAM. Tut, tut. [*He moves, nervously, over to* C.] Seen our
curios from the island, Emily? I should like you to examine
them.

LADY BROCKLEHURST. Thank you, Henry, I am glad you say
that, for I have just taken the liberty of asking two of them to
step upstairs.

> [*All register consternation by exchanging glances. Lady Mary
> gives her father a quick look. Lord Loam crosses to above
> the armchair* R.C. *Lady Mary turns away to the top of the
> table* L.C. *Enter Crichton with Tweeny in neat maid's
> dress—she is timid. They stand up* C.

LORD BROCKLEHURST. [*Stoutly.*] Loam, *I* have *no* hand in this.

> [*Lady Agatha crosses down in front of the settee* L. *and sits.*

LADY BROCKLEHURST. Pooh, what have I done? You always
begged me to speak to the servants, Henry, and I merely

wanted to discover whether the views you used to hold about equality were adopted on the island—it seemed a splendid opportunity, but Mr Woolley has not a word on the subject.

[All appeal to Ernest.

ERNEST. [*Crossing to* L.C.] The fact is——

> [*He backs to* R. *of Lady Agatha, seeing Lord Brocklehurst and Lady Brocklehurst exchange glances.*

LORD LOAM. [*Moving towards Lady Brocklehurst.*] I assure you, Emily——

LADY MARY. [*Boldly—crossing and putting her hand on Lord Loam's arm.*] Father, nothing whatever happened on the island of which I, for one, am ashamed, and I hope Crichton will be allowed to answer Lady Brocklehurst's questions.

LADY BROCKLEHURST. To be sure.

> [*Lady Mary, after a cold glance at Lady Brocklehurst, returns to up* L.C.

There's nothing to make a fuss about and we're a family party.

> [*Lord Loam sits in the chair* L. *of the settee* R.

Now——   [*She beckons.*

> [*Crichton comes down* C.

Truthfully, my man.

CRICHTON. I promise that, my lady.

LADY BROCKLEHURST. [*Sharply.*] Well, were you all equal on the island?

CRICHTON. No, my lady—I think I may say there was as little equality there as elsewhere.

LADY BROCKLEHURST. All the social distinctions were preserved?

CRICHTON. As at home, my lady.

LADY BROCKLEHURST. The servants?

CRICHTON. They had to keep their place.

LADY BROCKLEHURST. Wonderful! How was it managed?

> [*Suddenly beckoning to Tweeny, who now comes down* L. *of Crichton.*

You, girl, tell me that.

> [*There is general anxiety as Tweeny is seen to hesitate. Only Crichton is quite impassive.*

Come!

TWEENY. It was all the Gov.'s doing, your ladyship.

> [*Ernest sits beside Lady Agatha on the settee* L. *There is a pause in which they all give themselves up for lost.*

CRICHTON. In the regrettable slang of the servants' hall, my
lady, the master is usually referred to as the Gov.

LADY BROCKLEHURST. I see—you—— [*Looking at Lord Loam.*

LORD LOAM. Yes, I understand that is what they called me.
[*There is general relief.*

LADY BROCKLEHURST. You didn't even take your meals with the
family?

CRICHTON. No, my lady. I dined apart.

LADY BROCKLEHURST. You also—— [*To Tweeny, who is scared.*]
Come, did you dine with Crichton?

TWEENY. [*Terrified.*] No, your ladyship.

LADY BROCKLEHURST. [*Triumphant.*] With whom?

TWEENY. I took my bit of supper with—with Daddy and Polly
and—the rest.
[*A suppressed display of awful discomfort—Lady Brocklehurst
looks at Tweeny inquiringly.*

ERNEST. [*Brightly.*] Dear old Daddy—he was our monkey—
you remember our monkey, Agatha?

LADY AGATHA. Rather! What a funny darling he was!

LADY CATHERINE. [*Coming to above settee R.*] And don't you
think Polly was the sweetest little parrot, Mary?

LADY BROCKLEHURST. Ah! I understand—animals you had
domesticated?

LORD LOAM. Quite so—quite so. [*He is immensely relieved.*

LADY BROCKLEHURST. The servants' teas that used to take place
here once a month——

CRICHTON. They didn't seem natural on an island, my lady,
and were discontinued—by the Gov.'s orders.

LORD BROCKLEHURST. A clear proof, Loam, that they were a
mistake here.

LORD LOAM. [*Rises.*] I admit it frankly—I abandon them,
Emily, as the result of our experiences on the island. I think
of going over to the Tories.

LADY BROCKLEHURST. I am delighted to hear it.

LORD LOAM. [*Crossing up R.C.*] Thank you, Crichton, thank you
—that is all.
[*He motions to Crichton and Tweeny, who turn and go up stage.
Lady Mary crosses down L. of the table L.C.*

LADY BROCKLEHURST. One moment.
[*Crichton checks and turns to face her.*

One moment, Crichton.

  [*Crichton comes down* C. *Lady Mary sits in the chair* L.C.
Young people, Crichton, will be young people even on an
island—perhaps especially on an island—now, I suppose there
was a certain amount of—shall we say sentimentalizing going
on?

CRICHTON. Yes, my lady, there was.

LORD BROCKLEHURST. [*Angry.*] Mother!

LADY BROCKLEHURST. Which gentleman? [*To Tweeny.*] You,
girl, tell me.

TWEENY. [*Comes down.*] If you please, my lady——

ERNEST. [*Rises and moves forward—quickly.*] The fact is——

  [*He is stopped as before, by glances.*

TWEENY. [*Suddenly.*] It was him—Mr Ernest, your ladyship.

LADY BROCKLEHURST. With which lady?

LADY AGATHA. [*Rises.*] I have already told you, Lady Brocklehurst, that Ernest and I——

LADY BROCKLEHURST. Yes, now, but you were two years on the
island. [*To Tweeny.*] Was it this lady?

  [*Looking at Lady Mary.*

TWEENY. [*Candidly.*] No, your ladyship.

LADY BROCKLEHURST. Then I don't care which of the others
it was.

  [*Tweeny giggles.*

Well, I suppose that will do.

  [*Crichton bows and turns up, with Tweeny. All are relieved,
  and relax a little.*

LORD BROCKLEHURST. Do! I hope you are ashamed of yourself,
Mother. [*Taking a pace in to* R.C.] Crichton.

  [*Crichton checks and comes down* C.
You are an excellent fellow, and if after we are married you
ever wish to change your place, come to us.

LADY MARY. [*Rising.*] Oh no, impossible.

LADY BROCKLEHURST. Why impossible?

  [*Lady Mary cannot answer.*
[*To Crichton.*] Do you see why it should be impossible, my
man?

  [*General anxiety.*

CRICHTON. Yes, my lady.

  [*They wonder.*

[*Turning towards Lord Loam, who is up* C.] I had not told you, my lord, but as soon as your lordship is suited I wish to leave service.

LORD LOAM. Leave service?

CRICHTON. Yes, my lord.

TREHERNE. What will you do, Crichton?

[*Crichton shrugs his shoulders; 'God knows,' it may mean. All are relieved.*

CRICHTON. Shall I withdraw, my lord?

[*Lord Loam nods and turns away* L. *Crichton bows and withdraws without a tremor, Tweeny accompanying him. They can all breathe again; the thunderstorm is over.*

LADY BROCKLEHURST. [*Rising; thankful to have made herself unpleasant.*] Horrid of me, wasn't it? [*She crosses* C.] But if one wasn't disagreeable now and again, it would be horribly tedious to be an old woman. [*Moving towards Lady Mary.*] He will soon be yours, Mary, and then—think of the opportunities you will have of being disagreeable to me. On that understanding, my dear, don't you think we might——?

[*Their cold lips meet.*

LORD LOAM. [*Vaguely.*] Quite so—quite so. [*He moves to* C.]

[*Crichton announces dinner. Lord Loam gives Lady Brocklehurst his arm. The others file out. Lady Mary stays behind a moment and impulsively holds out her hand, meeting Crichton up* C.

LADY MARY. To wish you every happiness.

CRICHTON. [*An enigma to the last.*] The same to you, my lady.

LADY MARY. Do you despise me, Crichton?

[*The man who could never tell a lie makes no answer.*

You are the best man among us.

CRICHTON. On an island, my lady, perhaps. . . .

LADY MARY. Tell me one thing; you have not lost your courage?

CRICHTON. No, my lady.

[*Lady Mary exits. Crichton, impassive to the last, moves up and switches off the lights.*

CURTAIN

DEAR BRUTUS

A Comedy in Three Acts

COPYRIGHT BY J. M. BARRIE
COPYRIGHT A.77279, 1934, BY CHARLES SCRIBNER'S SONS

The copying by manuscript, typescript, photography or any other means of reproduction, of this play either in whole or in part is an infringement of the copyright.

All applications for a licence concerning the production of this play by amateurs must be made to:

SAMUEL FRENCH LIMITED,
26 SOUTHAMPTON STREET,
STRAND, LONDON, W.C.2.

The royalty fee payable for one performance is Five Guineas. No performance may be given unless the licence has first been obtained.

DEAR BRUTUS

Produced on 17th October, 1917, at Wyndham's Theatre, London, with the following cast of characters:

MR DEARTH	Mr Gerald du Maurier
MR PURDIE	Mr Sam Sothern
MR COADE	Mr Norman Forbes
MATEY	Mr Will West
LOB	Mr Arthur Hatherton
MRS DEARTH	Miss Hilda Moore
MRS PURDIE	Miss Jessie Bateman
MRS COADE	Miss Maude Millett
JOANNA TROUT	Miss Doris Lytton
LADY CAROLINE LANEY	Miss Lydia Bilbrooke
MARGARET	Miss Faith Celli

CHARACTERS

(in the order of their appearance)

MRS PURDIE
MRS COADE
MRS DEARTH
JOANNA TROUT
LADY CAROLINE LANEY
MATEY
LOB
MR COADE
MR PURDIE
MR DEARTH
MARGARET

SYNOPSIS OF SCENES

ACT I.—Lob's House.

ACT II.—The Wood.

ACT III.—The Same as Act. I

Act I

Scene: *Lob's house—the drawing-room of Sinister Warren, Lob's house in a remote part of England. It should be a shallow scene, because through open french windows at the back there must be a big view of the garden, not merely painted on cloth but occupying part of the stage. It is a beautiful flower-garden at midsummer. Nothing seen but flowers and a fountain. There is a door L. down stage, and another door into the dining-room R. This latter has two steps leading up to it, and the upper part is glass with a curtain across it. The drawing-room is pretty and quaint, but not so odd as it perhaps ought to be.*

There is a round table C., with chairs above it and on either side. A large settee down R. Above it, a small table with a bowl of flowers and a jug of water. Below the R. end of the windows, a stand with ashtray and matches. Up L., between the windows and the fireplace, a large armchair, facing diagonally up R. The fireplace in an angled recess up L. Below it, a desk and chair. There are bowls and vases of flowers on the table and the desk.

The Curtain rises on an empty stage, dark and unlit, though the time is late evening. This gives a striking view of the garden, which is bathed in moonlight. We see from the glass of the door R. that the dining-room is lit up. We have a glimpse of men standing at the table as this door is opened by Mr Purdie to let the ladies come into the drawing-room, and there is chatter and laughter as they do so.

First comes Mrs Coade, who is a delightful sunny lady of about sixty. Next Mrs Dearth, a woman of thirty-five, who can be fascinating and dangerous; who also is discontented, and despises her husband. Next a languid lady, Lady Caroline Laney. She has a drawling, rather insolent manner, and considers herself superior to the others. Then Mrs Purdie, a simple young wife, wistful, who knows her husband is fond of Joanna. Lastly, Joanna Trout, who is sentimental but a good sort. They are groping in the dark except for the light from the dining-room. There is the usual modesty about going first.

Mrs Purdie. [*In the background.*] Go on, Coady, lead the way.

MRS COADE. Oh dear, I don't see why I should go first.

MRS PURDIE. The nicest always goes first.

MRS COADE. [*Descending the two steps.*] It's a strange house if I'm the nicest!

MRS PURDIE. It *is* a strange house!

MRS DEARTH. Down with you, Mrs Coade. Make way for the second nicest.   [*Meaning herself.*

> [*Mrs Coade crosses to L.C. Mrs Dearth behind her. Mrs Purdie and Lady Caroline follow, the former to down R.C., and the latter to C. above the table.*

JOANNA. [*Entering after the others.*] I suppose that means I'm the nastiest.   [*She comes to R. of the table.*

> [*So far we have seen them in the light of the dining-room; now the dining-room door shuts and they are in darkness.*

LADY CAROLINE. Don't shut the door. I can't see where the switch is.

MRS DEARTH. [*Going up to L.*] Over here.

> [*Mrs Dearth switches on the lights. The ladies, now sure they cannot be overheard, flock together like conspirators.*

[*Moving down L.*] We mustn't waste another moment. We are all agreed, aren't we?

JOANNA. [*Above the chair R. of the table.*] Now is the time.

MRS COADE. [*To above the table, gleefully.*] Yes, now if at all. But should we?

MRS DEARTH. Certainly. And at once, before the men come in.

MRS PURDIE. [*Moving R., to the settee.*] You don't think we should wait for the men? They are quite as much in it as we are.   [*She sits on the settee.*

LADY CAROLINE. [*Languidly, moving down L.C.*] Lob would be with them. If the thing is to be done, it should be now.

> [*She sits on the chair L. of the table.*

MRS COADE. [*Though still beaming.*] Is it quite fair to Lob? After all, he is our host.

> [*Mrs Dearth turns to the desk and commences to write.*

JOANNA. [*Coaxingly.*] Of course it isn't fair to him. But let's do it, Coady.

MRS COADE. Yes, let's do it.

MRS PURDIE. [*Rising slightly, and looking L., seeing that Mrs Dearth is writing.*] Mrs Dearth *is* doing it!

> [*They all look at Mrs Dearth—Lady Caroline rising.*

MRS DEARTH. [*Writing.*] Of course I am. The men are not coming, are they?

> [*Joanna runs up* R. *and peeps through the glass of the dining-room door.*

JOANNA. No. [*Returning to* R. *of the table.*] Your husband is having another glass of port.

MRS DEARTH. [*Reading over what she has written.*] I'm sure he is. One of you ring, please.

> [*Joanna presses the bell* R. *of the windows.*

MRS COADE. Poor Matey!

LADY CAROLINE. He wichly desewves what he is about to get. (*Her 'r's' are thus pronounced throughout.*)

JOANNA. [*Glancing* L.] He's coming! Don't all stand huddled together like conspirators!

MRS COADE. It's what we are!   [*She sits above the table* C.

> [*Mrs Purdie tries to sit* R. *of the table, but as Joanna forestalls her, she snatches a book from the table, crosses* R., *and sits on the settee. Lady Caroline, who had moved to behind Mrs Dearth's chair, returns to* L. *of the table and sits. Mrs Dearth is still sitting* L., *at the desk.*
>
> [*Matey, a correct but furtive butler, enters down* L., *and is moving up towards the door* R. *when he is arrested, at* L.C., *by Mrs Dearth's voice.*
>
> [*The ladies, though pretending to be uninterested, are very on the alert.*

MRS DEARTH. [*Glancing up from her book, casually.*] Matey, I wish this telegram sent.

MATEY. [*Moving* R. *of Mrs Dearth.*] Very good, ma'am. The village post office closed at eight, but if it is important . . .

MRS DEARTH. It is. And you are so clever, Matey—I'm sure you can persuade them to oblige you.

MATEY. [*Pleased, taking the telegram.*] I will see to it myself, madam. You can depend on its going.

> [*There is a little gasp from Mrs Coade—the equivalent to dropping a stitch in needlework.*

MRS DEARTH. Thank you. [*Indifferently as Matey makes to go.*] Better read it, Matey, to be sure that you can make it out.

MATEY. [L.C.] Very good, ma'am.

> [*Matey reads the telegram and gets a shock. All are covertly watching.*

MRS DEARTH. [*In a purring voice.*] Read it aloud, Matey.

MATEY. [*Turning to her.*] Oh, ma'am!   [*He shudders.*

MRS DEARTH. [*Inexorably, without the purr.*] Aloud!

MATEY. [*Reading huskily.*] To Police Station, Great Commony. Send officer first thing tomorrow morning to arrest Matey, butler, for theft of rings.

MRS DEARTH. [*Calmly.*] Yes, that's quite right.
            [*She picks up her book again.*
            [*All resume their pretended occupations.*

MATEY. [*To Lady Caroline imploringly.*] My lady!

LADY CAROLINE. [*Languidly with her eyes on her book.*] Shouldn't we say how many rings?

MRS DEARTH. Yes, put in the number of rings, Matey.

> [*Matey makes mute appeals to one after the other but sees they are all relentless. He produces three rings from a secret place in his clothes and hands them in deathly silence to the various owners; one to Mrs Purdie, one to Joanna and one on desk to Mrs Dearth.*

MATEY. [R. *of Mrs Dearth.*] May I tear this up, ma'am?

MRS DEARTH. Certainly not.   [*She takes the form.*

LADY CAROLINE. I told you from the first that he was the culprit. I am never mistaken in faces, and I see broad arrows all over yours, Matey.

MATEY. It's deeply regretted.

MRS DEARTH. I'm sure it is.

JOANNA. [*Rising.*] We may as well tell him that it isn't our rings we are worrying about. [*To above Mrs Coade's chair.*] They are just a means to an end, Matey.

MRS DEARTH. Precisely. In other words, that telegram goes unless——

MATEY. [*Eagerly.*] Unless?

> [*They all suddenly abandon pretence of being otherwise occupied. Joanna runs again to the dining-room door and peeps through. Mrs Purdie comes to the chair R. of the table.*

JOANNA. [*Returning to above and R. of Mrs Coade, and speaking with great emphasis.*] Unless—unless—you can tell us instantly what peculiarity it is that all we ladies have in common.

> [*All ladies now have their eyes on Matey, in whose face an uneasiness begins to grow.*

MRS PURDIE. Not only the ladies, the gentlemen as well. All Lob's guests in this house.

MRS DEARTH. [*With emphasis.*] We have been here a week, and we find that when he invited us he knew us all so little that we began to wonder why he asked us. And now from word he has let drop we know that we were invited because of something—he thinks—we have—in common.

MRS PURDIE. But he won't say what it is.

MRS COADE. [*Gurgling.*] And we can't sleep at night, Matey, till we find out.

JOANNA. And we are sure you know, and if you don't tell us— quod!

[*All these sentences have been fired at him quickly like pistol shots.*

MATEY. [*Whose uneasiness has increased.*] I don't know what you mean, ladies.

[*We can see, however, that he does know.*

MRS DEARTH. Oh yes, you do.

MRS COADE. You must admit that your master is a very strange person.

MATEY. [*With a gasp.*] He is a little—odd, ma'am. That's why everybody calls him just Lob—not Mr Lob.

JOANNA. He is so odd that it has got on my nerves that we have been invited here for some sort of horrid experiment.

[*Matey starts. All look at him.*
[*To Matey.*] You look as if you thought so too!

MATEY. Oh no, miss. I—he—you shouldn't have come, ladies —you didn't ought to have come.

LADY CAROLINE. [*Turning in her chair.*] Shouldn't have come? [*She motions him to step down* L.C.] Now, my man, what do you mean by that?

MATEY. [*Taking a pace down.*] Nothing, my Lady—I—I just mean—why did you come if you are the kind he thinks?

MRS PURDIE. The kind he thinks?

MRS DEARTH. What kind does he think? Now we're getting at it.

MATEY. [*Wriggling.*] I haven't a notion, ma'am.

LADY CAROLINE. Then it isn't necessarily our virtue that makes Lob interested in us?

MATEY. No, my lady—oh no, my Lady.

[*Mrs Dearth laughs.*

MRS COADE. And yet, you know, he's rather lovable.

MATEY. [*Eagerly.*] He is, ma'am. He's the most lovable old devil I ever—I beg your pardon, my Lady.

JOANNA. And yet it's true. I have seen him among his flowers, petting them, talking to them, coaxing them till they simply had to grow.

[*They look out at the garden.*

MRS DEARTH. It certainly is a divine garden.

MRS COADE. [*Looking out through the windows.*] How lovely it is in the moonlight. Roses, roses, all the way. . . . [*Dreamily.*] It is like a hat I had once when I was young. . . .

MRS DEARTH. Lob is such an amazing gardener, I believe he could even grow hats.

LADY CAROLINE. He's a wonderful gardener, but is one sure that that is nice at his age? What is his age, man?

MATEY. [*Scared.*] He won't tell, my Lady. I think he's frightened that the police would step in if they knew how old he is. [*Uneasily.*] They do say in the village that they remember him seventy years ago, looking just as he does today.

MRS DEARTH. Rubbish!

MATEY. Yes, ma'am; but there are his razors.

LADY CAROLINE. Razors!

MATEY. [*Turning to her, a trifle maliciously.*] You won't know about razors, my Lady, not being married—as yet—excuse me. But a married lady can tell a man's age by the number of his razors. [*A little scared.*] If you saw his razors—there's a little world of them, from patents of the present day back to implements so horrible you can picture him with them in his hand—scraping his way through the ages.

LADY CAROLINE. Ages? You amuse one to an extent. [*She motions him back.*] Was he ever married?

MATEY. He has quite forgotten, my Lady. How long ago is it since Merrie England?

MRS PURDIE. In Queen Elizabeth's time, wasn't it?

MATEY. He says he's all that's left of Merrie England, that little man!

MRS DEARTH. Fiddle-de-dee!

MRS PURDIE. Lob! I think there is a famous cricketer called Lob.

MRS COADE. Wasn't there a Lob in Shakespeare?

[*Nobody knows or cares.*

No, of course I'm thinking of Robin Goodfellow.

LADY CAROLINE. The names are so alike.

JOANNA. Robin Goodfellow was Puck.

MRS COADE. [*Triumphant.*] That's what was in my head. Lob was another name for Puck.

JOANNA. [*Moving down* R.C.] Well, he's certainly rather like what Puck might have grown into if he had forgotten to die. [*Turning.*] And, by the way, I remember now he does call his flowers by the old Elizabethan names.

MATEY. He always calls the nightingale Philomel, miss—if that is any help.

MRS DEARTH. None whatever. Tell me this. Did he specially ask you all for Midsummer week?

LADIES. Yes, yes.

MATEY. He would!

MRS COADE. What do you mean?

MATEY. He always likes them to be here on Midsummer night, ma'am.

MRS DEARTH. [*Rising.*] Them? Whom?
          [*A tiny pause. Then Matey speaks slowly and sombrely.*

MATEY. Them who have that in common.

MRS PURDIE. What can it be?

MATEY. [*Dissembling.*] I don't know.

LADY CAROLINE. I hope we are all nice women. We don't know each other very well. Does anything startling happen at these times?

MATEY. [*Doggedly.*] I don't know.

JOANNA. Why, I believe this is Midsummer Eve!

MATEY. Yes, miss, so it is. [*Grimly.*] The villagers know it. They are all inside their houses tonight—with the doors barred.

LADY CAROLINE. Because of—oh, *him*?

MATEY. He frightens them. There are—stories.

MRS DEARTH. What alarms them? Tell us—or——
          [*She brandishes the telegram.*

MATEY. I know nothing for certain, ma'am; I've never done it myself. He's wanted me to, but I wouldn't.

MRS PURDIE. Done what?

MATEY. [*With fine appeal.*] Oh, ma'am, don't ask me. [*To Mrs Dearth and thoroughly believing what he says.*] Be merciful to me, ma'am. I'm not bad naturally. It was just going into service that did for me! The accident of being flung among bad companions. It's touch and go how the poor turn out in this world; all depends on your taking the right or the wrong turning.

MRS COADE. [*Commiserating.*] I dare say that's true.

MATEY. [*Turning to Mrs Coade.*] When I was young, ma'am, I was offered a clerkship in the City. If I had taken it there wouldn't be an honester man alive today. I would give the world to be able to begin over again!

MRS COADE. It's very sad, Mrs Dearth.

MRS DEARTH. I'm sorry for him, but still——

MATEY. [*Appealing to Lady Caroline.*] What do you say, my Lady?

LADY CAROLINE. As you ask me, I should certainly say jail!

MATEY. [*To Mrs Dearth.*] If you'll say no more about this, ma'am—[*indicating the telegram*]—I'll give you a tip that's worth it.

MRS DEARTH. Ah, now you're talking!

LADY CAROLINE. Don't listen to him!

MATEY. You're the one that's hardest on me.

LADY CAROLINE. Yes, I flatter myself I am.

MATEY. You might take a wrong turning yourself, my Lady.

LADY CAROLINE. I? How dare you?

[*Joanna turns again to the dining-room door up R.*

JOANNA. They're rising!   [*She returns to R.C.*

MRS DEARTH. Very well, we agree—if the tip is good enough!

LADY CAROLINE. You'll regret this!

MATEY. [*To Mrs Dearth.*] Thank you, ma'am! It's this: [*with sombre emphasis*] I wouldn't go out tonight if he asks you. Go into the garden, if you like. The garden's all right. I wouldn't go farther—tonight.

MRS COADE. But he never proposes to us to go farther. Why should he tonight?

MATEY. I don't know, ma'am, but don't any of you go—[*to Lady Caroline, vindictively*]—except you, my Lady. I should like you to go.

LADY CAROLINE. Fellow!

[*They all look at one another and nod.*

MATEY. Is that all, ma'am?

MRS DEARTH. I suppose so.   [*She tears up the telegram.*

MATEY. Thank you.   [*He moves down* L.

LADY CAROLINE. You should have sent that telegram off.

JOANNA. You are sure you have told us all you know, Matey?

MATEY. [*Checking at* L.] Yes, miss.

> [*Mrs Dearth rises and moves to above and* L. *of the table.
> Matey is about to exit, but turns at the door, coming in a
> pace.*

[*Impressively.*] Above all, ladies, I wouldn't go into the wood.

MRS PURDIE. [*Rising.*] The wood? Why, there is no wood within a dozen miles of here.

MATEY. No, ma'am. But—all the same—[*very slowly*]—I wouldn't go into it, ladies—not if I was you!

> [*Matey turns and exits* L., *leaving the ladies puzzled.*

JOANNA. [*Up* R.C.] Here's Lob!

> [*Joanna moves down* R. *Mrs Purdie and Mrs Dearth move
> up, below the* R. *window up* C. *Lady Caroline goes up
> below the* L. *window. Mrs Coade is above the table* C.

> [*Lob enters from the dining-room. He is rather unearthly, very
> small and exceedingly old, but very light and vivacious.
> He enters with portentous gravity, his hands behind his
> back, his head bent, and he crosses thus down to* L.C. *All
> withdraw a little as he enters. At* L.C. *he suddenly jumps
> completely round to face them, which gives them a start.
> He peers at them to see if they are amused. It has amused
> him vastly.*

LOB. [*To Mrs Coade.*] Standing, dear lady? Pray be seated.

> [*Lob draws out the chair* L. *of the table, and as Mrs Coade is
> about to sit in it he pulls it away, almost from under her.
> She saves herself from falling by gripping the table. He
> sinks in the desk chair in a paroxysm of delight, kicking
> one leg in the air, which is a characteristic way of express-
> ing delight in himself. Joanna is at* R.C. *Mrs Dearth moves
> down* R. *to the settee. Mrs Coade, much amused, aims a
> playful blow at Lob with her finger.*

MRS COADE. You monkey!

LOB. [*Chuckling gleefully, and bringing her the flowers from the
desk.*] It's quite a flirtation, isn't it?

> [*Lob crosses below the table and sits* R. *of it, with his legs
> beneath him, as like a ball as possible. Outside, the moon-
> light deepens, slowly and imperceptibly.*

[*Joanna and Mrs Dearth sit on the settee and eye Lob's back, suspiciously. Mrs Purdie and Lady Caroline watch him from the windows.*

[*Mr Coade, a happy, lazy old man, enters from the dining-room up* R., *smoking a cigarette.*

COADE. Hope you've been missing us! [*To the ladies.*] You are sure you don't mind?   [*Indicating his cigarette.*

MRS DEARTH. You know we like it, Mr Coade.

[*Mr Purdie enters* R. *after Coade. He is a young barrister, and is modestly sure that he is of a deeply passionate nature.*

Is my husband still sampling the port, Mr Purdie?

PURDIE. [R.C.] Do you know, I believe he is—are the ladies willing, Coade?

COADE. [C.] I hadn't told them. [*Crossing to Mrs Coade solicit-ously.*] The fact is that I'm not sure whether it wouldn't tire my wife too much. Do you feel equal to a little exertion, Coady, tonight, or is your foot troubling you?

MRS COADE. [*Beaming as usual, for they are a happy pair.*] No, Coady, I have been resting it.

COADE. That's right. [*He gets a footstool for her from the fireplace, and places it for her.*] There! Don't disturb it for a while, as we are going out for a walk presently.

[*He gets the chair from the desk, and sits* L. *of her.*

MRS COADE. Yes, let's go into the garden.

PURDIE. No, not the garden tonight. [*Towards the settee.*] We are going farther afield. [*Jocular, mysterious.*] We have an adven-ture on for tonight.

MRS DEARTH. Oh?

PURDIE. Get thick shoes and a wrap, Mrs Dearth—indeed, all of you.

LADY CAROLINE. Where do you propose to take us?

PURDIE. To find a mysterious wood.

LADIES. A wood?

[*Mrs Purdie and Lady Carlone come down above the table* R.C. *quickly. They take a sharp look at Lob, who is exagger-atedly innocent.*

JOANNA. Is it your fun, Mr Purdie? You know quite well that there are not any trees for miles around. You have said your-self that it is the one blot on the landscape.

COADE. [*Jocularly solemn.*] Ah, on ordinary occasions, but allow

me to point out to you, Miss Joanna, that this is Midsummer
Eve.

[*The ladies again look sharply at Lob, who is wickedly innocent.*

PURDIE. Tell them what you told us, Lob.

[*At the back of Lob, pulling his ears.*

LOB. It's all nonsense, of course—just foolish talk of the
villagers. [*Like one pitying their credulity.*] They say that on
Midsummer Eve there is a strange wood in this part of the
country.

MRS PURDIE. Where?

PURDIE. Ah, that is one of its most charming features. It is never
twice in the same place, apparently. It has been seen on
different parts of the Downs and on More Common—once it
was close to Radley village and another time about a mile from
the sea! Oh, a sporting wood!

LADY CAROLINE. [*Moving a little* L.C.] Lob is anxious we should
all go and look for it?

[*She comes down* L. *of Coade, and turns.*

COADE. Oh no, Lob's the only sceptic in the house. Says it's all
rubbish, and we'll be sillies if we go. But we believe, eh, Purdie?

PURDIE. [*Moving to above the table* R. *of Mrs Purdie.*] Rather!

[*Mrs Purdie moves to* L. *of the chair* C.

LOB. Just wasting the evening. Let's have a round game at cards
here instead.

PURDIE. No, sir, I am going to find that wood.

JOANNA. What's the good of it when it's found?

PURDIE. [*A pace or two* R.C.] We shall wander in it deliciously,
listening to a new sort of bird called the Philomel.

MRS DEARTH. Ah!   [*Another sharp look at Lob.*

JOANNA. [*Rising.*] All together?

[*She crosses to Purdie* R. *of the table.*

PURDIE. No, in pairs.   [*He gives her significant look.*

[*Mrs Purdie moves up* L. *to the fireplace.*

JOANNA. [*Demurely.*] I think it would be rather fun. Come on,
Coady, I'll lace your boots for you, I'm sure your poor foot
will carry you nicely.   [*Crossing to the door* L.

MRS DEARTH. [*Rises, still suspicious.*] Miss Trout, wait a
moment! [*She moves to* R. *of Lob's chair.*] Lob, has this wonderful wood any special propeties?

LOB. Pooh! There's no wood.

LADY CAROLINE. [*Moving up* C., *above the table.*] You've never seen it?

LOB. Not I. Don't believe in it.

MRS DEARTH. Have any of the villagers ever been in it?

LOB. So it's said; so it's said.

MRS DEARTH. What did they say were their experiences?

LOB. That isn't known. They never came back.

JOANNA. Never came back!   [*She moves from the door to* L.C.

LOB. Absurd, of course. You see, in the morning the wood was gone, and so they were gone too.   [*This is rather creepy.*

JOANNA. [*To above, and between Mr and Mrs Coade.*] You know, I don't think I like this wood.

MRS COADE. It certainly is Midsummer Eve.

COADE. Of course if you ladies are against it we'll drop the idea. It was only a bit of fun.

MRS DEARTH. [*With a malicious eye on Lob.*] Better give it up— to please Lob.

PURDIE. Oh, all right, Lob. What about that game of cards?

COADE. Yes, yes.   [*He rises.*

[*Here Lob bursts into tears and sobs with disappointment. They don't know what to do. He falls on his knees* R. *of the table, and then creeps under it, where he sits down forlorn.*

LOB. [*Under the table.*] I wanted you to go. I had set my heart on your going. It's the thing I wanted, and it isn't good for me not to get the thing I want.

MRS COADE. Good gracious! He's wanted it all the time! You wicked Lob!   [*Looking under the table.*

MRS DEARTH. Now, you see there is something in it!

COADE. Nonsense, Mrs Dearth, it's all a joke!

MRS PURDIE. [*Kneeling,* R. *of the table, and coaxing Lob.*] Don't cry, Lobby.

LOB. Nobody cares for me—nobody loves me. And I need to be loved.

[*Mrs Coade and Mrs Purdie, joined by Joanna, bend down and make much of him.*

JOANNA. Yes, we do, we all love you. Nice, nice Lobby.

MRS PURDIE. Dear Lob, I'm so fond of you.

JOANNA. Dry his eyes with my own handkerchief.

LADY CAROLINE. Don't pamper him!

LOB. I need to be pampered!

MRS COADE. You funny little man! Let us go at once and look for his wood.

MRS PURDIE. Yes, let's.

JOANNA. Rather! Shoes, cloaks, and hats forward! [*Crossing* L.] Come on, Lady Caroline, just to show you're not afraid of Matey.

> [*Lady Caroline, Purdie, Mrs Purdie, the Coades and lastly Mrs Dearth follow Joanna off gaily* L., *chatting, dragging the reluctant ones. Coades, before his exit, replaces his chair at the desk.*

> [*Lob, left alone, gloats over his success in an uncanny way. Mrs Dearth goes last, the only one who really suspects Lob. He suddenly sees her down* L., *watching him, and drops the flowers from the vase which he has taken from the table,* C. *To him this is a tragedy. He utters long-drawn moans, then goes down on the floor, picking up the flowers, individually examining their hurts, pressing them to him as if they were children.*

> [*Mrs Dearth exits* L.

LOB. [*To the flowers.*] Poor bruised one, it was I who hurt you. Lob is so sorry. Lie there! [*To another.*] Pretty, pretty, let me see where you have a pain?—you fell on your head—is this the place? Now I make it better. [*To another.*] Oh, little rascal, you are not hurt at all, you just pretend. [*To another, whose stem is broken.*] Oh, dear oh dear, sweetheart, don't cry. You are now prettier than ever. You were too tall. Oh, how beautiful you smell now that you are small. [*He rises with them in his arms.*] Drink, drink! [*He puts them in another vase* R., *which has already some flowers in it.*] Now you are happy again. The little rascal smiles! All smiles, please—and nod heads—aha! aha! You love Lob—Lob loves you!

> [*Mr Purdie and Joanna come in rather secretly by the window. Lob behaves as if he had caught them love-making; he beckons to the flowers as if he had something funny to tell them, whispers some merry jest to them.*

JOANNA. [*Up* C., L. *of Purdie.*] What were you saying to them, Lob?

LOB. [*Turning, and going down* L.] I was saying 'Two's company, three's none!'

> [*Lob exits grinning,* L., *with a final nod to the flowers.*

JOANNA. That man—he suspects!   [*She goes* L.

PURDIE. [*Following her to* L.C.] Who minds him? [*Lovingly; above her.*] Joanna!

JOANNA. [*Moving to below the chair* L. *of the table.*] And Mabel? She saw you kiss my hand. I can't quite make her out. She was so deadly quiet about it. [*Facing Purdie, who is now on her* L.] Oh, Jack, if Mabel suspected!

PURDIE. There's nothing for her to suspect!

JOANNA. [*Comforted.*] No, there isn't, is there? Jack, I'm not doing anything wrong, am I?

PURDIE. [*Taking her hand fondly.*] You?

JOANNA. [*Giving him her other hand also.*] Mabel is your wife, Jack. I should so hate myself if I did anything that was disloyal to her.

PURDIE. Those eyes could never be disloyal—my lady of the nut-brown eyes!

JOANNA. Ah, Jack! All I want is to—to help her and you.

                    [*Both are believing all they say.*

PURDIE. I know—how well I know—my dear brave love!

JOANNA. I'm very fond of Mabel, Jack. I should like to be the best friend she has in the world.

PURDIE. [*Pressing her to him.*] You are, dearest! No woman ever had a better friend.

JOANNA. [*In his embrace.*] And yet I don't think she really likes me—I wonder why?

PURDIE. It's just that Mabel doesn't understand. Nothing would make me say a word against my wife——

JOANNA. I wouldn't listen to you if you did.

PURDIE. I love you all the more, dear, for saying that. But Mabel is a cold nature and she doesn't understand.

JOANNA. She doesn't appreciate your finer qualities.

PURDIE. That's it. [*He kisses her hand and crosses below her to* R.C., *speaking with gloomy satisfaction.*] I often think, Joanna, that I am rather like a flower that has never had the sun to shine on it nor the rain to water it.

                    [*He sits on the lower arm of the chair* R. *of the table.*

JOANNA. [*Sitting* L. *of the table.*] You almost break my heart.

PURDIE. [*Almost cheerful at the thought.*] I suppose there is no more lonely man than I walking the earth today.

JOANNA. It's so mournful!

PURDIE. It is the thought of you that sustains me, elevates me. You shine high above me like a star.

JOANNA. No, no! I wish I was wonderful, but I'm not.

PURDIE. You have made me a better man, Joanna.

JOANNA. I am so proud to think that.

PURDIE. You have made me kinder to Mabel.

JOANNA. I am sure you are always kind to her.
                                        [*She sits* C. *of the table.*

PURDIE. Yes, I hope so. [*He rises and turns up* R.C.] But I think now of special little ways of giving her pleasure. [*With sudden vehemence crossing to* L.C., *above the table.*] That never-to-be-forgotten day when we first met, you and I!
                        [*He comes down and kneels* L. *of her chair.*

JOANNA. That tragic, lovely day by the weir! Oh, Jack!

PURDIE. [*Carried away by the beauty of his conduct.*] Do you know how in gratitude I spent the rest of that day?

JOANNA. Tell me.

PURDIE. I read to Mabel aloud for an hour. I did it out of kindness to her, because I had met you. .

JOANNA. It was dear of you.

PURDIE. Do you remember that first time my arms—your waist—you are so fluid, Joanna. [*The fluidity of her is so great that it is almost a pain to think of it.*] I gave her a ruby bracelet for that.

JOANNA. It is a gem. You have given that lucky woman many lovely things.

PURDIE. It's my invariable custom to go straight off and buy her something whenever you have been sympathetic to me. Those new earrings of hers—they are in memory of the first day you called me Jack. Her gown—the one with the beads—was because you let me kiss you.

JOANNA. I didn't exactly let you.

PURDIE. No, but you have such a dear way of giving in.

JOANNA. [*Suddenly faintly disturbed.*] Jack, she hasn't worn that gown of late.

PURDIE. Nor the jewels either. I think she has some sort of idea now that when I give her anything nice it means that you have been nice to me. She has rather a suspicious nature, Mabel; she never used to have it, but it seems to be growing on me. I wonder why, I wonder why, Joanna?
                                        [*He kisses her solemnly.*

* E 148

[*Mrs Purdie passes outside the french windows, sees them, and passes off sadly*, L. *to* R.

JOANNA. [*Rising.*] Who was that?

PURDIE. [*Rises, and going up to the window.*] There's no one.

JOANNA. Yes, there was. [*Crossing* R., *and turning to face up* C.] If it were Mabel! [*Purdie comes down* R.C.] Oh, Jack, if she saw us she will think you were kissing me.

PURDIE. [*Kissing her again.*] No, no!

[*Purdie's arms are about her when enter Mrs Purdie quietly at the french windows up* C.

MRS PURDIE. [*Quietly.*] I am so sorry to interrupt you, Jack, but please wait a moment before you kiss her again. Excuse me, Joanna.

[*Mrs Purdie pulls the curtains and the garden is hidden from view, but she leaves the windows open.*

I don't want the others to see. [*Crossing down* L.] They mightn't understand how noble you are, Jack. [*Turning at the door.*] You can go on now.

[*Mrs Purdie exits* L.

[NOTE: *At this point, change the exterior setting to the wood.*

JOANNA. How extraordinary! Of all the—— [*She crosses* L. *below the table.*] Oh, how contemptible! [*She calls.*] Mabel!

[*Mrs Purdie comes back* L. *Purdie comes down* R.

MRS PURDIE. Did you call me, Joanna?

JOANNA. I insist on an explanation. [*Rather haughty.*] What were you doing out there, Mabel?

MRS PURDIE. I was looking for something I have lost!

PURDIE. Anything important?

MRS PURDIE. I used to fancy it, Jack. It is my husband's love. You didn't happen to have picked it up, Joanna? If you don't value it very much I should like it back—the pieces, I mean.

JOANNA. Mabel—I—I will not be talked to in that way. To imply that I—that your husband—oh, shame!

[*She turns up* L.C.

PURDIE. I must say, Mabel, that I am a little disappointed in you. I certainly understood that you had gone upstairs to put on your boots.

MRS PURDIE. Poor old Jack! [*Bitingly.*] A woman like that!

JOANNA. [*Above the table.*] I forgive you, Mabel! You will be sorry for this afterwards.

PURDIE. Not a word against Joanna, Mabel. If you knew how
nobly she has spoken of you.

JOANNA. [*To above the chair* R. *of the table.*] She does know.
She has been listening.

[*There is a gasp and a movement from Mrs Purdie. The two
ladies glare at each other, and for a moment there is danger
of the scene degenerating into something worse; but
Purdie intervenes.*

PURDIE. [*Crossing to* L.C. *below the table.*] This is a man's business.
I must be open with you, Mabel. It is the manlier way. If you
wish it, I shall always be true to you in word and deed. It is
your right. But I cannot pretend that Joanna is not the one
woman in the world for me. If I had met her before you—
it's Fate, I suppose.

[*He turns up above the chair* L. *of the table.*

JOANNA. [*Moving to below the chair* R. *of the table.*] Too late!
Too late!   [*She sits in the chair.*

MRS PURDIE. I suppose you never knew what true love was till
you met her, Jack?

PURDIE. You force me to say it. Joanna and I are as one person.
We have not a thought at variance. We are one rather than
two.

MRS PURDIE. [*Looking at Joanna.*] Yes, and that's the one!
[*Scornfully.*] I am so sorry to have marred your lives.

PURDIE. [*Thinking himself rather fine.*] If any blame there is, it
is all mine, she is as spotless as—as—the driven snow. The
minute I mentioned love to her she told me to desist.

MRS PURDIE. Not she! [*She goes to the door* L. *and pauses.*]

JOANNA. [*Rising.*] So you *were* listening! [*She moves up* R.C.]
Mabel, don't you see how splendid he is!

MRS PURDIE. Not quite, Joanna.   [*Mrs Purdie exits* L.
                                             [*Purdie moves up to the fire* L.

JOANNA. [*Crossing up* L.C. *to Purdie.*] How fine of you, Jack,
to take it all upon yourself.

PURDIE. [*Nobly.*] It is the man's privilege.

JOANNA. Mabel has such a horrid way of seeming to put people
in the wrong.

PURDIE. Have you noticed that? Poor Mabel, it's not an enviable
quality!

JOANNA. [*Turning away, above the table* C. *Despondently.*] I don't

think I care to go out now. She has spoilt it all. She has taken
the innocence out of it, Jack.

PURDIE. [*Moving towards her.*] You'll come, dear, surely, and
we'll give the others the slip.

[*They move together a little* L.C.

JOANNA. If we do, Mabel will say we did it intentionally.

PURDIE. We must be brave and not mind her. Oh, Joanna, if we
had met in time! If only I could begin again! To be doomed
for ever just because I once took the wrong turning—it isn't
fair.

JOANNA. The wrong turning! Now, who was saying that a
moment ago—about himself? Why, it was Matey.

[*They hear something.*

PURDIE. Is that her come back again? It's too bad.

[*Purdie puts his arm around Joanna to face Mrs Purdie boldly,
but they look foolish when Mrs Dearth enters* L. *in her
cloak, etc.*

Ah! It's you, Mrs Dearth.

MRS DEARTH. Yes, it is, but thank you for telling me, Mr
Purdie.

[*Joanna escapes from Purdie's arm, but he keeps it extended,
not knowing that it does not still enfold her. She pulls it
down.*

I don't intrude, do I?   [*She crosses below the table to* R.

JOANNA. [*Barking.*] Why should you?

PURDIE. Rather not. We were—hoping it would be you. I can't
think what has become of the others. We have been looking for
them everywhere. . . .

[*He glances vaguely round the room, as if they might so far
have escaped detection.*

MRS DEARTH. [*Moving up* R.C.] Well, do go on looking—
[*pointing to the table*]—under that flowerpot would be a good
place. It's my husband I am in search of.

[*She moves to down* R.

PURDIE. [*Moving* R.] Shall I rout him out of the dining-room?

[*He checks at* R.C.

MRS DEARTH. [*With mock seriousness.*] How too unutterably
kind of you, Mr Purdie. I hate to trouble you, but it would
be the sort of service one never forgets.

PURDIE. You know I believe you are chaffing me.

MRS DEARTH. No, no, I am incapable of that!

PURDIE. [*Glancing up* L.C. *at Joanna.*] I won't be a moment.

MRS DEARTH. Miss Trout and I will await your return with ill-concealed impatience. [*She sits* R. *of the table.*

[*Purdie exits up* R., *into the dining-room.*

[*Mrs Dearth looks at Joanna up* L.C., *who tosses her head.*

[*As if reading Joanna's thoughts.*] Yes, I suppose you're right. I daresay I am.

JOANNA. I didn't say anything. [*Ready for a quarrel.*

MRS DEARTH. I thought I heard you say, 'That hateful Dearth woman coming butting in where she's not wanted.'

JOANNA. [*Tartly.*] You certainly have good ears.

MRS DEARTH. Yes, they have always been admired.

JOANNA. By the painters for whom you sat when you were an artist's model?

MRS DEARTH. So that has leaked out, has it?

JOANNA. [*Rather ashamed.*] I shouldn't have said that.

MRS DEARTH. Do you think I care whether you know or not?

JOANNA. I'm sure you don't. Still, it was cattish of me.

MRS DEARTH. It was.

JOANNA. [*Flaring up.*] I don't see it!

[*Mrs Dearth laughs.*

[*Joanna stamps and exits* L.

[*Mr Dearth comes in* R. *He is a man of forty. An artist, his appearance gone a little to seed. He is not in the least intoxicated, but he is flushed with wine. A good man who has gone wrong, and in his heart despises himself for it. He is, in a quiet way, rather a wreck.*

DEARTH. [*Coming to* C. *above the table.*] I'm uncommon flattered that you should want me, Alice. It quite takes me aback.

MRS DEARTH. [*Who despises him.*] It isn't your company I want, Will.

DEARTH. You know, I felt that Purdie must have delivered your message wrongly.

MRS DEARTH. It is something to do with Lob. I want you to come with us on this mysterious walk and keep an eye on him.

DEARTH. On poor little Lob. Oh, surely not!

MRS DEARTH. I can't make the man out. I want you to tell me something. When he invited us here, do you think it was you or me he especially wanted?

Dearth. Oh, you. He made no bones about it—said there was something about you that made him want uncommonly to have you down here.

Mrs Dearth. Will, try to remember this. Did he ask us for any particular time?

Dearth. Yes. [*To above the chair* L. *of the table.*] He was particular about its being Midsummer week.

Mrs Dearth. Ah! I thought so. Did he say what it was about me that made him want to have me here in Midsummer week?

Dearth. No, but I presumed it must be your fascination.

Mrs Dearth. Nonsense! Well, I want you to come out with us tonight and watch him.

Dearth. Spy on my host! And such a harmless little chap, too! Excuse me, Alice. Besides, I have—an engagement!

Mrs Dearth. An engagement—with the port decanter, I presume.

Dearth. [*Moving back to above the table,* C.] A good guess, but wrong. The decanter is now but an empty shell. Still, how you know me! My engagement is with a quiet cigar in the garden.

Mrs Dearth. Your hand is so unsteady, you won't 'be able to light the match.

Dearth. I shall just manage.

Mrs Dearth. A nice hand for an artist!

Dearth. One would scarcely call me an artist nowadays.

Mrs Dearth. Not so far as any work is concerned.

Dearth. [*Moving a little up* L.] Not so far as having any more pretty dreams to paint is concerned. [*A pause as he comes down* L.C.] Wonder why I've become such a waster, Alice?

[*He sits* L. *of the table.*

Mrs Dearth. I suppose it was always in you!

Dearth. I suppose so, and yet I was rather a good sort in the days when I went courting you.

Mrs Dearth. Yes, I thought so. Unlucky days for me, as it has turned out.

Dearth. [*Quite sincere.*] Yes, a bad job for you. I didn't know I was a wrong 'un at the time. Thought quite well of myself. Thought a vast deal more of you. How I used to leap out of bed at 6 a.m. all agog to be at my easel. Blood ran through my veins in those days. And now I'm middle-aged and done for—funny! Don't know how it has come about, nor what has made the music mute. [*A slight pause.*] When did you begin to despise me, Alice?

Mrs Dearth. When I got to know you really, Will—a long time ago.

Dearth. Yes, I think that's true. It was a long time ago, and before I had begun to despise myself. It wasn't till I knew you had no opinion of me that I began to go downhill. You'll grant that, won't you?—and that I did try for a bit to fight on. If you had cared for me I wouldn't have come to this, surely?

Mrs Dearth. Well, I found I didn't care for you, and I wasn't hypocrite enough to pretend I did. That's blunt, but you used to admire my bluntness.

Dearth. The bluntness of you—the adorable wildness of you, you untamed thing. [*He pauses, remembering.*] There were never any shades in you. You could only love or hate. Kiss or kill was your motto, Alice. I felt from the first moment I saw you that you would either love me or knife me.

Mrs Dearth. I didn't knife you!

Dearth. No, I suppose that was where you made the mistake. It's hard on you, old lady. I suppose it's too late to try to patch things up, Alice?

Mrs Dearth. Let's be honest. It's too late, Will.

Dearth. Perhaps if we had had children! [*He pauses.*] Pity!

Mrs Dearth. A blessing, I should think, seeing what sort of a father they would have had!

Dearth. I dare say you're right. [*He rises, and moves round above the table.*] Well, Alice, I know that somehow it's my fault. I'm sorry for you.

Mrs Dearth. I'm sorry for myself. If I hadn't married you, what a different woman I should be! What a fool I was!

Dearth. Ah! Three things, they say, come not back to man nor woman—the spoken word, the past life and the neglected opportunity. Wonder if we should make any more of them, Alice, if they did come back to us.

Mrs Dearth. You wouldn't.

Dearth. I guess you're right.

Mrs Dearth. But I——

Dearth. [*Coming down above her chair.*] Yes, I dare say it would have been a boon for you, but I hope it's not 'The Honourable Freddy Finch-Fallowe' you would put in my place. I know he is following you about again.

MRS DEARTH. He followed me about, as you put it, before I knew you. I don't know why I quarrelled with him.

DEARTH. Your heart told you that he was no good.

MRS DEARTH. My heart told me that you were. So it wasn't of much service to me, my heart!

DEARTH. Freddy Finch-Fallowe is a rotter, Alice.

MRS DEARTH. You are certainly an authority on the subject.

DEARTH. You have me there. Poor old Alice. After which brief, but pleasant little connubial chat he pursued his dishonoured way into the garden.

[*Dearth crosses up towards the windows. But he is prevented from doing so by the arrival of all the others. Purdie enters from the dining-room, others from L. headed by Lob, attired for the walk. Cries of* 'Here we are!' 'I'm quite excited!' 'Mr Coade, you lead the way!' *The idea is that they are going off by the door* L. *Mrs Dearth rises, and turns* R. *to the settee.*

LOB. [*Excited—to Mr and Mrs Dearth and Purdie.*] Come on, come on!

MRS COADE. Are you not coming, Mr Dearth?

DEARTH. Alas! Unavoidably detained. You'll find me in the garden when you come back.

JOANNA. [*Humorously.*] If we ever do come back!

DEARTH. Precisely! [*To his wife.*] Should we never meet again, Alice, fare thee well. Purdie, if you find the tree of knowledge in the wood, bring me back an apple.

PURDIE. I promise.

[*He crosses* L. *to the door, and is checked by Lob.*

LOB. [*On needles.*] Don't speak so loud. Matey might hear you.

LADY CAROLINE. [*Up* L.C. *Always ready to pounce on him.*] Matey! That man again! What difference would that make, Lob?

LOB. He would take me off to bed. It's past my time.

[*All are amused.*

COADE. You know, old fellow, you make it very difficult for us to embark upon this adventure in the proper eerie spirit.

[*A movement to go.*

DEARTH. [*Turning up* C.] I'm for the garden.

> [*Dearth goes to the window, is pulling aside the curtain when he turns back. Something he has seen has startled him, though this must not be too greatly emphasized. He looks at the others, comes in and places his cigar on the ash tray up* R.

PURDIE. How now, Dearth?

DEARTH. [*Who has turned very quiet—coming down to the table,* C.] What is it we get in that wood, Lob?

MRS DEARTH. Ah, he won't tell us that.

LOB. [*Trying to get them to door* L.] Come on!

MRS DEARTH. Tell us first.

> [*They all look at Lob. A pause. All are silent and still.*

LOB. [*Compelled to tell.*] They say—that in the wood—you get what nearly everybody here is longing for—a second chance.

> [*He moves softly to the chair* L. *of the table, and sits.*
>
> [*A slight pause, as the ladies exchange glances.*

JOANNA. [*To* L. *of the chair above the table.*] So that's what we have in common!

ALL. [*Softly, looking at each other.*] Ah!

COADE. [L.C., *to Mrs Coade.*] You know, I've often thought, Coady, that if I had a second chance, I could be a useful man instead of just a lazy one.

MRS DEARTH. A second chance!

PURDIE. A second chance!

LOB. [*Rising.*] Come on!

> [*Endeavouring to push them all towards the door* L.
>
> [*A general movement towards* L.

DEARTH. [*Still quiet.*] Stop! [*They all check, and face him.*] Why not go this way?

> [*Dearth's manner has not been such as to rouse any suspicion in the audience. He pulls the window curtains and, instead of a garden, we now see close up to window and extending into the far distance a wood of great beech trees. It is very mysterious, with black splashes relieved by streaks of moonlight. Everybody is startled, most of all Lob, on whom all eyes gradually turn.*

LOB. [*In terror.*] Matey! Call Matey!

> [*He sits* L. *of the table, staring at the windows.*
>
> [NOTE: *Mrs Dearth has risen. The other ladies take one step*

  to the men for protection, but it should be still eerie, not
  funny.

DEARTH. [*Up* C.] Anyone ready to risk it?

              [*There is silence.*

PURDIE. [*Coming forward to up* L.C.] Of course there's nothing
it it—just—er—just——

DEARTH. Of course. Going out, Purdie?

          [*Purdie shrinks back—silence.*

MRS DEARTH. [*After the pause.*] A second chance.

        [*Facing Dearth across the table.*

DEARTH. I'll be back in a moment—probably.

  [*Dearth goes out and is lost in the wood. As he steps into it he*
   puts his hands to his ears as if something strange came
   over him at that moment.

  [*The others look at one another. There is another pause.*

LADY CAROLINE. He doesn't come back.

        [*She crosses to the* R. *of windows.*

MRS COADE. It's horrible! I'm going to my room. [*To Coade.*]
Come, dear.

           [*Mrs Coade exits* L.

COADE. Yes, yes.

   [*Coade takes a step after her, then comes back, to* L.C.
  [*Suddenly Mrs Purdie crosses up* C., *walks out of the window*
   and is lost.

  [NOTE: *She does the same business with her hands and ears as*
   Dearth had done, and this is repeated by all who go into
   the wood.

PURDIE. [*Taking a step after her.*] Mabel!

MRS DEARTH. You'll have to go now, Mr Purdie.

  [*Purdie moves up to the windows slowly. Joanna crosses to him.*
   He looks at Joanna and they go out together.

LOB. [*Imploringly.*] That's enough. Don't you go. Mrs Dearth.
Stay with me. You'll catch it if you go.

MRS DEARTH. [*Moving up* C.] A second chance!

      [*Mrs Dearth walks out into the wood.*

LADY CAROLINE. [*Moving up to the window. Slowly.*] One—
would like—to know. [*Lady Caroline follows Mrs Dearth.*

MRS COADE. [*Calling from off* L.] Coady!

  [*Coade hesitates between the door and the window. Then he*
   tiptoes up C., *and exits into the wood.*

[*Lob rises slowly and back a pace or two to* L.C.

[*Matey enters, up* R., *from the dining-room with a tray with coffee and cake. He does not see the window.*

MATEY. [*Coming to above the chair* R. *of the table.*] It's past your bedtime, sir. [*Putting down the tray.*] Say good night to the ladies and come along.

LOB. [*Pointing up* C.] Matey—look!

[*Matey wheels round and looks at the windows. He is speech-less. Then he turns to face down, slowly, and they look at each other, quaking.*

MATEY. Great Heavens! It's true, then!

LOB. Yes, but I—I wasn't sure!

[*Matey, shuddering, goes up to the windows to peer, but not to go out. He is backing a pace down, when Lob, who has gone up behind him, pushes him out. Matey disappears into the wood, putting up his hands as the others have done.*

[*Lob is terrified still, and backs to* L. *of the windows—yet he gloats also. He stretches his hand to the switch and turns out the lights, and stands, with his back to the audience, silhouetted against the moonlight, as—*

THE CURTAIN FALLS

ACT II

SCENE: *The Wood*

The scene is the wood, in the glory of a moonlight night. It is the same scene as the wood we saw from the windows, but now we have its full depth and wealth of trees.

The ground is mossy and leaf-strewn, and there are small twigs and branches here and there.

When the Curtain rises, the stage is almost dark and the moonlight fades in slowly.

Bright, strange music is heard at the beginning suggesting the 'Light that never was on sea or shore'. The nightingale is heard and continues singing until the lights are full up. Until then there is no talk.

Seated together on the sward a little R. of C., are a pair whom we have known in different conditions. We don't yet see who the man is; he is lying on his back with a handkerchief over his face and his head on the lady's lap. He is dressed in a motor-coat, rather loudly, in the manner of an affluent City man. The lady is Lady Caroline Laney, in an elegant country attire, suggestive of motoring. Her manner is quite changed. She neither drawls her words nor calls herself a person. She is rather jolly. We are to discover that the second chance has converted these two into man and wife.

There is a long pause before speaking as the lights are brought up.

LADY CAROLINE. [*Sentimental and very unlike her old self.*] Isn't it a lovely night, Jim? Listen to Philomel.

> [*The nightingale is heard again. Lady Caroline imitates its note sentimentally.*

It's saying it is lately married. [*To the unseen bird.*] So are we, you ducky thing! [*To her husband.*] I feel, Jim, that I am Rosalind, and that you are my Orlando.

MATEY. [*Sitting up and leaning on his elbow and disclosing himself—taking handkerchief off his face.*] What do you say I am, Caroliney?

LADY CAROLINE. My own one, don't you think it would be fun

if we were to write poems about each other and pin them on the tree trunks?

MATEY. [*Tolerantly.*] Poems! I never knew such a lass for high-flown language.

LADY CAROLINE. Your lass, dearest—Jim's lass!

MATEY. And don't you forget it!

LADY CAROLINE. What would you do if I were to forget it, great bear? [*Archly.*

MATEY. Take a stick to you.

LADY CAROLINE. I love to hear you talk like that. It's so virile. I always knew that it was a *master* I needed.

MATEY. It's what you all need.

LADY CAROLINE. It is—it is! You knowing wretch!

MATEY. Listen, Caroliney! [*He rattles his pocket.*] That's what gets the ladies.

LADY CAROLINE. How much have you made this week, you wonderful man?

MATEY. [*Blandly.*] Another five hundred or so. [*Getting out a cigar.*] That's all—just five hundred or so.

LADY CAROLINE. My dear golden fetter, listen to him! [*Looking at her wedding ring.*] Kiss my fetter, Jim.

MATEY. [*Bus. with matches.*] Wait till I light this.

LADY CAROLINE. Let me light the darling match.
[*She daintily does so while he continues.*

MATEY. Tidy-looking Petitey Corona this! There was a time when one of that sort would have run away with two days of my screw!

LADY CAROLINE. How I should have loved, Jim, to know you when you were poor! Fancy your having once been a clerk!

MATEY. We all have our beginning. [*Puffing his cigar.*] But it wouldn't have mattered how I began, Caroliney. I would have come to the top just the same. [*Proudly.*] I am a climber, and there's nails in my boots for the parties beneath me. Boots! I tell you if I had been a bootmaker, I would have been the first bootmaker in London.

LADY CAROLINE. [*Archly.*] I'm sure you would, Jim; but would you have made the best boots?

MATEY. [*As if she had paid him a compliment.*] Ha, ha! Very good, Caroliney; that's the neatest thing I've heard you say. But it's late. We have best be strolling back to our Rolls.

LADY CAROLINE. [*She rises and helps him up*.] I do hope the
ground wasn't damp!   [*Her hand on his arm.*
MATEY. Don't matter if it was. I was lying on your rug.
  [*Lady Caroline, however, has been on the bare ground. She
  picks up the rug. Joanna comes on R. in a country dress
  which should suggest that she is miserable; she is no longer
  the jolly, high-spirited girl we have known, but sad and
  crushed. They don't know each other. She passes to L.
  in front of them.*
Who's the mournful party?
JOANNA. [*Turning at R. of the L: lower tree.*] I wonder, sir,
whether you happen to have seen my husband? I have lost
him in the wood.   [*She is sobbing.*
  [*Gay woodland music is heard softly off stage.*
MATEY. [*At C.*] We are strangers in these parts ourselves,
missis. Have we passed anyone, Caroliney?
LADY CAROLINE. [*R.C., coyly.*] Should we have noticed, dear?
Might it be the old gent over there?   [*Looking R.
                          [*The music is nearer.*
MATEY. [*To Joanna, who has moved up L.C.*] Is that him?
JOANNA. Oh, no! My husband is quite young.
  [*Coade, fancifully attired in a light summer suit and panama,
  is passing along happily at the back, playing on a whistle
  he has cut from a twig, and dancing to it as he goes. They
  survey Coade as he frisks along R. to L.*
MATEY. Seems a merry old cock. [*Calling.*] Hi, sir!
              [*Coade comes back from up L., to down L.C.*
Evening to you, sir. Do you happen to have seen a young
gentleman in the wood lately, all by himself, and looking for
his wife?
  [NOTE: *Coade only seems to be playing. The music is really
  from an oboe off stage and ceases when Coade speaks. The
  special gramophone record should be used if possible.*
COADE. [*L.C.*] Can't say I have.
JOANNA. [*Faltering.*] He isn't necessarily by himself—and I
don't know that he's looking for me. There may be a—a young
lady with him.
LADY CAROLINE. Oho!
JOANNA. [*Flashing and nearly blubbering.*] What do you mean
by 'Oho'?

Lady Caroline. Pooh! If you like that better.

Matey. Now, now, now—your manners, Caroliney.

Coade. Would he be singing or dancing?

Joanna. Oh, no!—at least, I hope not.

Coade. [*To whom this is a strange hope.*] Hope not? Odd! Then I'm not likely to notice him. But if I do—what name shall I say?

Joanna. Purdie. I am Mrs Purdie.

Coade. I'll try to keep a look out, and if I see him . . . But I am rather occupied at present.

> [*Coade dances a whimsical sword dance over his whistle and another stick crossed, and then goes off up* L., *playing and dancing.*

Joanna. [*To Matey.*] I'm sorry I troubled you. I see him now.
> [*Looking* R. *up stage.*

Lady Caroline. [*Without looking.*] Is he alone?
> [*Joanna glares at her.*

Ah! I see he isn't!

Matey. Caroliney, no awkward questions! [*Moving up stage.*] Evening, missis, and I hope you'll get him to go along with you quietly. [*Looking after Coade.*] Look at the old codger dancing.

> [*Caroline, behind him, looks off in the same direction. The whistle is heard in the distance. They go off, skipping like Coade, and singing, to* L., *up stage.*

> [*The music ceases.*

> [*Joanna, the jealous, hides behind the tree down* L. *as Mr and Mrs Purdie enter up* R. *in smart country clothes. He now thinks that Joanna is his wife and Mabel his only love. Mabel is now bright and vivacious. It is as if she and Joanna had changed characters. It is Mrs Purdie who is the pursued now, instead of having to pursue. She banters him, which makes him hotter in the chase.*

> [*Purdie enters* R., *looks round carefully, and turns at* C.

Purdie. [*Calling.*] It's all right. She's gone.

> [*Mrs Purdie comes on gaily at* R., *eludes his advance, hides behind the tree* R. *and is pursued by Purdie round the tree, down, and gets to* R. *of the* R. *tree.*

[*After the above bus.*] Now, will you? Please do!

Mrs Purdie. [*Bantering.*] No, and no, and *no!* I don't know you nearly well enough for that. Besides, what would your

wife say? I shall begin to think you are a very dreadful man,
Mr Purdie.

Purdie. [*Who is as sincere as ever; below and to* L. *of the tree.*]
Surely you might call me Jack by this time?

Mrs Purdie. [*Also sincere.*] Only if you are very good—Jack.
[*To Purdie.*

Purdie. If only Joanna were more like you!

Mrs Purdie. Like me? You mean her face—it's a—well, if it's
not precisely pretty, it's a good face. *I* don't mind her face at
all. I'm glad you've got such a dependable little wife, Jack.

Purdie. [*Gloomily.*] Thanks!   [*He leans against the tree.*
[*Mrs Purdie crosses to* L. *of him and he goes to kiss her. Joanna
    peeps at them at times and we understand her feelings from
    her face.*

Mrs Purdie. [*Eluding him, to* C.] . . . No, you stand over there
—and behave. What would Joanna have said if she had seen
you just now?   [*She reclines on the ground down* C.

Purdie. [*On her* R., *and below her.*] A wife should be incapable
of jealousy.

Mrs Purdie. [*Pretending innocence.*] Joanna jealous! But has
she any reasons? Jack, tell me, who is the woman?

Purdie. Shall I, Mabel, shall I?   [*He kneels by her.*

Mrs Purdie. [*Faltering.*] I can't think who she is. Have I ever
seen her?

Purdie. [*As if it were an original remark.*] Every time you look
in a mirror.

Mrs Purdie. [*Thoughtfully.*] How odd! Jack, that can't be.
When I look in the mirror I only see myself.

Purdie. [*Believing her.*] How adorably innocent you are, Mabel!
Joanna would have guessed at once.

Mrs Purdie. [*Startled.*] Oh! Oh! I believe I . . . Oh, Jack.

Purdie. Shall I tell you now? The old, old story.
[*A little cry from Joanna, behind her tree down* L.

Both. What's that?

Purdie. It's only that robin. Shall I tell you . . . ?
[*He leans a little towards her and pauses.*

Mrs Purdie. [*Faltering.*] I don't know, I'm sure. Jack, try not
to say it, but if you feel you must, say it in such a way that it
would not hurt the feelings of Joanna if she happened to be
passing by—as she nearly always is.

PURDIE. I'd rather not say it at all than that way. I don't know, Mabel, whether you have noticed that I am not like other men?

MRS PURDIE. Yes.

PURDIE. All my life I have been a soul that has had to walk alone.

MRS PURDIE. How tragic!

PURDIE. I do so still. Then I met Joanna——

                    [*Joanna sniffs—he looks up.*

MRS PURDIE. Ah!

PURDIE. Foolishly, as I now see, I thought she would understand that I was far too deep a nature really to mean the little things I sometimes said to her.

MRS PURDIE. And so you married her.

PURDIE. And so I married her. [*A sob from Joanna.*] But still my soul walked alone.

MRS PURDIE. Then you met me?

PURDIE. Then—I met you.   [*He draws a little closer.*

MRS PURDIE. Too late—never—for ever—for ever—never! They are the saddest words in the English tongue.

PURDIE. At the time I thought a still sadder word was Joanna——

MRS PURDIE. What was it you saw in me that made you love me?

PURDIE. [*His arms round her.*] I think it was the feeling that you were so like myself.

    [*Purdie murmurs something to himself. She draws away from him.*

MRS PURDIE. You are saying something to yourself, Jack. What is it? Don't keep anything from me.

PURDIE. [*Fervently.*] I was repeating a poem, dear. It is in two words— 'Mabel Purdie'.

MRS PURDIE. Oh!

PURDIE. [*Kneeling.*] Mabel Purdie! If it could only be! Say 'Mabel Purdie' to me. Say it once, dear.

MRS PURDIE. If I were to say it, Jack. [*She is practically in his arms now.*] I should be false to Joanna—

                    [*They embrace.*

—and that I swear I shall never be.

PURDIE. [*Rising.*] Mabel!

MRS PURDIE. Let us go on.   [*She rises.*

PURDIE. Say it, Mabel, say it!

MRS PURDIE. I'll whisper it.   [*She does so.*

    [*The nightingale is heard again. Purdie and Mrs Purdie move up, his arm round her waist, and off up* L. *Joanna, bedraggled and miserable, moves up* C. *and turns. Before following them off, she looks up at the tree* R., *and addresses the unseen bird.*

JOANNA. That's all you know—you *bird!*

[*Joanna turns and exits up* L.

[*But the nightingale is really singing for another pair he has espied below. Apparently they are racing to the spot, and there is a prize for the one who finds where the easel was put up last night.*

[*The winner is Margaret, who enters* R., *a boyish figure of a girl not yet grown to womanhood. Brambles adhere to her dress. One boot has been in the water. Her hair is short and unruly, and she has many freckles. Yet she is as lovely as you think she is, and she is aged the moment when you like your daughter best.*

[*A hoot of triumph from her brings her father to the spot. We have already heard him as he approached, singing a song picked up in the Latin Quarter.*

MARGARET. [*Calling to him off* R.] Daddy—Daddy! I've won! Here's the place! Crack-in-my-eye, Tommy!

[*Her father enters. It is Dearth. But he is now an engaging fellow in tweeds, ablaze in happiness and health, and carrying easel and paint-box. He looks around, and nods approvingly, setting his easel up at* L.C. *as he speaks.*

DEARTH. Yes, that's the tree I stuck my easel under last night— [*in burlesque, pointing to the sky*]—and behold the blessèd moon behaving more gorgeously than ever. I'm sorry to have kept you waiting, old lady, but you ought to know by now how time passes. [*Setting up his materials.*] Now, keep still, while I hand you down to posterity.

[NOTE: *The moon is supposed to be down stage* R., *not visible to the audience.*

MARGARET. [C., R. *of Dearth.*] She's rather pale tonight, isn't she?

[*Margaret puts her cap in his pocket. Now and again throughout the scene she makes use of his pockets as receptacles for her various articles.*

DEARTH. Comes of keeping late hours.

MARGARET. [*To the moon, gaily coming down a little.*] Daddy, watch me—look at me! [*To the moon.*] Please, sweet moon, a pleasant expression—No, no—not as if you were sitting for it—that's too professional. That's better. [*She drops the moon a curtsy.*] Thank you. Now keep it. [*Turning up to Dearth.*] That's the sort of thing you say to them, Dad!

DEARTH. [*Getting to work.*] You're a monkey! You know I oughtn't to have brought you out so late. You should be tucked up in your cosy bed at home.

MARGARET. With the pillows, anyhow.
[*Throwing beech nuts off* L.

DEARTH. Except in its proper place!

MARGARET. And the sheet over my face.
[*A pace or two towards* R.C.

DEARTH. Where it oughtn't to be.

MARGARET. [*Turning to face Dearth.*] And daddy tiptoeing in to take it off.

DEARTH. Which is more than you deserve.

MARGARET. [*A pace to* C.] Then why does he stand so long at the door? And before he's gone she bursts out laughing, for she has been awake all the time.   [*Back of him.*
[*She is now above him, glancing at the picture.*

DEARTH. That's about it! What a life. But I oughtn't to have brought you here. Best to have the sheet over you when the moon's about. Moonlight's bad for little daughters.

MARGARET. Daddy . . . [*To* C.] I can't sleep when the moon's at the full. She keeps calling to me to get up. Perhaps I'm *her* daughter too.

DEARTH. Gad, you look it tonight!

MARGARET. [*Pleased.*] Do I? Then can't you paint me into the picture as well as Mamma? You could call it 'A mother and daughter', or simply, 'Two ladies', if the moon thinks that calling me her daughter would make her seem too old.

DEARTH. *O mater pulchra filia pulchrior!* That means, 'O Moon—more beautiful than any twopenny-ha'penny daughter'!

MARGARET. [*Mischievously, pouting.*] Daddy, do you really prefer her?
[*To him, he kisses her lightly.*

DEARTH. [*In stage whisper.*] H'sh! She's not a patch on you. It's the sort of thing we say to our sitters to keep them in good humour. [*Struck by something on her frock.*] Come here. [*Examines it—evidently it is a stain. He sighs.*] I wish to heaven, Margaret, you and I weren't both so fond of apple tart! [*Catching hold of her skirt.*] And what's this?

MARGARET. It's a tear!

DEARTH. I should think it is a tear!

MARGARET. [*Sliding a little* R. *and turning.*] It was that boy at the farm. He kept calling Snubs after me, but I got him down and kicked him in the stomach. He's rather a jolly boy.

[*She goes up, above and to* R. *of Dearth.*

DEARTH. Ye gods! What a night!

MARGARET. [*Looking at the picture.*] And what a moon! Dad, she's not quite so fine as that.

DEARTH. 'Sh! I've touched her up!

[*Coade's music is heard again. He dances in up* L., *and across up stage to* R.

MARGARET. [*As Coade reaches* C.] Dad, Dad—what a funny man!

[*Margaret gaily dances behind Coade, imitating him. He disappears up* R., *but his whistling is still heard. Dearth joins Margaret in a wild dance. She ends in his arms, at* C., *suddenly sad and fearful.*

Hold me tight, Daddy, I'm frightened. I think they want to take you away from me.

DEARTH. Who, gosling?

MARGARET. I don't know. It's too lovely, Daddy. I won't be able to keep hold of it.

DEARTH. What is?

MARGARET. The world—everything—and you, Daddy, most of all. Things that are too beautiful can't last.

DEARTH. [*Who knows it.*] Now, how did you find that out?

MARGARET. [*Still in his arms.*] I don't know, Daddy. Am I sometimes stranger than other people's daughters?

DEARTH. More of a mad-cap, perhaps.   [*He kisses her.*

MARGARET. Do you think I am sometimes *too* full of gladness?

DEARTH. You are sometimes running over with it.

[*He goes to the easel.*

MARGARET. To be very gay, dearest dear, is so near to being very sad.

DEARTH. [*Who knows this also.*] How did you find that out, child?

MARGARET. I don't know. From something in me that's afraid.

[*She sits on the ground* C.] Daddy, what is a 'might-have-been'?

DEARTH. [*To easel.*] A 'might-have-been'? They're ghosts, Margaret! I dare say I 'might-have-been' a great swell of a painter, instead of just this uncommonly happy nobody—or again I might have been a worthless idle waster of a fellow.

MARGARET. [*Incredulous, sitting up.*] You?

DEARTH. Who knows? Some little kink in me might have set me off on the wrong road. And that poor soul I might so easily have been might have had no Margaret. I'm sorry for *him.* [*He sits at the easel.*

MARGARET. [*Sitting back.*] And so am I! [*Playing with twigs.*] The poor old daddy, wandering about the world without me.

DEARTH. And there are other 'might-have-beens'—lovely ones, but intangible. *Shades*, Margaret, made of sad folks' thoughts.

MARGARET. [*Gaily.*] I'm so glad I'm not a shade. How awful it would be, Daddy, to wake up and find one wasn't alive.

DEARTH. It would, dear.

MARGARET. Daddy, wouldn't it be awful? [*A slight pause.*] I think men need daughters.

DEARTH. They do.

MARGARET. Especially artists.

DEARTH. Especially artists.

MARGARET. Especially artists.

DEARTH. Especially artists.

MARGARET. Fame is not everything.

DEARTH. [*In same spirit.*] Fame is rot! Daughters are the thing!

MARGARET. Daughters are the thing.

DEARTH. Daughters are the thing.

MARGARET. I wonder if sons would be even nicer?

DEARTH. Not a patch on daughters. The awful thing about a son is that never—never—at least, from the day he goes to school—can you tell him that you rather like him. By the time he's ten you can't even take him on your knee. Sons are not worth having, Margaret, Signed, W. Dearth.

MARGARET. [*Still on the ground.*] But if you were a mother, Dad, I dare say he would let you do it.

DEARTH. Think so?

MARGARET. I mean, when no one was looking. Sons are not

so bad. Signed, M. Dearth. But I'm glad you prefer daughters. [*Coming to him on her knees.*] At what age are we nicest, Daddy? [*But he is engrossed in his moon.*] Hie, Daddy, at what age are we nicest? [*He seems not to hear.*] Daddy—hie! Hie—at what age are we nicest?

DEARTH. [*Rising.*] Eh? [*Jocular and tender at the same time.*] That's a poser! I think you were nicest when you were two and knew your alphabet up to 'G' but fell over at 'H'. [*He paints a stroke or two.*] No, you were best when you were half past three—or just before you struck six—or in the mumps year, when I asked you in the early morning how you were and you said solemnly, 'I haven't tried yet.' [*He moves back a pace, viewing the picture.*] I'm not sure that chicken-pox doesn't beat mumps. [*Down* L.C. *and turns.*] Oh, Lord! I'm all wrong. The nicest time in a father's life is *now*, the year before she puts up her hair.

MARGARET. [*Thoughtfully.*] I suppose that is a splendid time for fathers. But there's a nicer year coming to you, Daddy, the year she *does* put up her hair.

DEARTH. Suddenly puts it up for ever? You know, I am afraid that when the day for that comes I won't be able to stand it, it will be too exciting. My poor heart, Margaret!

MARGARET. [*Still on the ground.*] No, no, it will be *lucky* you, for it isn't to be a bit like that. I'm to be a girl and woman day about, for the first year. You'll never know which I am till you look at my hair. And even then you won't know, for if it's down I'll put it up, and if it's up I'll put it down. [*Importantly.*] And, so my daddy will gradually get used to the idea.   [*She rises.*

DEARTH. I see you have been thinking it out.
                                   [*He moves up to the easel again.*

MARGARET. I have been doing more than that. Shut your eyes, Daddy, and I'll give you a glimpse into the future.

DEARTH. I don't know that I want that. The present's so good.

MARGARET. Shut your eyes at once.

DEARTH. No, Margaret.

MARGARET. Please, Daddy.

DEARTH. Oh, all right. [*Doing so.*] They are shut!

MARGARET. Don't open them till I tell you. What finger is that?
                                   [*Holding up a thumb.*

DEARTH. The dirty one.

[*Dearth hums a French song. She begins to put up her hair, using as mirror a little pool of water on the ground,* L. *of the middle tree at* R.

MARGARET. [*Kneeling by the pool.*] Daddy, now I am putting up my hair. I have got such a darling of a mirror. It's such a darling mirror I've got, Dad. Dad, don't look. It's such a darling mirror. I'll tell you about it. It's a little pool of water. I wish we could take it home and hang it up. Of course the moment my hair is up there will be other changes also. For one thing, I shall talk quite differently.

DEARTH. Pooh! Where are my matches, dear?

[*Feeling his pockets with his eyes shut.*

MARGARET. Top pocket, waistcoat.

DEARTH. [*Trying to light his pipe, eyes closed.*] You were trying to frighten me just now.

MARGARET. [*Still kneeling at the pool.*] No, I am just preparing you. You see, darling, I can't call you Daddy when my hair is up. I think I shall call you—[*reflects*]—I shall call you—parent. Parent dear, do you remember the days when your Margaret was a slip of a girl, and sat on your knee? How foolish we were, Parent, in those distant days!

DEARTH. Shut up, Margaret.

MARGARET. Now I must be more distant to you—more like the boy who couldn't sit on your knee any more.

DEARTH. See here, I want to go on painting. Shall I look now?

MARGARET. [*Rather quaking now.*] No—no—no—— [*She looks in pool.*] I am not quite sure whether I want you to. It makes such a difference. Perhaps you won't know me. Even the pool is looking a little scared. [*She comes* C., *anxiously.*] Look, Daddy. What do you think? Will I do?

DEARTH. Stand still, dear, and let me look my fill. [*He looks long at her.*] The Margaret that is to be.

MARGARET. You'll see me often enough, Daddy, like this, so you don't need to look your fill. You are looking as long as if this were to be the only time.

DEARTH. Was I? Surely it can't be that?

MARGARET. Be gay, Dad. [*She moves to him, and puts her arms round him.*] You will be sick of Margaret with her hair up before you are done with her.

DEARTH. I expect so.

MARGARET. Shut up, Daddy! [*She moves a little* R., *letting her hair down.*] Daddy, I know what you are thinking of. You are thinking what a handful she is going to be.

DEARTH. [*Humorously.*] Well, I guess she is!

MARGARET. [*Grave.*] Daddy, now you are thinking about—about my being in love some day.

DEARTH. Rot!

MARGARET. [*Reassuringly.*] I won't, you know, no, never! [*Coming nearer to him.*] Oh, I've quite decided, so don't be afraid, Daddy. [*At back of him* L.C.—*whispers.*] Will you hate him at first, Daddy?

DEARTH. Whom?

                   [*During the following lines, Dearth paints assiduously.*

MARGARET. Well, if there was!

DEARTH. If there was what, darling?

MARGARET. You know the kind of thing I mean, quite well. Would you hate him at first?

DEARTH. I hope not. I should want to strangle him, but I wouldn't hate him.

MARGARET. *I* would. [*Moving to* C.] That is to say, if I liked him.

DEARTH. If you liked him, how could you hate him?

MARGARET. [*Up* C.] For daring!

DEARTH. Daring what?

MARGARET. You know! [*Sighing half humorously.*] But of course *I* shall have no say in the matter.

DEARTH. Why?

MARGARET. [*Reproachfully.*] *You* will do it all. You do everything for me.

DEARTH. [*With a groan.*] I can't help it.

MARGARET. [*Sauntering to* L.C., *kicking twigs and leaves.*] You will even write my love-letters, if I ever have any to write—which I won't.

DEARTH. [*Properly alarmed.*] Surely to goodness I'll leave you alone to do that!

MARGARET. [*Standing by the tree, behind the easel.*] Not you. You'll try to, but you won't be able.

                                        [*Dearth stops painting.*

DEARTH. I want you, you see, to do everything exquisitely. [*Remorseful.*] I wish I could leave you to do things a little more

for yourself. [*As he paints a few strokes.*] I suppose it's owing
to my having to be father and mother both. I knew nothing
practically about the rearing of children—and of course I
couldn't trust you to a nurse.

MARGARET. [*Severely—crossing down* C., *below and* R. *of the
easel.*] Not you. So sure you could do it better yourself.
That's you all over. [*Turning, and shaking her head solemnly
at him.*] Of course I know you can't help it. [*Moving up* C. *to*
R. *of Dearth.*] If I ever *should* marry—not that I will—but if I
should—will you let *me* be the one who says 'I do'?

DEARTH. [*Groaning.*] I suppose I deserve this!

MARGARET. [*Sitting* C.] Daddy, do you remember how you taught
me to balance a biscuit on my nose, like a puppy?

DEARTH. [*Sadly.*] Did I?

MARGARET. And when you said 'snap' I caught it in my mouth?

DEARTH. Horrible!

MARGARET. [*Kneeling up, and whispering.*] Daddy! I can do it
still. [*Producing a biscuit.*] Here is the last of my supper. [*She
puts it on her nose.*] Say 'snap', Daddy.

DEARTH. Not I.

MARGARET. Say 'snap', please.

DEARTH. No, Margaret.

MARGARET. Daddy!

DEARTH. Snap!

[*Margaret catches the biscuit in her mouth.*
Let that be the last time, Margaret. [*He resumes his painting.*

MARGARET. Except just once more.

DEARTH. [*Putting down his brush.*] No, darling.

MARGARET. [*Sitting back.*] Not now. [*Wheedling and shy.*] But
if I should ever have a—a Margaret of my own, come in and
see me, Daddy, in my bed, and say 'snap'—and I'll have the
biscuit ready.

DEARTH. [*Turning away his head.*] Right-o.

MARGARET. *You* think I'm pretty, don't you, Daddy, whatever
other people say? [*Sitting by him.*

DEARTH. [*Taking up his brush.*] Not so bad.

MARGARET. I *know* I have nice ears.

DEARTH. [*Painting.*] They are all right now, but I had to work
on them for months.

MARGARET. You don't mean to say that you did my *ears*?

DEARTH. Rather!

MARGARET. [*Entreating.*] My dimple's my own, isn't it?

DEARTH. [*Drawing back and regarding the painting.*] I'm glad you think so. I wore out the point of my little finger over that dimple.

MARGARET. Even my dimple! Have I anything that's really mine? A bit of my nose or anything?

DEARTH. [*Sighing.*] When you were a babe you had a laugh that was all your own.

MARGARET. Haven't I it now?

DEARTH. It's gone. [*He is a good deal moved, and rises, moving up* C.—*sadly.*] I'll tell you how it went. We were fishing in a stream—that is to say, I was wading and you were sitting on my shoulders doing the fishing. We didn't catch anything. Somehow or another—I can't think how I did it—you irritated me, and I answered you sharply.   [*He shudders.*

MARGARET. [*Who is on ground* C. *below him.*] I can't believe that.

DEARTH. [*Behind her, moving about.*] Yes, I did. It gave you a shock, and, for the moment, the world no longer seemed a safe place to you. Your faith in me had always made it safe till then. You were suddenly not even sure of your bread and butter, and a frightened tear came to your eyes. I was in a nice state, I can tell you.   [*He looks down at her.*

MARGARET. [*Looking up at him.*] But what has that to do with my laugh, Daddy?

DEARTH. The laugh that children are born with lasts just so long as they have perfect faith. To think it was I who robbed you of yours. I expect I am not the only parent in that plight, though they may not remember the doing of it. [*He is crushed.*

MARGARET. Don't, dear! I'm sure the laugh just went off with the tear to comfort it, and they have been playing about that stream ever since. They have quite forgotten us, so why should we remember them? Shall I tell you my farthest-back recollection?

                 [*He nods—and strolls to down* R.C.

[*She speaks in some awe.*] I remember the first time I saw the stars.

                 [*He nods again.*

I had never seen the *night*, and then I saw *it*, and the *stars*, together. Crack-in-my-eye, Tommy!—not everyone can boast of such a lovely recollection for their earliest!

DEARTH. I was determined your earliest should be a good one.

MARGARET. Do you mean to say *you* planned it.

DEARTH. [*To her—at* C.] Rather! Most people's earliest recollection is of some trivial thing; how they cut their finger or lost a piece of string. I was resolved my Margaret's should be something bigger. I was poor, but I could give her the stars.

MARGARET. [*Impulsively, she clasps his knee.*] Oh, how you do love me, Daddy!

DEARTH. Yes, I do rather.

> [*It is the climax of their scene of affection. Margaret releases Dearth, and he returns to his easel.*

> [*Mrs Dearth enters down* R. *She is poor in dress and worn in appearance, but with the simpering airs and touches of the fine lady—though she is almost a vagrant. They do not know each other.*

MARGARET. [*Nicely.*] Good evening.

MRS DEARTH. Good evening, missy. Evening, mister.

> [*She is looking about among the roots of the trees.*

DEARTH. [*At the easel—at work.*] Lost anything?

MRS DEARTH. Sometimes when the tourists have had their sandwiches there's bits left over, and they squeeze them between the roots to keep the place tidy. I'm looking for bits.

DEARTH. You don't tell me you are as hungry as all that?

MRS DEARTH. Try me.

MARGARET. [*Feeling his pocket.*] Daddy, that was my last biscuit!

DEARTH. We must think of something else.

MARGARET. [*Up* L., *to Mrs Dearth.*] Wait a bit, we're sure to think of something. Daddy, think of something.

> [*She puts her hand on Mrs Dearth's shoulder.*

MRS DEARTH. Your father doesn't like you to touch the likes of me.

MARGARET. Oh yes, he does! [*Smiling defiantly.*] And if he didn't, I'd do it all the same. This is a bit of *myself*, Daddy.

DEARTH. That's all *you* know.

MRS DEARTH. [*Sulky.*] You needn't be angry with her, mister, I'm all right.

DEARTH. I'm not angry with her. I'm very sorry for you.

MRS DEARTH. If I had my rights, I would be as good as you— and better.

DEARTH. I dare say.

MRS DEARTH. I've had menservants and a motor.

DEARTH. Margaret and I never rose to that.

MARGARET. I've been in a taxi several times, and Dad often gets telegrams.

DEARTH. Margaret!

MARGARET. I'm sorry I boasted.

MRS DEARTH. That's nothing. I have a town house—at least, I had. . . . At any rate, he said there was a town house.

MARGARET. Fancy his not knowing for certain.

MRS DEARTH. The Honourable Mrs Finch-Fallowe—that's who I am.

MARGARET. It's a lovely name.

MRS DEATH. Curse him!

MARGARET. Don't you like him?

DEARTH. [*To Mrs Dearth.*] We needn't go into these matters, I have nothing to do with your past. I wish we had some food.

MRS DEARTH. You haven't a flask?

DEARTH. No, I don't take anything myself. But let me see . . .

MARGARET. [*Sparkling.*] I know. You said we had five pounds. [*To Mrs Dearth.*] Would you like five pounds?

DEARTH. Darling, don't be stupid. We haven't paid our bill at the inn.

MRS DEARTH. [*Rising.*] All right. I never asked you for anything.

DEARTH. Ah, don't take me up in that way. I've had my ups and downs too. Here's ten bob, and welcome.

> [*He hands a ten shilling note to Margaret.*

MARGARET. And I have half a crown. [*Giving it to Mrs Dearth with the note.*] It's quite easy for us. Dad will be getting another fiver any day. You can't think how exciting it is when the fiver comes in. We dance, and then we run out and buy chops.

DEARTH. Margaret!

MRS DEARTH. It's kind of you. I'm richer this minute than I've been for many a day.

DEARTH. It's nothing. I'm sure you'd do the same for us.

MRS DEARTH. I wish I was as sure!

DEARTH. Of course you would. Glad to be of any help. You get some food as quick as you can. Best of wishes and may your luck change.   [*He goes to the easel.*

MRS DEARTH. Same to you and may yours go on.

MARGARET. [*Giving her hand.*] Good night.

MRS DEARTH. [*Turning Margaret round—and moving to* L. *of her.*] What's her name, Mister?

DEARTH. Margaret!

MRS DEARTH. [C.] Margaret—— You drew something good out of the lucky bag when you got her, mister.

DEARTH. Yes.

MRS DEARTH. Take care of her. They're easily lost.

[*She wanders off up* R.

DEARTH. Poor soul! I guess she has had a rough time, and that some man is to blame for it—partly, at any rate. That woman rather affects me, Margaret. I don't know why.

[*Margaret moves thoughtfully* L., *below the easel, as Dearth goes on painting, talking in his pauses in which he surveys his work, mixes paint, etc.*

I say, Margaret, we lucky ones, let's swear always to be kind to people who are down on their luck, and then when we're kind, let's be a little kinder.   [*He puts down his brush.*

MARGARET. [*Moving up to his* L., *gleefully.*] Yes, let's.

DEARTH. [*Taking her hand.*] Margaret, always feel sorry for the failures, the ones who are always, always failures—especially in my sort of calling. Wouldn't it be lovely, to turn them on the thirty-ninth year of failure into glittering successes?

MARGARET. Topping.

DEARTH. Topping.

MARGARET. Oh, topping. How could we do it, Daddy?

DEARTH. [*Returning to his painting.*] By letter. 'To poor old Tom Broken Heart, Top Attic, Garret Chambers, S.E. Dear Sir: His Majesty has been graciously pleased to purchase your superb picture of Marlow Ferry.'

MARGARET. 'PS. I am sending the money in a sack so as you can hear it chink.'   [*She crosses to* R.C.

DEARTH. [*Putting down his brush and palette.*] What could we do for our friend who passed just now? I can't get her out of my head.   [*He comes to* C., *on* R. *of the easel.*

MARGARET. [*Troubled.*] Oh, you have made me forget! [*Plaintively.*] Daddy, I didn't like it.   ·   [*She clings to him.*

DEARTH. What is it now, dear? Didn't like what?

MARGARET. [*With a little shudder.*] I didn't like her saying that about your losing me.

DEARTH. I'll not lose you!

MARGARET. It would be hard for me if you lost me, but it would be worse for my daddy! I don't know how I know that, but I do know it. What would you do without me?

DEARTH. [*Almost sharply.*] Don't talk like that, dear. It's wicked and stupid, and naughty. [*He relents, giving her a little hug. He is moved.*] Somehow that poor woman—I won't paint any more tonight.

> [*He turns to the easel and begins to pack up his things.*

MARGARET. Let's get out of the wood. It frightens me.

DEARTH. And you loved it a moment ago. [*He goes on packing, whistling as he does so. Then, as he turns to glance up* C.] Hallo!

> [*He has seen something strange. Part of a house has imperceptibly appeared in the background, a gauze effect. The curtained window of Act I is seen as from outside—the house is small and some distance away. He is only mildly surprised, thinking he has been unobservant.*

I hadn't noticed there was a house there!

MARGARET. [*Agitated, looking in the same direction.*] Nor I. [*Going up to him.*] Daddy, I feel sure there wasn't a house there.

> [*The moonlight commences to fade very slowly.*

DEARTH. Goose! It's just that we didn't look. Our old way of letting the world go hang! So interested in ourselves. Nice behaviour for people who had been boasting about what they would do for other people! That gives me an idea.

MARGARET. [*Gripping his arm.*] Let's get out of the wood!

> [*She draws him towards* R.C.

DEARTH. [*Disengaging.*] Yes, but my idea first. It is to rouse these people and get food from them for our friend.

MARGARET. [*Clutching his coat.*] She's too far away now.

DEARTH. [*Drawing away.*] I can overtake her in a jiffy.

> [*Only a light between the chinks of the curtain can be seen now.*

MARGARET. [*In a frenzy.*] Don't go into that house, Daddy! I'm afraid of it! I don't know why, but I'm afraid of that house!

> [*He waggles a reproving finger at her.*

DEARTH. [*Giving her three kisses.*] There's a kiss for each moment until I come back.

> [*She wipes them from her face.*

Oh, naughty! Go and stand in the corner.

> [*She stands against the tree down* R., *but stamps her foot.*

Who has got a nasty temper!

[*She tries hard not to smile, but she has to, and he smiles too; and they make comic faces at each other as they have done a thousand times before in similar circumstances.*

I shall be back before you can count a hundred.

[*He turns and goes off up* C. *to* L., *humming his gay French song.*

[*The wood is now growing dark, and the trees more obscure. The nightingale is heard again, though farther off than before.*

[*Margaret tries dutifully to count her hundred, but her fear returns. She runs panic-stricken up* C., *and then from tree to tree, calling.*

MARGARET. Daddy! [*To up* C.] Daddy! [*Running from* L. *to* R.] Daddy! [*To come* C., *and backing to down* R.] Daddy, come back! Come back, Daddy! [*She turns* L. *of the lower* R. *tree, to face down. There is no light but a faint moonbeam upon her face.*] I don't want to be a might-have-been!

[*The moonbeam fades.*

CURTAIN

ACT III

SCENE: *As in Act I. The drawing-room is in darkness. The curtains are drawn across the windows. Outside, the wood has been replaced by the garden, but this too is in darkness and cannot be seen when the curtains are parted.*

Lob is asleep in the armchair up L., *which is still turned to face up* R., *diagonally, so that only one of his legs can be seen, and no more.*

There is a knocking at the window and then Purdie and Mrs Purdie enter as intruders. They are dressed (like those who follow) as at the end of Act I, but they still regard each other as in Act II. They do not see Lob yet, and are unaware that their clothes have changed.

PURDIE. [*In the darkness.*] I feel rather like a burglar.

                                       [*He gropes up* L.C.

MRS PURDIE. [*Up* R.C.] It's quite creepy, sweetheart.

PURDIE. Ah! It's extraordinary how helpless one is in a dark room.

MRS PURDIE. Yes, even if you know the room, and this one being strange to us makes it worse.

                         [*Purdie knocks against some furniture.*

PURDIE. One minute. I think I've fallen down a cellar.

MRS PURDIE. Beloved, are you hurt?

PURDIE. How awful if Joanna were following us! Here's a switch.

                    [*He turns on the light and they look around.*

Ah! A pretty room. I wonder who is the owner?

MRS PURDIE. [*Suddenly, pointing to Lob.*] There's a man!

PURDIE. Hallo, he's asleep!   [*He moves* L. *to Lob.*

MRS PURDIE. [*Moving to* C., *on* R. *of Purdie.*] Do you know him?

PURDIE. Never set eyes on him before. [*To Lob.*] Excuse me, sir! Hi!

    [*Purdie shakes Lob in vain, though Lob makes sufficient movement to show that he is alive.*

Darling, how extraordinary! I suppose he is the owner.

MRS PURDIE. [*Drawing Purdie to* C.] After all, precious, have

152

we any right to wake up a stranger, just to tell him that we are runaways hiding in his house?

PURDIE. I think he would expect it of us. [*Turning to Lob.*] Hi! [*Slight pause.*] There's no budging him.

MRS PURDIE. Well, at any rate, we've done the civil thing. [*She crosses to* R. *of the table, and looks at the tiny tray with the coffee.*] There have evidently been people here, but they haven't drunk their coffee. [*Drinks.*] Ugh! Cold as a deserted egg in a bird's nest. [*To below the chair* R. *of the table.*] Jack, if you were a clever detective you could construct those people out of their deserted coffee-cups. I wonder who they are, and what has spirited them away?

PURDIE. [*Beautifully.*] What does it matter? [*Moving towards her.*] There's just one cup I want to drink, and its name is Mabel!   [*He comes above and to her* R.

MRS PURDIE. [*Sitting* R. *of the table.*] Dear! I suppose we have run away, Jack—meaning it?

PURDIE. Irrevocably! [*Passionately, he kneels* R. *of her chair.*] Mabel, if the dog-like devotion of a lifetime . . . [*He checks, and glances over at Lob.*] He's not shamming, is he?

MRS PURDIE. Shake him again.

> [*Purdie rises, goes up to Lob, returns and kneels again. Lob, unseen by them, gives his kick in the air.*

PURDIE. If the dog-like devotion of a lifetime . . .

MRS PURDIE. Poor little Joanna! Still, if a woman will be a pendulum round a man's neck!

PURDIE. Do give me a chance, Mabel! If the dog-like devotion of a lifetime . . .

> [*Joanna enters at the window up* C., *and stands a little melo-dramatically, up* L.C.

You know this is just a little too thick, Joanna!

> [*He remains kneeling absurdly at Mabel's side.*

JOANNA. So, sweet husband, your soul is still walking alone, is it?

MRS PURDIE. Joanna! How can you sneak about in this way! Have you no pride?

JOANNA. Please to address me as Mrs Purdie, madam. [*Looking at Lob.*] Who is this man?   [*She goes up to Lob's chair.*

PURDIE. We don't know. There's no waking him. But you can try if you like. [*Joanna shakes Lob, without result.*] It's no good.

* F 184

JOANNA. [*Moving to* L. *of the table.*] You were saying something about the devotion of a lifetime? Please go on!

[*She sits* L. *of the table.*

PURDIE. [*Rising diffidently.*] I don't like to before you, Joanna.

JOANNA. [*Tossing her head.*] Oh, don't mind me!

PURDIE. [*Moving above the table.*] I should certainly like to say it.

MRS PURDIE. [*Defying Joanna.*] And I shall be proud to hear it.

PURDIE. [*To Joanna.*] I should have liked to spare you this. You wouldn't put your hands over your ears?

JOANNA. No, sir.

MRS PURDIE. Fie, Joanna! Surely a wife's natural delicacy . . .

PURDIE. As you take it in that spirit, Joanna, I can proceed with a clear conscience.   [*He returns to Mrs Purdie.*

JOANNA. Fox!

MRS PURDIE. Sneak!

PURDIE. 'If the dog-like devotion of a lifetime . . .' [*He stops, dazed.*] I'm feeling very funny!

[*All rise.*

JOANNA. So am I. [*She turns up* L., *her hand to her forehead.*

MRS PURDIE. [*Bewildered.*] I think I have been in this room before.   [R.C.

PURDIE. There's something coming rushing back to me.

MRS PURDIE. I seem to know that coffee-set. If I do, the lid of the milk-jug is chipped. [*She goes and examines it.*] It is.

JOANNA. [*Now* R. *of Lob's chair, staring down at him.*] I can't remember this man's name, but I am sure it begins with L.

MRS PURDIE. [*Triumphantly.*] Lob!

ALL. Lob!

[*Joanna comes down* L.C.

PURDIE. [*Above and* L. *of the table.*] Mabel, your dress!

MRS PURDIE. [*Looking down.*] Gracious! How on earth——!

JOANNA. My dress! [*To Purdie.*] You were in flannels in the wood.

PURDIE. And so I am now. [*He looks down.*] Good heavens—— What's this? Where did I change? The wood! Let me think! [*Turning to the windows, and then down* C., *above the table.*] The wood . . . the wood, certainly. But the wood wasn't the wood.

JOANNA. My head's going round.

MRS PURDIE. Lob's wood! I remember it all! [*She turns up* R.] We were here. We did go! [*To* R. *of Purdie.*

PURDIE. [*Moving a little* L.C.] So we did! But how could . . . ? Where was . . . ?

[*They speak almost simultaneously.*

JOANNA. [*To* L. *of Purdie.*] And who was . . .?

MRS PURDIE. [*To* R. *of Purdie.*] And what was . . .?

PURDIE. [*Excitedly, stretching a hand to each.*] Don't let go. Hold on to what we were doing, or we'll lose grip of ourselves. [*Bewildered, passing his hands over his face.*] Devotion! Something about devotion . . . Hold on to devotion . . . 'If the dog-like devotion of a lifetime . . .' [*Dropping his hand, and looking from one to the other.*] Which of you was I saying that to?

MRS PURDIE. To me.

PURDIE. Are you sure?

MRS PURDIE. I'm not quite sure.

PURDIE. Joanna! What do you think? Good heavens! [*Sudden increase of uneasiness.*] Which of you is my wife?

JOANNA. I am. [*Starts back a pace.*] No, I'm not.

PURDIE. What?

JOANNA. It's Mabel who is your wife.

MRS PURDIE. [*Retreating a little* R. *and down.*] Me?

[*They slowly take it in.*

PURDIE. Why, of course you are, Mabel.

MRS PURDIE. What? I believe I am! [*She sits* R. *of the table.*

PURDIE. [*Above the table.*] How can it be? I was running away with you!

JOANNA. You needn't do it now. [*She sits* L. *of the table.*

PURDIE. [*Almost with a grievance.*] Why have I been making all this fuss? [*He turns a little up* C.] The wood . . . hold on to the wood . . . it's the wood that explains it. Yes, I see the whole thing. [*He gazes at Lob.*] You infernal old rascal! [*He shakes his fist at Lob.*] Let's try to think it out. [*He sits above the table.*] Don't anyone speak for a moment. Think first! Love . . . ! Hold on to love. . . .

[*A pause, during which all three are very still. Then suddenly.*

I say! I believe I'm not a deeply passionate chap, at all! I believe I'm just . . . a philanderer!

MRS PURDIE. [*Nearly crying.*] It's what you are! You made

love to me in the wood, because you thought I wasn't your
wife.   [*She rises, and crosses* R. *to the settee.*

JOANNA. Mabel, what about ourselves? I believe you and I are
both cats.

MRS PURDIE. Speak for yourself, Joanna!   [*She sits* R.

JOANNA. A pair of rank sentimentalists.

PURDIE. That's of no importance . . . Just a philanderer! And
if people don't change, I suppose we'll begin all over again
now!

JOANNA. I dare say, but not with each other. I may philander
again—but not with you!

                [*They look at each other, and give way to shame.*

PURDIE. [*Rising.*] Oh, John Purdie, John Purdie! Barrister-at-
law! [*He turns up* R. *of his chair, to* R.C.] The wood has taught
me one thing, at any rate.

MRS PURDIE. What, Jack?

PURDIE. That it isn't accident that shapes our lives.

JOANNA. No, it's Fate.

PURDIE. It's not Fate, either. Fate is something outside us.
What really plays the dickens with us is *something in ourselves*.
Something that would make us go on doing the same sort of
fool thing however many chances we get.

JOANNA. How ignominious! But I believe you're right.

MRS PURDIE. Can't we guide it? Isn't that what we're here for?

PURDIE. I dare say, if we try hard enough. But I have for the
moment an abominably clear perception that the likes of me
never really tries. I was just being the same twaddler over
again! Yes, I see it clearly now; I'll forget it, I suppose, by
morning. Forgive me, Joanna—no, Mabel . . . I'm mixed up
still.   [*He sits in the chair* R. *of the table.*

JOANNA. I could forgive anybody anything tonight. It's so
lovely not to be married to you, Jack!

PURDIE. [*Lugubrious.*] I do feel small.

JOANNA. You'll soon swell up again.

PURDIE. That's the awful thing. But at present, at any rate, I
am a rag at your feet, Joanna—no, at yours, Mabel. [*To Mrs
Purdie.*] Are you going to pick me up?

MRS PURDIE. [*Not to be mollified.*] I don't know about that,
Jack. To begin with, which of us is it your lonely soul is in
search of?

JOANNA. Which of us is the fluid one, or the fluider one?

MRS PURDIE. Are you and I one? Or are you and Joanna one? Or are the three of us two?

JOANNA. [*In burlesque of the sentimental lover.*] He wants you to whisper in his ear the entrancing poem 'Mabel Purdie'. Do it, Mabel! There will be nothing wrong in it now!

PURDIE. [*Rising, and crossing up* R.C.] Rub it in!

MRS PURDIE. [*Firmly.*] I understand you better now, Jack, at any rate. And when I meet Joanna's successor . . .

PURDIE. [*Quailing.*] No, no, Mabel! [*Earnestly, coming down* R.C.] There will never be another woman! I swear it by all that's . . .

JOANNA. [*In her excellent imitation of a sheep.*] Baa! He's off again! [*She moves up* L. *to the fireplace recess.*
[*Lob here—and once or twice later—indulges in his favourite kick.*

PURDIE. Oh, Lord! So I am! [*He moves up to the chair* C.] In my present state of depression—which won't last—I feel there's something in me that will make me go on being eternally the same ass, however many chances I get. [*He rises from the arm of the chair.*] Shakespeare knew what he was talking about . . .
[*Quoting.*

'The fault, dear Brutus, is not in our stars
    But in ourselves, that we are underlings.'

JOANNA. [*Moving in a little towards* L.C.] For 'dear Brutus' we are to read 'dear audience', I suppose?

PURDIE. You have it.
[*He moves* R.C., *between the table and the settee.*
[*Joanna sits* L. *of the table.*
[*Sincere for the moment, moving towards the settee.*] Mabel, try to help me. If you catch me at it again have the goodness to whisper to me in passing 'Lob's Wood'. That may cure me for the time being.

MRS PURDIE. [*Sadly.*] Perhaps I will . . . as long as I care to bother, Jack. It depends on you how long that is to be.

JOANNA. Hear, hear! There's hope in that as well as a warning. Perhaps the wood may prove to have been useful after all.
[*They are looking lugubrious. Purdie turns to the chair* R. *of the table.*
You know, we are not people worth being sorrowful about—so let's laugh!

[*They laugh, at first on the wrong side of their mouths, then heartily at themselves.*

PURDIE. [*Pointing at Lob.*] Queer! I thought I saw him smile.

MRS PURDIE. [*Suddenly, rising.*] Stop! I forgot.   [*To* R.C.

JOANNA. What?

MRS PURDIE. We have forgotten the others. I wonder what is happening to them?

PURDIE. By Jove, yes! Have *they* changed?

MRS PURDIE. I didn't see any of them in the wood, did you?

JOANNA. No. [*She rises.*] Or perhaps we did see them without knowing them. [*Turning up* C.] We didn't know Lob!

[*Looking at Lob.*

PURDIE. That's true.

JOANNA. [*Turning to the others.*] I say! Won't it be delicious to be here to watch the others when they come back, and see them waking up, or whatever it was we did!

PURDIE. How do we know they'll come back?

JOANNA. [*Startled.*] We don't know! [*To above the table.*] How awful!   [*She sits* C.

MRS PURDIE. Listen!

PURDIE. Sh-sh! [*He moves down below the table.*] I distinctly hear someone on the stairs.

MRS PURDIE. Matey!   [*She turns* R. *to the settee.*

PURDIE. [*Turning back.*] I say!   [*He moves* R. *of the table.*
[*Mrs Purdie sits on the settee.*
Don't tell him we had any, any . . . odd experiences.

[*Enter Mrs Coade,* L., *in her dressing-gown with a muffler in her hand.*

MRS PURDIE. [*Rising.*] It's Coady!

MRS COADE. So you're back at last! A nice house, I must say! Where's Coady?   [*She goes up towards the window.*

PURDIE. What! [*Going up* C. *to meet Mrs Coade.*] Did he go into the wood too?

MRS COADE. He must have. I've been down several times to look for him.

MRS PURDIE. Coady too!

JOANNA. I wonder . . . [*Suddenly, rising and moving* L.] Oh, how dreadful!

MRS COADE. [*Coming down* R. *of Joanna.*] What is dreadful, Joanna?   [*Mrs Purdie sits* R., *on the settee.*

JOANNA. Nothing. I was just wondering what he is doing.

MRS COADE. Doing? What should he be doing? [*Looking from one to the other, moving to* C.] Did anything odd happen to you in the wood?

[*Purdie moves down* R.C.

ALL. [*Hurriedly.*] No, no, nothing.

JOANNA. [*Moving up* L.C.] We just strolled about and came back. [*Looking at Lob.*] Have you seen him?

MRS COADE. Oh yes, he has been like that all the time. [*She sits above the table,* C.] A sort of stupor, I think, and sometimes the strangest grin comes over his face.

PURDIE. Grin?

MRS COADE. Just as if he were seeing amusing things in his sleep.

PURDIE. [*Behind the chair* R. *of the table.*] And I dare say he is! Oughtn't we to get Matey to him?

MRS COADE. Matey's gone too.

PURDIE. [*Retreating a pace.*] Wha-at?

[*He turns to look at Mrs Purdie, and then moves up* R.

MRS PURDIE. Into the wood?

MRS COADE. I suppose so. He's not in the house.

JOANNA. [*Coming down* L.C.] Matey! [*Looking across at Purdie.*] I wonder who's with him?

MRS COADE. [*Anxious.*] Must somebody be with him?

JOANNA. Oh no, not at all.

[*There is a knock at the window. They all look in that direction.*

MRS COADE. Listen! I hope it's Coady.

MRS PURDIE. [*Sorry for her, rising.*] Oh, I hope not!

MRS COADE. Why, Mrs Purdie?

[*Going up above Mrs Coade's chair and bending over.*

JOANNA. Dear Mrs Coade, whoever he is with and whatever he does, I beg you not to be surprised. We feel that though *we* had no unusual experiences in the wood, others may not have been so fortunate.

MRS PURDIE. [*Moving to* R. *of Mrs Coade.*] And be cautious, you dear, what you say to them before they come to.

MRS COADE. 'Come to'? You alarm me. And Coady didn't have his muffler.

[*Joanna moves down* L. *of the table. Purdie goes up to* R. *of the windows and peeps out. Mrs Purdie moves down* R. *to the settee. Mrs Coade pushes her chair slightly* L., *turned to face* R., *as Purdie draws back.*

PURDIE. Sh-sh! [*Coming to* R.C.] Matey!

> [*He moves to above the settee and sits.*

[*Matey enters at the windows* C. *Though in his butler's clothes —of which he is unaware—he retains his aggressive business-man manner.*

JOANNA. Do come in!

MATEY. With apologies, ladies and gents . . . May I ask who is host?

PURDIE. [*Seated on the upper arm of the settee.*] A very reasonable request. Third on the left.

> [*He points delightedly to Lob, and turns* R., *above the settee.*

MATEY. [*Crossing to* R. *of Lob's chair.*] Only to ask, sir, if you would direct me to my hotel. I . . . the gentleman seems to be reposing.   [*He returns to* R.C.

MRS COADE. It's Lob!

MATEY. [R. *of Mrs Coade.*] What is Lob, ma'am? . . .

MRS COADE. Surely you haven't forgotten!

PURDIE. Sh-sh! Anything we can do for you? Just give it a name.

JOANNA. I hope you are not alone. Do you say have some lady friend with you.

MATEY. My wife is with me.

JOANNA. His wife! You *have* been quick!

MRS PURDIE. I am so glad! I love a bride!

MRS COADE. I didn't know you were married!

MATEY. Why should you? You talk as if you knew me.

MRS COADE. Good gracious! Do you really think I don't?

> [*Matey stares at Mrs Coade.*

PURDIE. Sit down, won't you, and make yourself comfy?

MATEY. Thank you, but my wife . . .

JOANNA. Yes, please bring her in. We are simply dying to make her acquaintance.

MATEY. You are very good. I'm much obliged.   [*He exits* C.

MRS PURDIE. [*Crossing up to* R. *of the windows.*] Who can she be?

> [*She comes* C.

JOANNA. Who? Who? Who?

MRS COADE. [*Rising.*] But what an extraordinary wood! [*She moves to* L. *of the table.*] He doesn't seem to know who he is at all.

MRS PURDIE. Don't worry about that, Coady. He will know soon enough.

[*She turns up to the windows and peeps out, through the curtains.*

JOANNA. And so will the little wife. [*Moving up* C., *to* L. *of the windows.*] By the way, whoever she is, I hope she's fond of butlers.

MRS PURDIE. [*Peeping through window.*] It's Lady Caroline!
[*She hurries back down* R.

JOANNA. [*Following Mrs Purdie down* R.] Oh, hurray! And she was so sure she couldn't take the wrong turning!

[*They both stand down* R., *in front of the settee, as Matey and Lady Caroline enter* C. *Lady Caroline is all graciousness.*

MATEY. [*On her* L.] May I present my wife—Lady Caroline Matey.

PURDIE. [*Crossing to* R. *of Lady Caroline.*] How do you do, Lady Caroline?

MRS COADE. [*Aghast.*] Lady Caroline Matey! You!

LADY CAROLINE. Charmed, I'm sure.
[*Mrs Coade sits above the table* C.

JOANNA. Very pleased to meet any wife of Mr Matey.

PURDIE. [R.C.] Allow me. [*Introducing Mrs Coade.*] The Duchess of Candelabra. [*Introducing Joanna and Mrs Purdie.*] The Ladies Helena and Matilda McNab. I am Mr Justice Purdie.

LADY CAROLINE. How d'you do? How d'y' do!
[*She sits* R. *of the table.*

MRS PURDIE. [*Sitting on lower end of the settee.*] I have wanted so long to make your acquaintance.

LADY CAROLINE. Charmed!

JOANNA. These informal meetings are so delightful . . . don't you . . . ? [*She sits on the upper end of the settee.*

LADY CAROLINE. Yes, indeed!

MATEY. [*Looking at Lob.*] And your friend by the fire?

PURDIE. I'll introduce you to him when you wake up—I mean when he wakes up. [*He sits on the upstage arm of the settee.*

MATEY. Perhaps I ought to have said that I am *James* Matey.

LADY CAROLINE. *The* James Matey.

MATEY. A name not perhaps unknown in the world of finance.

JOANNA. Finance! Oh! So you did take that clerkship in the city?

MATEY. I began as a clerk in the city, certainly, and I'm not ashamed to admit it.

MRS COADE. [*Muddled with wonder.*] Fancy that, now. And did it save you?

MATEY. Save me, madam?

JOANNA. Excuse us—we ask odd questions in this house—we only mean, did that keep you honest? Or are you still a pilferer?

LADY CAROLINE. [*To Matey.*] Husband mine! What does she mean?

JOANNA. No offence. I mean a pilferer on a large scale.

MATEY. [*Blustering, to* R.C.] If you are referring to that Labrador business—or the Working Women's Bank . . .

PURDIE. O-oh! Got him!

JOANNA. [*Delighted.*] Yes, those are what I meant!

MATEY. [*Stoutly.*] There was nothing proved.

JOANNA. [*Rising.*] Mabel! Jack! Here's another of us. [*She goes up to Matey.*] You've gone just the same way again, my friend! There's more in it, you see, than taking the wrong turning! *You* would always take the wrong turning. Tra-la-la!

> [*Joanna trips back to the settee. Lady Caroline rises and goes up*, R.C.

LADY CAROLINE. If you are casting any aspersions on my husband, allow me to say that a prouder wife than I does not today exist.

MRS COADE. My dear, do be careful.

MRS PURDIE. [*Down* R.] So long as *you* are satisfied, dear Lady Caroline! But I thought you hated all men, and had a contempt for love.

LADY CAROLINE. [*Indignant.*] I? I beg to assure you that I adore my Jim. [*She turns to Matey, her hand on his arm.*]

JOANNA. [*To Mrs Purdie.*] Jim!

> [*They are amused.*
> [*But Matey has come upon the tray containing the coffee-cups. He lifts it and moves about* L.C. *with it puzzled, but in correct butler manner.*

LADY CAROLINE. [*Moving towards him.*] Whatever are you doing, Jim?   [*There is a pause. Then:*

MATEY. I don't understand it, Caroliney, but somehow I feel at home with this in my hands!

MRS PURDIE. Caroliney!

MRS COADE. Look at me well. Don't you remember me?

MATEY. [*Staring at her.*] I don't remember you; but I seem to associate you with hard-boiled eggs. [*With conviction, putting down the tray.*] You like your eggs hard-boiled?

PURDIE. [*Crossing to* R.C.] Hold on to hard-boiled eggs. She used to tip you especially to see to them! [*He crosses to Matey.*
                                            [*Matey's hand goes to his pocket.*
Yes, that was the pocket.

LADY CAROLINE. [*Indignantly.*] Tip? James?
                                            [*She comes down* R.C.

MATEY. [*Dwelling pleasantly on the word.*] Tip!
                                            [*Lady Caroline is looking around.*

PURDIE. Jolly word, isn't it?

MATEY. It seems to set me thinking.

LADY CAROLINE. [*Crosses to the desk* L.—*suddenly seeing it.*] Why is my work-basket in this house?

MRS COADE. You are living here, you know.
                                   [*Joanna and Mrs Purdie rise slowly.*

LADY CAROLINE. [*To* L.C.] That's what a person feels. But when did I come? It's very odd, but one feels one ought to say when did one go.

PURDIE. She's coming to with a 'wush'!

MATEY. [*Up* C.] Mr . . . Purdie!

LADY CAROLINE. Mrs Coade!

MATEY. [*Turning to look at Lob.*] The guv'nor.

LADY CAROLINE. One is in evening dress!

MATEY. Oh, Moses!
                                   [*They are startled by their clothes.*

JOANNA. You will understand clearly in a minute, Caroliney. You didn't really take that clerkship, Jim. You went into domestic service. But in the essentials you haven't altered.

PURDIE. [*To up* R.C.] I'll have my shaving water at seven-thirty sharp, Matey.   [*He turns back to Mrs Purdie.*

MATEY. [*In servant manner.*] Very good, sir.
                                   [*His hands stray unconsciously to the tray.*

LADY CAROLINE. [*Crossing to* L. *of Matey.*] Sir! You . . . You . . . You . . . Midsummer Eve! The wood.

PURDIE. [*Turning to her.*] Yes, hold on to the wood.

MATEY. You are . . . you are . . . you are Lady Caroline Laney.

LADY CAROLINE. It's Matey, the butler!

MRS PURDIE. You seem quite happy with him, you know, Lady Caroline.

JOANNA. [*Nicely.*] We won't tell.

>   [*A pause. Purdie sits on the upstage arm of the settee.*

LADY CAROLINE. Caroline Matey! And I seem to like it! [*A pause of horror.*] How horrible.

>   [*Lady Caroline sits abruptly, L. of the table. Matey is bewildered.*

MRS COADE. It's rather difficult to see what we should do next!

MATEY. [*Superbly controlling himself, the tray still in his hands. To Lady Caroline L.*] Coffee, my Lady?

LADY CAROLINE. [*Also rather superbly.*] No!   [*A pause.*

MATEY. [*Tentatively.*] Perhaps if I were to go downstairs?

PURDIE. It would be conferring a personal favour on us all.

>   [*Matey crosses down L. correctly with the tray, and exits.*
>   [NOTE: *The cake on the plate has been left on the table.*
>   [*Lob again gives his kick.*

LADY CAROLINE. [*Rising, and going up L. to the R. of Lob's chair.*] It's all that wretch's doing. . . .

>   [*Lady Caroline shakes his chair, but Lob does not waken. The playing of Coade's whistle is heard off.*

JOANNA. [*Up at the window, and peeping.*] It's Coady!

>   [*Joanna goes down L. of the chair C. Lady Caroline to L.C.*

MRS COADE. [*Rising.*] Coady! [*Moving to R.C.*] Why is he so happy?   [*She moves, troubled, to the settee, R., and sits.*

JOANNA. [*Moving down to Mrs Coade.*] Dear, take my hand.

>   [*Joanna sits L. of Mrs Coade, taking her left hand. Mrs Purdie takes her right hand. She looks from one to the other. Lady Caroline sits L. of the table.*

LADY CAROLINE. [*To L. of Mrs Coade.*] Dear, hold my hand.

>   [*She takes Mrs Coade's left hand.*
>   [*They are both very nice to her.*

MRS COADE. Won't he know me?

JOANNA. [*Apprehensive, still holding Mrs Coade's hand.*] Oh dear, I wish Coady hadn't gone out.

>   [*Purdie moves to behind the settee.*

MRS COADE. We that have been happily married these thirty years.

[*Coade comes in inquiringly with a skip and jump, wearing his Act I clothes like the others.*

COADE. [*Up* R.C.] May I introduce? My name is Coade. The fact is I was playing about in the wood on a whistle, and I saw your light.

[*The others uncomfortably let Mrs Coade have most to say.*

MRS COADE. Playing about in the wood with a whistle! You!

COADE. [*Moving down a pace, with mild dignity.*] And why not, madam?

MRS COADE. Madam! [*Wistful.*] Don't you know me?

COADE. [*Taking a pace or two towards her down* R.] I don't know you . . . [*Looking at her.*] But I wish I did.

MRS COADE. Do you? Why?

COADE. If I may say so, you have a very soft, lovable face.

[*Mrs Coade looks at the others with the smile of a pleased child. They nod encouragingly. Joanna gives her hand a reassuring pat, rises quietly and moves up, and across to above the chair* R. *of the table.*

MRS COADE. Who was with you playing whistles in the wood!

[*Everybody is very tense.*

COADE. No one was with me.

[*General relaxation.*

MRS COADE. No . . . lady?

COADE. Certainly not!

[*Mrs Coade beams.*
[*Moving nearer the upper end of the settee.*] I am a bachelor.

MRS COADE. [*Quaking.*] A bachelor?

JOANNA. [*Moving to* R. *of the* R. *chair.*] Don't give way, dear! It—might—be much worse.

MRS COADE. And you're sure you never spoke to me before? Do think!

COADE. Not to my knowledge, Never . . . except in dreams.

MRS PURDIE. What did you say to her in dreams?

COADE. [*Reflecting.*] I said, 'My dear'. [*He is surprised himself.*] Odd!

JOANNA. The darling man!

MRS COADE. [*Trembling.*] How could you say such things to an old woman?

COADE. Old? [*Puzzled.*] I didn't think of you as old. No, no! Young! With the morning dew on your face, coming across the lawn in a black and green silk dress, and such a pretty parasol.

MRS COADE. That was how he first met me. He used to love me in black and green. And it was a pretty parasol. Look! I'm old. So it can't be the same woman.

COADE. Old! Yes, I suppose so. But it is the same soft, lovable face, and the same kind beaming smile that children could warm their hands at.

MRS COADE. [*With a child's smile to the others.*] He always liked my smile.

[*There is a tiny pause.*

PURDIE. So do we all.

COADE. Emma!

MRS COADE. He hasn't forgotten my name.   [*To the others.*

COADE. It's sad that we didn't meet long ago. I think I've been waiting for you. I suppose we have met too late? You couldn't overlook my being an old fellow, could you? No!

JOANNA. How lovely! [*She turns up* C., *to above the table.*] He is going to propose to her again! Coady, you happy thing! He is wanting the same soft face after thirty years.   [*She sits* C.

MRS COADE. [*After beaming again.*] We mustn't be too sure. I think that's it. I hope it is. Perhaps I'm wrong, Joanna. What is it exactly you want, *Mr* Coade?

COADE. I want to have the right to hold the parasol over you. Won't you be my wife, my dear? And so give my long dream of you a happy ending?

[*Mrs Coade rises and smooths his arms, then looking triumphantly at the others.*

MRS COADE. Kisses are not called for at our age, Coady, but here's a muffler for your old neck.

COADE. [*Simply.*] Thank you, dear, I've missed it. [*He is tying it in a matter-of-fact way round his neck when he becomes conscious of his evening clothes. He looks round him, blinking.*] Why . . . why . . . what . . . who . . . how is this?

[*He wanders up* R.C.

PURDIE. He's coming to!

COADE. [*Looking at the chair, then remembering, after an effort, in which the others are in suspense.*] Lob!

[*Lob gives his kick.*

PURDIE. You've got it, old man!

COADE. [*Returning down* R. *to Mrs Coade.*] Bless me, Coady! I went into that wood.

MRS COADE. And without your muffler.

[*Mrs Coade sits on the settee, and then notices Coade is feeling his pockets.*

What are you feeling for?

COADE. [*Up* C.] The whistle! Gone! Of course it is! It's rather a pity, but . . . [*Anxiously coming to* R.C.] Have I been saying awful things to you?

MRS PURDIE. You have been making her so proud. You had a second chance, and it's her again.

COADE. Of course! It would be! But I see I was just the same nice old lazy Coady as before! And I had thought that if I had a second chance I could *do* things! I've often said to you, Coady, that it was owing to my being cursed with a competency that I didn't write my great book. But I had no competency this time, and I haven't written a word.

PURDIE. [*To* R. *of Coade, with a fellow feeling.*] That needn't make you feel lonely in this house.

[*Mrs Purdie rises and turns down and behind the settee.*

MRS COADE. You seem to have been quite happy as an old bachelor, dear!

COADE. I'm surprised at myself, but I'm afraid I was.

MRS COADE. I wonder if what it means is that you don't especially need even me. I wonder if it means that you are just the sort of amiable creature that would be happy anywhere and anyhow.

COADE. Oh dear, can it be as bad as that?

JOANNA. Certainly not! It's a romance, and I won't have it looked upon as anything else.

[*Purdie moves up to the windows.*

MRS COADE. Thank you, Joanna. You'll try not to miss that whistle, Coady!

COADE. [*Moving towards Mrs Coade.*] Not while I have your smile to make the music for me, Emma. You are all I need.

[*Kissing her hand.*

MRS COADE. Yes, but I'm not so sure as I used to be that it's a great compliment.

JOANNA. Coady, behave! [*She rises and turns up* L.

[*There is a knock at the window. Lady Caroline rises. Purdie goes up and peeps out.*

PURDIE. [*Turning to the others.*] Mrs Dearth—alone!
  [*Lady Caroline turns* L. *to the desk, Joanna drops down above and on her* R.
  [*Moving to* L.C.] Who would have expected it of *her*!
                              [*Coade moves to* R. *of the windows.*
JOANNA. She's rather a dear, and I do hope she's got off cheaply.

                              [*Coade moves across to* R. *of Purdie.*
  [*Mrs Dearth enters at the windows, in her evening dress and cloak. She simpers to show that she is the equal of these fine ladies.*
PURDIE. Pleased to see you, stranger!
MRS DEARTH. [C.] I was afraid such an unceremonious entry might startle you.
PURDIE. Not a bit.
MRS DEARTH. I usually enter a house by the front door.
PURDIE. I've heard that's the swagger way.
MRS DEARTH. So stupid of me, I lost myself in the wood . . . and . . .
JOANNA. Of course you did, but never mind that. Do tell us your name.
LADY CAROLINE. Yes, yes, your name!
MRS DEARTH. Of course. I'm the Honourable Mrs Finch-Fallowe.
MRS PURDIE. Of course, of course.
LADY CAROLINE. Who can he be?
PURDIE. I hope Mr Finch-Fallowe is very well. We don't know him personally; but may we have the pleasure of seeing him pop in presently?
MRS DEARTH. No, I'm not sure where he is.
LADY CAROLINE. I wonder if the dear clever police know?
MRS DEARTH. No, they don't!
PURDIE. Phew!
MRS DEARTH. So awkward! I gave my sandwiches to a poor girl and her father whom I met in the wood, and now . . . [*Faltering.*] Isn't that a nuisance? I'm quite hungry myself. [*Seeing the cake.*] May I?
  [*She sits* R. *of the table, and falls to without waiting for permission. She wolfs the cake.*
MRS COADE. The poor thing!

PURDIE. [*Moving to* C., *above the table, referring to the cake.*] Like it?

MRS DEARTH. Delicious!

[*Coade closes in to* L. *of Purdie, at* L.C. *Joanna moves in below and* L. *of Coade. Lady Caroline rises and moves in a pace.*

JOANNA. [*To Lady Caroline.*] Finch-Fallowe.

LADY CAROLINE. Dear Mrs Finch-Fallowe, we are so anxious to know whether you met a friend of ours in the wood—a Mr Dearth? Perhaps you know him too?

MRS DEARTH. Dearth? I don't know any Dearth.

MRS COADE. Oh dear! What a wood!

[*Mrs Purdie moves to* L. *of the upper end of the settee.*

PURDIE. He is quite a front-door sort of man. Knocks and rings as cool as you like.

MRS DEARTH. I meet so many, you see, and go out a great deal. I have visiting cards—printed ones.

[*Lady Caroline turns and sits at the desk.*

MRS PURDIE. [*Moving a pace towards Mrs Dearth.*] Perhaps he has painted your portrait? He is an artist.

MRS DEARTH. [*Over her shoulder.*] Very likely. [*Eating.*] I dare say that is the man I gave my sandwiches to.

MRS COADE. But I thought you said *he* had a daughter.

MRS DEARTH. Such a pretty girl! I gave her half a crown.

COADE. A daughter. [*Looking from one to the other.*] That can't be Dearth.

PURDIE. Don't be too sure. [*To Mrs Dearth.*] A rather melancholy, gone-to-seed sort of man?

MRS DEARTH. No, I thought him such a jolly attractive man.

COADE. Dearth, jolly attractive? Oh, no! [*Coming a little down* L.] Did he say anything about his wife?

LADY CAROLINE. Yes, do try to remember if he mentioned *her*?

MRS DEARTH. No, he didn't.

[*Coade moves up below the fireplace.*

PURDIE. He was far from jolly in her time.

MRS DEARTH. [*Simpering.*] Perhaps that was the lady's fault.

[*She goes on eating.*

[*Purdie is amused, and crosses to* R. *of Coade. Dearth is heard singing a French song off. Mrs Purdie moves down* R., *and sits above Mrs Coade.*

COADE. Dearth singing. He seems quite gay!

JOANNA. [*Moving up to* L. *of Mrs Dearth.*] You poor thing!
PURDIE. H'sh! H'sh!

> [*Joanna moves* R., *to above and* L. *of the settee. Dearth comes in at the windows dressed as at end of Act I. Purdie and Coade are at* L., *below the fireplace.*

DEARTH. [*Still a happy man.*] I'm sorry to bounce in on you in this way, but really I have an excuse. I'm a painter of sorts, and . . .

> [*He checks, up* C., *seeing that he had brought some strange discomfort here.*

MRS COADE. I must say, Mr Dearth, I am delighted to see you looking so well. Like a new man, isn't he?

> [*No one dares to answer. Glances are exchanged.*

DEARTH. I'm certainly very well, if you care to know. But did I tell you my name?

JOANNA. [*Turning up* R.C. *to Dearth.*] No, but we have an instinct in this house.

DEARTH. [*Facing Joanna.*] Well, it doesn't matter. Here's the situation. My daughter and I have just met in the wood a poor wretched woman famishing for want of food.

> [*Here Mrs Dearth rises slowly, and backs below and to* R. *of her chair.*

We were as happy as grigs ourselves, and the sight of her distress rather cut us up. Can you give me something for her? [*Checking.*] Why are you looking so startled? [*He turns to the table and sees the remains of the cake.*] May I have this?

> [*A slight movement from Mrs Dearth attracts his attention, and for the first time he sees her. He recognizes her as the woman in the wood and her dress astonishes him. The others are beginning to understand the situation. He frowns, and takes a step* R.C. *towards her.*

I feel I can't be mistaken. It *was* you I met in the wood. Have you been playing some trick on me? [*To the others.*] It was for her I wanted the food.

MRS DEARTH. [*Putting her hand to her dress, to protect his gift.*] Are you going to take back the money you gave me?

DEARTH. Your dress! You were almost in rags when I saw you outside.

> [*Mrs Dearth looks down and is startled by her attire.*

MRS DEARTH. I don't . . . understand . . .

COADE. [*Crossing Purdie to up* L.C.] For that matter, Dearth, I dare say you were different in the wood, too.

DEARTH. [*He becomes aware of his dress clothes.*] What . . . What . . . Am I crazy?

MRS DEARTH. [*Looking around, bewildered and no longer a comedy figure.*] Where am I? I seem to know you . . .
                        [*She crosses to Mrs Coade, down* R.

MRS COADE. [*Kindly.*] Yes, you do. Hold my hand, and you'll soon remember all about it.

JOANNA. [*Moving a pace or two to Dearth, kindly.*] I'm afraid, Mr Dearth, it's harder for you than the rest of us.

MRS PURDIE. [*Seated down* R.] We're awfully sorry. Don't you remember . . . Midsummer Eve!
                        [*Coade turns slowly back to Purdie up* L.

DEARTH. Midsummer Eve! This room! Yes, this room . . . You . . . was it you . . . were going out to look for something . . . The tree of knowledge, wasn't it? Somebody wanted me to go, too . . . Who was it? A lady, I think . . . Why did she ask me to go? What was I doing here? I was smoking a cigar . . . I laid it down, there . . . [*He goes straight to the ash-tray stand up* R., *where he had put his cigar, and lifts it up. He looks around, puts it back on the stand, and shivers a little.*] Who was the lady?   [*He moves to* R.C.

MRS DEARTH. [*Slowly—staring out front.*] Something about a second chance.

MRS COADE. Yes, you poor dear. You thought you could make so much of it.

DEARTH. A lady who didn't like me . . . she had good reasons, too; but what were they . . . ?

MRS DEARTH. [*Swinging round to face* L.] Lob. He did it! [*To* R.C.] What did he do?

DEARTH. [*A tragic figure.*] I'm . . . it's coming back! [*To above the table* C.] I'm not the man I thought myself . . .

MRS DEARTH. I'm not Mrs Finch-Fallowe! Who am I?
        [*The husband and wife stare at each other, and then realize.*

DEARTH. [*To above the chair* R. *of the table.*] You were that lady!

MRS DEARTH. [*Retreating a step* R.] It's you—my husband!

DEARTH. Alice!
        [*There is very little movement, but they are overcome.*

MRS COADE. My dear, you are much better off, so far as I can
see, than if you *were* Mrs Finch-Fallowe.

MRS DEARTH. [*Generously.*] Yes. [*With passionate knowledge.*]
Yes, indeed! *But he isn't!*

DEARTH. [*Taking a step towards Mrs Dearth.*] Alice . . . I . . .
[*He tries to smile.*] I didn't know you when I was in the wood
with Margaret! She . . . she . . . [*He realizes his greatest loss.*]
Margaret! Oh, my God!

    [*Dearth sits* R. *of the table burying his face in his hands. No
    one can do anything. Mrs Dearth goes to him. A pause.*

MRS DEARTH. I should have liked to have been her mother, Will.

    [*He does not look up. She presses his shoulder fiercely and goes
    out* L. *He remains with his head in his hands; the others
    don't know what to do.*

PURDIE. [*Below and* L. *of Lob's chair.*] You old ruffian!!!

DEARTH. [*Looking up.*] No, I'm rather fond of him. [*Rising.*]
Our lonely, friendly host. [*Crosses up* L. *to* R. *of Lob's chair.*]
Lob, I thank thee for that hour! [*He goes down and opens the
door* L., *pauses, and calls.*] Alice!

               [*Dearth goes out* L., *closing the door.*

JOANNA. [*Moving to the table.*] If one could only change!

               [*She sits in the chair* R. *of the table.*

MRS PURDIE. [*Rising.*] Who knows? Perhaps the brave ones can.
[*Moving up* R.C.] You know I feel sorry for her, as well as for
him.

JOANNA. She's really a good sort.

PURDIE. [*Moving across up* C.] I dare say there's nothing the
matter with her except that she would always choose the wrong
man. Good man or bad; but the wrong man for her. I think
we had best all toddle off to bed. Hold on to bed.

    [*Lady Caroline rises, moving to* L. *of the table. All brighten up.*

MRS PURDIE. And try a little reflection before we fall asleep.

COADE. Yes, yes! [*Crossing to above the table.*] It must be quite
late!

MRS COADE. That's my candle, Coady.

    [*Coade lights the candle. Matey enters from the dining-room,
    up* R.

MATEY. Breakfast is quite ready.   [*There is pleasant excitement.*

ALL. Breakfast! Breakfast!

               [*Mrs Coade rises and moves up.*

LADY CAROLINE. [*Looking at her watch.*] My watch has stopped.

COADE. [*Looking at his.*] And mine.

JOANNA. Just as well, perhaps. [*She rises and goes up.*

COADE. [*Moving across* R.C.] You know, now that I think of it, I feel quite peckish!

MRS COADE. There's a smell of coffee.

[*They go towards the dining-room.*

COADE. [*Taking her arm.*] Come along, Coady! I do hope you haven't been tiring your poor foot too much!

MRS COADE. I shall give it a good rest tomorrow, dear.

MATEY. [*As they pass.*] I have given your egg six minutes, ma'am.

[*Mr and Mrs Coade exit* R.
[*Purdie exits with Mrs Purdie to the dining-room.*
[*Lady Caroline crosses up* R. *She and Matey have a self-conscious look at each other; getting in each other's way. He draws aside, and Lady Caroline goes out* R. *and closes the door.*

JOANNA. [*Reflectively coming down to above the table.*] A strange experience! [*She calls.*] Matey.

MATEY. Yes, miss? [*Coming* C.

JOANNA. Does it ever have any permanent effect, Matey?

MATEY. Not often, miss, but once in a while. If you want to know whether it will have any on you, he could show you if he liked.

JOANNA. Catch me risking it! [*She turns* R.] But I should like to know about the Dearths. Breakfast! [*She exits* R.

MATEY. [*Setting the chairs into the table.*] Did you hear what the lady said, you mischievous, innocent old devil? . . .

[*Lob kicks, and withdraws his leg from view. Matey goes to his chair and seizes it, leaning well over it as he speaks.*

You've diddled me again and again, but I think I've got you now. . . .

[NOTE: *During the above line and bus., Lob makes a trick exit through the wall above the chair.*
[*Matey pulls the chair round to face down, and finds it empty. He shakes his head tolerantly as one who knows Lob's ways, then switches off the lights. He then goes up and draws aside the curtains.*
[*We now see the garden in full daylight. Lob is standing there*

with his back to us. He jumps round to startle Matey, who
goes off to the dining-room with a tolerant smile.

[Lob remembers what Joanna had said about wanting to know
the future of the Dearths. He works a spell with his hands.
A lark is heard singing in the garden. Lob hides behind the
curtain, retreating to L. of the windows.

[Dearth in a tweed suit, carrying easel and canvas, humming
a French song and smoking a pipe, happy again, comes
into view. He looks up at the lark and smiles. He beckons,
and Mrs Dearth comes, dressed rather like Margaret.
They look happily at each other, kiss and pass on. There
is a moment's pause and then Margaret, as she was in the
wood, gaily dances after them. The lark sings on. Lob,
looking very old, but pleased, sinks into his chair and has
a final kick. But he is really very tired of it all. Perhaps
he is a sprite who has lost his way among the mortals.

CURTAIN

SHALL WE JOIN THE LADIES?

COPYRIGHT 1926 BY J. M. BARRIE
COPYRIGHT A.76997, 1934, BY CHARLES SCRIBNER'S SONS

The copying by manuscript, typescript, photography or any other means of reproduction, of this play either in whole or in part is an infringement of the copyright.

All applications for a licence concerning the production of this play by amateurs must be made to:

SAMUEL FRENCH LIMITED,
26 SOUTHAMPTON STREET,
STRAND, LONDON, W.C.2.

The royalty fee payable for each performance is One Guinea. No performance may be given unless the licence has first been obtained.

SHALL WE JOIN THE LADIES?

Presented at the opening of the Theatre of the Royal Academy of Dramatic Art, on 27th May 1921, with the following cast of characters:

SAM SMITH	*Mr Dion Boucicault*
LADY JANE RAYE . . .	*Miss Fay Compton*
MR PREEN	*Mr Charles H. Hawtrey*
LADY WRATHIE . . .	*Miss Sybil Thorndike*
SIR JOSEPH WRATHIE . .	*Mr Cyril Maude*
MRS PREEN . . .	*Lady Tree*
CAPTAIN JENNINGS . .	*Mr Leon Quartermaine*
MRS CASTRO . . .	*Miss Lillah McCarthy*
MR VAILE	*Mr Nelson Keys*
MRS BLAND . . .	*Miss Madge Titheradge*
MR GOURLAY . . .	*Sir Johnston Forbes-Robertson*
MISS ISIT	*Miss Irene Vanbrugh*
MISS VAILE . . .	*Miss Marie Lohr*
A POLICEMAN . . .	*Mr Norman Forbes*
LUCY (MAID) . . .	*Miss Hilda Trevelyan*
DOLPHIN	*Mr Gerald du Maurier*

The Scene is the dining-room of Sam Smith's country house in the late evening.

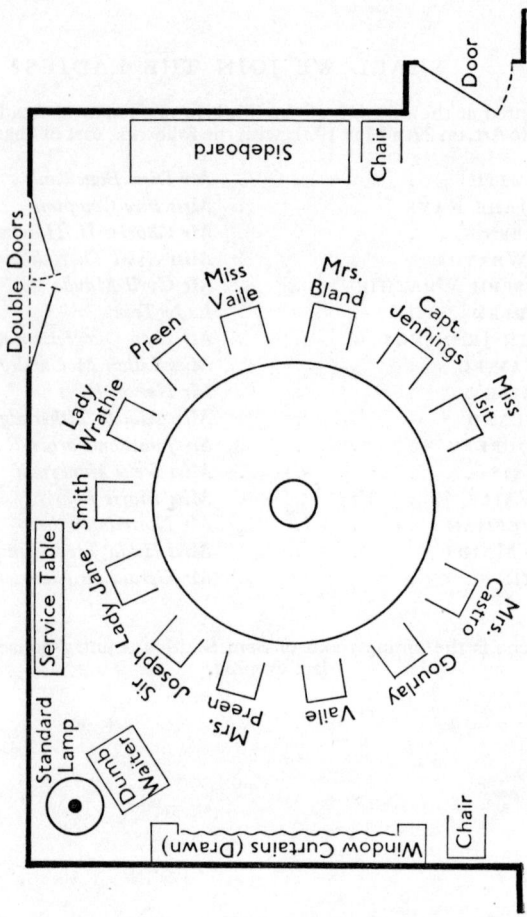

The SCENE *is the dining-room of Sam Smith's country house. The time is late evening.*

It is a spacious, dark-panelled room, the furniture is very fine and solid, the lighting discreet. In the C., *a large mahogany table. The silver and glass are very beautiful.*

When the Curtain rises dessert is being served by Dolphin, a silent and incredibly efficient butler on the R., *with the assistance of a Maid who is down* L.

Seated around the table are Sam Smith and his twelve guests in the positions indicated in the diagram. They are:

LADY JANE. *Young and very beautiful.*

SIR JOSEPH WRATHIE. *An elderly and arrogant financier.*

MRS PREEN. *Middle aged and somewhat neurotic.*

MR VAILE. *About forty, and a perfect little gentleman, if socks and spats can do it.*

MR GOURLAY. *An artist, but not a very attractive one.*

MRS CASTRO. *A mysterious widow from Buenos Aires. In the late thirties.*

MISS ISIT. *Younger than the widow, but her name obviously needs to be queried.*

CAPTAIN JENNINGS. *A typical young officer, probably in the Guards.*

MRS BLAND. *In her thirties. We hear nothing of a Mr Bland. She is inclined to be gushing, especially to her host.*

MISS VAILE. *Vaile's sister, so she says. But there is something wrong here.*

MR PREEN. *Of middle age, self-indulgent, but well liked by the rest.*

LADY WRATHIE. *Sir Joseph's wife. She probably has ambitions of her own to match those of her husband.*

Sam Smith is a little old bachelor, who beams on his guests like an elderly Cupid. That is how his guests regard him, but they are to be undeceived.

The windows, heavily curtained, are in the R. *wall. There is a door down* L. *and double doors back stage to the* L. *of* C. *There is a massive sideboard against the* L. *wall, and a serving table up* R.

179

On each are the wines, glasses, and other details ready for appropriate moments.

As the Curtain rises, there is hilarious laughter over some quip we are just too late to catch. But we notice that Lady Jane is not laughing, for she is scanning the table and counting the company. As the laughter subsides:

LADY JANE. [*Appalled; rising.*] We are thirteen at table!

GOURLAY. What's that?

[*Many fingers begin to count.*

LADY JANE. We are thirteen.

[*She looks down at Smith.*

LADY WRATHIE.			Fourteen.
CAPTAIN JENNINGS.	[*Almost together.*]		Twelve.
PREEN.			Surely not!

LADY JANE. [*To Smith.*] We are thirteen.

SMITH. Oh dear, how careless of me. Is there anything I can do?

SIR JOSEPH. [*As at a board meeting.*] Leave this to me. All keep your seats. [*He rises.*

MRS PREEN. I am afraid Lady Jane has risen.

[*Lady Jane sits.*

LADY WRATHIE. Joseph, you have risen yourself.

[*Sir Joseph sits.*

MRS CASTRO. [*With an air of mystery.*] Were we thirteen all those other nights?

MRS PREEN. [*Reassuring herself and the company.*] We always had a guest or two from outside, you remember.

MISS ISIT. [*Brightly.*] All we have got to do is to make our number fourteen.

VAILE. [*Leaning forward.*] But how, Miss Isit?

MISS ISIT. Why, Dolphin, of course!

MRS PREEN. It's too clever of you, Miss Isit. [*To her host.*] Mr Smith, Dolphin may sit down with us, mayn't he?

LADY JANE. Please, dear Mr Smith; just for a moment. That breaks the spell.

SIR JOSEPH. [*With a look at Dolphin, who is behind and just below him.*] We won't eat you, Dolphin.

[*But he has crunched some similar ones.*

SMITH. Let me explain to him. [*To Dolphin, who turns to Smith respectfully.*] You see, Dolphin, there is a superstition that if thirteen people sit down at table, something staggering will happen to one of them before the night is out. [*To the others.*] That is it, isn't it?

MRS BLAND. [*Darkly.*] Namely, death.

SMITH. [*Brightly.*] Yes, namely, death.

LADY JANE. But not before the night is out, you dear; before the year is out.

SMITH. I thought it was before the night was out.

GOURLAY. [*Making to shift his chair.*] Sit here, Dolphin.

　　　　　　　　　　[*Dolphin makes a reluctant movement.*

MISS VAILE. No, I want him.

MISS ISIT. It was my idea, and I insist on having him.

MRS CASTRO. [*Moving her chair towards Gourlay.*] Yes, here between us.

　　　　[*Dolphin moves down. The Maid smoothly slides a chair between Mrs Castro and Miss Isit. Dolphin sits, so that he is now facing Smith. The Maid retires to* L.

MRS PREEN. [*With childish abandon.*] Saved!

SMITH. As we are saved, and he does not seem happy, may he resume his duties?　　　　[*Dolphin rises and is checked by :*

LADY WRATHIE. Yes, yes; and now we ladies may withdraw.

PREEN. First, a glass of wine with you, Dolphin.

VAILE. [*Ever seeking to undermine Preen's popularity.*] Is this wise?

PREEN. [*Ignoring him.*] To the health of our friend, Dolphin.

　　　　[*The company drink Dolphin's health without rising. He gives a slight stiff bow and goes up* L. *A moment later he is discreetly noting who needs a glass refilled. There is a slight stir among the ladies, who would now rise but for a detaining gesture from Sir Joseph, who stands.*

SIR JOSEPH. One moment. Another toast. Fellow guests, tomorrow morning, alas, this party has to break up, and I am sure you will all agree with me that we have had a delightful week. It has not been an eventful week; it has been too happy for that.

CAPTAIN JENNINGS. [*Rising, with a smile at Lady Jane.*] I rise to protest. When I came here a week ago I had never met Lady Jane. Now, as you know, we are engaged.

　　　　[*The Maid commences an ecstatic sigh which is quelled by a glance from Dolphin.*

I certainly call it an eventful week.

LADY JANE. [*Very prettily.*] Yes, please, Sir Joseph.

SIR JOSEPH. I stand corrected. And now we are in the last evening of it. We are drawing to the end of a perfect day. . . .

PREEN. [*Who is also an orator.*] In seconding this motion . . .

VAILE. Pooh!

> [*His lack of good manners checks Preen, and Sir Joseph continues, addressing Smith.*

SIR JOSEPH. Though I have known you intimately but for a short time, I already find it impossible to call you anything but Sam Smith.

MRS CASTRO. [*With a dazzling smile.*] In our hearts, Mr Smith, that is what we ladies call you also.

> [*Smith gives a little smile and bow in her direction.*

PREEN. If I might say a word . . .

VAILE. Tuts.

> [*Preen is speechless.*

SIR JOSEPH. [*Ignoring all this, and indicating their host with an expansive gesture.*] Ladies and gentlemen, is he not like a pocket edition of Mr Pickwick?

GOURLAY. Exactly. That is how I should like to paint him.

MRS BLAND. [*Leaning in his direction—very gushing.*] Mr Smith, you love, we think that if you were married you could not be so nice.

SIR JOSEPH. At any rate, he could not be so simple. [*This amuses everybody at the table.*] For you are a very simple soul, Sam Smith. Well, we esteem you the more for your simplicity. [*He picks up his glass.*] Friends all, I give you the toast of—Sam Smith.

> [*The toast is drunk with acclamation. Dolphin, who has been quite impassive throughout the speech, refills Preen's glass. The Maid is busy for a moment at the sideboard, then returns to her place. There are cries of 'Sam Smith!' and 'Speech!'*

SMITH. [*Rising; with his Pickwickian smile.*] Ladies and gentlemen, you are very kind, and I don't pretend that it isn't pleasant to me to be praised. Tell me—[*a tiny pause*]—have you ever wondered why I invited you here?

MISS ISIT. Because you like us, of course, you muddled-headed old darling.

SMITH. [*Blandly.*] Was that the reason?

SIR JOSEPH. [*Inclined to be playful.*] Take care, Sammy, you are
not saying what you mean!

[*The guests all display great interest.*

SMITH. Am I not? Kindly excuse. I dare say I am as simple as
Sir Joseph says. And yet, do you really know me? Does any
person ever know another absolutely? Has not the simplest
of us a secret drawer inside him with . . . with a lock to it?

MISS ISIT. If you have, Mr Smith, be a dear and open it to us.

MRS CASTRO. How delicious! He is going to tell us of his first
and only love. [*This is to Miss Isit.*

SMITH. Ah, Mrs Castro, I think I had one once—very nice—
but I have forgotten her name. The person I loved best was—
my brother.

PREEN. I never knew you had a brother.

SMITH. I suppose none of you knew. He died two years ago.

SIR JOSEPH. Sorry, Sam Smith.

MRS PREEN. [*Drawing the chocolates nearer her.*] We should like
to hear about him if it isn't too sad.

SMITH. Would you? [*There is a murmur of assent, and he
continues.*] He was many years my junior and as attractive as
I am commonplace. [*A murmur of deprecation.*] He died in a
foreign land. [*Gravely.*] Natural causes were certified. But—
there were suspicious circumstances, and I went out there to
probe the matter to the full. [*To Mrs Bland.*] I did, too.

PREEN. You didn't say where the place was.

[*Miss Isit drinks.*

SMITH. It was—Monte Carlo.

[*He pauses. As Miss Isit's glass is lowered it slips from her
hand to the floor. No one notes it, apparently, but Smith
and Dolphin, and the Maid, who instantly remove the
pieces.*

Dolphin, another glass for Miss Isit.

[*Almost before the request is made, Dolphin is gliding smoothly
to Miss Isit with another glass. He fills it without the
slightest expression on his face.*

LADY JANE. Do go on.

[*Everybody is most intent.*

SMITH. My inquiries were slow, but I became convinced that
my brother had been poisoned.

MRS BLAND. How dreadful. You poor man.

GOURLAY. I hope, Sam Smith, you got on the track of the criminals?

SMITH. [*Blandly.*] Oh, yes. [*A chair creaks.*] Did you speak, Miss Isit?

MISS ISIT. Did I? I think not. What did you say about the criminals?

SMITH. Not criminals; there was only one.

PREEN. Man or woman?

SMITH. We are not yet certain.

> [*Preen nods understandingly, and empties his glass.*

What we do know is that my brother was visited in his rooms that night by someone who must have been the murderer. It was someone who spoke English and who was certainly dressed as a man, but it may have been a woman. There is proof that it was someone who had been to the tables that night. I got in touch with every 'possible', though I had to follow some of them to distant parts.

> [*Dolphin quietly refills Preen's glass.*

LADY WRATHIE. It is extraordinarily interesting.

SMITH. [*Replying direct to her.*] Outwardly, many of them seemed to be quite respectable people.

SIR JOSEPH. Ah, one can't go by that, Sam Smith.

SMITH. I didn't. I made the most exhaustive inquiries into their private lives. [*Smoothly.*] I did it so cunningly that not one of them suspected why I was so anxious to make his or her acquaintance; and then—when I was ready for them, I invited them to my house for a week, and—[*with a gentle embracing sweep of the hands*]—they are all sitting round my table this evening.

> [*For a moment a horrified silence; then a low murmur of indignation which dies down as he resumes.*

You wanted to know why I had asked you here, and I am afraid that in consequence I have wandered a little from the toast; but I thank you, Sir Joseph, I thank you all, for the too kind way in which you have drunk my health.

> [*He sits down as modestly as he had risen, but it is noted that the smile has gone from his face and that he is licking his lips. A confused babel breaks out, during which Dolphin, who has displayed no emotion whatever, goes about refilling glasses.*

PREEN. In the name of every one of us, Mr Smith, I tell you that this is an outrage.

SMITH. I was afraid you wouldn't like it.

SIR JOSEPH. May I ask, sir, whether all this week you have been surreptitiously ferreting into our private affairs, perhaps even rummaging our trunks?

SMITH. [*Brightening.*] That was it. You remember how I pressed you all to show your prowess on the tennis courts and the golf links while I stayed at home? That was my time for the trunks.
[*He sips his wine.*

LADY JANE. [*Braving it out.*] Was there ever such a man? Did you open our letters? [*The company is now very still.*

SMITH. [*To Lady Jane.*] Every one of them.
[*Dolphin refills his glass and retires to up* R.
And there were some very queer things in them. [*Speaking to the company generally.*] There was one about a luncheon at the Ritz. 'You will know me', the man wrote, 'by the gardenia I shall carry in my hand.' Perhaps I shouldn't have mentioned that. But the lady who got that letter needn't be frightened. She is married, and her husband is here with her, but I won't tell you any more.

MISS ISIT. [*Resentfully.*] I think he should be compelled to tell.

PREEN. Wrathie, there are only two ladies here with their husbands.

SIR JOSEPH. [*Meeting the challenge.*] Yours and mine, Preen.

LADY WRATHIE. [*In a tone brooking no further argument.*] Joseph, I don't need to tell you it wasn't your wife.

MRS PREEN. [*For Lady Wrathie's benefit.*] It certainly wasn't yours, Willie.

PREEN. Of that I am well assured.

SIR JOSEPH. Take care what you say, Preen. That is very like a reflection on my wife. [*His voice rises in cold anger.*

GOURLAY. [*Contemptuous of these anxieties.*] Let that pass. The other is the serious thing—so serious that it is a nightmare. [*To Smith.*] Whom do you accuse of doing away with your brother, sir? Out with it.

SMITH. [*Looking around at his guests.*] You are not all turning against me, are you? I assure you I don't accuse any of you— yet. I know that one of you did it, but I am not sure which one. I shall know soon.

* G 184

VAILE. Soon? How soon?

SMITH. Soon after the men join the ladies tonight. I ought to tell you that I am to try a little experiment tonight, something I have thought out which I have every confidence will make the guilty person fall into my hands, like a—ripe plum.

> [*His right hand closes slowly, and rather horribly.*

LADY JANE. [*Hitting the hand.*] Don't do that.

> [*Vaile empties his glass. There is a disturbed murmur and restless movement. Dolphin, during this, comes down and refills Vaile's glass.*

SIR JOSEPH. We insist, Smith, on hearing what this experiment is to be.

SMITH. That would spoil it. But I can tell you this. My speech had a little pit in it, and all the time I was talking I was watching whether any of you would fall into that pit.

MRS PREEN. [*Rising; nervously.*] I didn't notice any pit.

> [*Sir Joseph and Lady Wrathie exchange a contemptuous smile of triumph.*

SMITH. [*Courteously.*] You weren't meant to, Mrs Preen.

> [*Mrs Preen sits rather suddenly. Dolphin moves up to* R.

PREEN. May I ask, without pressing the personal note, did anyone fall into your pit?

SMITH. [*With a private smile.*] I think so.

> [*The Maid makes a slight movement. She is watching Mrs Preen very anxiously.*

CAPTAIN JENNINGS. Smith, we must have the name of this person.

LADY WRATHIE. Mrs Preen has fainted!

> [*There is instant commotion. Mrs Preen is lying back in her chair. Sir Joseph and Vaile are attentive but futile. Preen hurries round to up* R., *and takes a glass of water from Dolphin, who has brought it from the table up stage. Lady Jane has risen. But Mrs Preen recovers very quickly. Sir Joseph puts down the napkin with which he has fanned her. Lady Jane sits.*

MRS PREEN. Why—what—who—I am all right now. Willie, go back to your seat. Why are you all staring at me so?

MISS ISIT. [*Insincerely.*] Dear Mrs Preen, we are so glad you are better. I wonder what upset you?

> [*She exchanges a smile with Mrs Castro.*

PREEN. [*To the company, returning to his place.*] I never knew her faint before.   [*He instantly regrets his words.*

MISS ISIT. [*As before.*] I expect it was the heat.

PREEN. [*From behind his chair.*] Say it was the heat, Emily.

MRS PREEN. No, it wasn't the heat, Miss Isit. It was Mr Smith's talk of a pit.

PREEN. [*Distressed.*] My dear. . . .   [*He sits.*

MRS PREEN. [*In a curious tone.*] I suddenly remembered how, as that man mentioned that the place of the crime was Monte Carlo, some lady let her wineglass fall. That was why I fainted. [*With assumed vagueness.*] I can't remember who she was.

LADY WRATHIE. It was Miss Isit.

MRS PREEN. [*Casually.*] Really?

MISS ISIT. There is a thing called the law of libel. If Lady Wrathie and Mrs Preen will kindly formulate their charges . . .

GOURLAY. Oh, come, let us keep our heads.

SMITH. That's what I say.

GOURLAY. What about a motive? Scotland Yard always seeks for that first.

SMITH. I see two possible motives. If a woman did it—well, they tended to run after my brother, and you all know of what a woman scorned is capable.

PREEN. [*Reminiscently.*] Rather.   [*Then he is confused.*

SMITH. Then again, my brother had a large sum of money with him, which disappeared.

SIR JOSEPH. If you could trace that money if might be a help.

SMITH. [*Leaning forward keenly.*] All sorts of things are a help. The way you are all pretending to know nothing about the matter is a help. It might be a help if I could find out which of you has a clammy hand that at this moment wants to creep beneath the table.

      [*Not a hand creeps, but several glance at others' hands.*] I'll tell you something more.

        [*Mrs Castro stiffens. The Maid glances at her.*] Murderers' hearts beat differently from other hearts. [*Raising a finger.*] Listen! [*There is complete stillness. He almost whispers.*] Whose was it?

    [*A cry from Miss Vaile. All look at her, and she shows confusion.*

MISS VAILE. I thought I heard it. It seemed to come from across the table.

> [*A resentful murmur from those on the* R.

Please don't think because this man made me scream that I did it. I never was on a yacht in my life, at Monte Carlo or anywhere else.

> [*The murmur assumes a triumphant tone.*

VAILE. [*Sharply.*] Bella!

MISS VAILE. [*Still more confused.*] Have I said—anything odd?

GOURLAY. [*Very pleased.*] A yacht? There has been no talk of a yacht.

> [*Vaile suppresses fury.*

MISS VAILE. [*Shrinking back.*] Hasn't there?

SMITH. [*Indulgently.*] Perhaps there should have been. It was on his yacht my brother died.

MRS CASTRO. You said 'in his rooms'.

SMITH. Yes, that is what I *said*. I wanted to find out which of you knew better.

LADY JANE. And Miss Vaile . . .

MISS VAILE. I can explain it all if—if——

MISS ISIT. [*Sneering.*] Yes, give her a little time.

SMITH. Perhaps you would all like to take a few minutes.

MISS VAILE. I admit I was at Monte Carlo—with my brother—when an Englishman died there rather mysteriously on a yacht. When Mr Smith told us of his brother's death, I concluded that it was probably the same person.

VAILE. I presume that you accept my sister's statement?

MISS ISIT. Ab—so—lute—ly.

SMITH. She is not the only one of you who knew that yacht. You all admit having been at Monte Carlo two years ago, I suppose?

CAPTAIN JENNINGS. One of us wasn't. Lady Jane was never there.

SMITH. [*His eyes gleaming.*] What do you say to that, Lady Jane?

> [*Lady Jane falters.*

CAPTAIN JENNINGS. Tell him, Jane.

SMITH. Yes, tell me.

CAPTAIN JENNINGS. You never were there; say so.

LADY JANE. [*With a touch of defiance.*] Why shouldn't I have been there?

CAPTAIN JENNINGS. No reason. But when I happened to mention

Monte Carlo to you the other day I certainly understood——
Jane, I never forget a word *you* say, and you did say you had
never been there.

LADY JANE. So you—you, Jack—you accuse me—you—me——

CAPTAIN JENNINGS. I haven't—I haven't!

LADY JANE. [*Suddenly very cold.*] You have all heard that Captain
Jennings and I are engaged. I want you to understand that we
are so no longer.

CAPTAIN JENNINGS. Jane!

> [*Lady Jane has removed her engagement ring as he speaks.
> For a moment she holds it, hesitant; but by this time
> Dolphin has come smoothly to her right, with a salver on
> which she deposits the ring. In silence he conveys it up and
> across* L. *to the Captain, who takes it sullenly. There is an
> audible gurgle of sympathy from the Maid. This is a
> breach of etiquette, and Dolphin, with stony disapproval,
> opens the door down* L. *and the Maid makes a shameful
> exit. Dolphin then refills Captain Jennings's glass.*

SMITH. [*In a kindly tone.*] Take comfort, Captain. If Lady Jane
should prove to be the person wanted—mind you, perhaps
she isn't—why then, the ring is a matter of small importance,
because you would be parted in any case. I mean by the handcuffs. I forgot to say that I have them here.

> [*He gropes at his feet, and brings to light the handcuffs. Dolphin
> is instantly at his* L. *with the salver, on which they are
> deposited.*

Pass them round, Dolphin. [*To the guests.*] Perhaps some of
you have never seen them before.

> [*Dolphin moves from Smith with the salver, going around the
> table clockwise, displaying the handcuffs to each as if
> proffering some dish. It is coldly rejected by all.*

PREEN. [*As this is in progress.*] A pocket edition of Pickwick we
called him; he is more like a pocket edition of the devil.

SMITH. [*In mild and smiling reproof.*] Please, a little courtesy.
After all, I am your host.   [*Dolphin has reached Miss Vaile.*
Do take a look at them, Miss Vaile; they are an adjustable
pair in case they should be needed for small wrists.

> [*Miss Vaile is furious. Mrs Bland smiles at the handcuffs.
> Dolphin passes on to Captain Jennings, who ignores them.
> Miss Isit gives them a brief look.*

Would you like to try them on, Mrs Castro? They close with a click—a click.

[*Mrs Castro sits rigid.*

SIR JOSEPH. We quite understand.

[*Dolphin shows the handcuffs to Gourlay, who smiles at them sardonically. Vaile will not look at them. Dolphin passes on.*

MRS BLAND. [*Rising.*] How stupid of us. We have all forgotten that he said the murderer may have been a woman in man's clothes, and I have just remembered that when we played the charade on Wednesday he wanted the ladies to dress up as men. Was it to see whether one of us looked as if she could have passed for a man that night at Monte Carlo?

SMITH. You've got it, Mrs Bland.

SIR JOSEPH. Well, none of you did dress up, at any rate.

MRS BLAND. [*Distressed.*] Oh, Sir Joseph. Some of us did dress up, in private, and we all agreed that—of course, there's nothing in it, but we all agreed that the only figure which might have deceived a careless eye was Lady Wrathie's.

PREEN. I say!

LADY WRATHIE. Joseph, do you sit there and permit this?

[*Dolphin replenishes her glass.*

SMITH. Now, now! There is nothing to be touchy about. Have I not been considerate?

SIR JOSEPH. Smith, I hold you to be an impudent scoundrel.

SMITH. [*Mildly.*] May not I, who lost a brother in circumstances so painful, appeal for a little kindly consideration from those of you who are innocent—shady characters though you be?

PREEN. I must say that rather touches me. Some of us might have reasons for being reluctant to have our past at Monte inquired into, without being the person you are asking for.

SMITH. [*Glass in hand and sitting back.*] Precisely. I am presuming that to be the position of eleven of you.

LADY WRATHIE. [*Rising; imperiously.*] Joseph, I must ask you to come upstairs with me to pack our things.

MISS ISIT. For my part, after poor Mr Smith's appeal I think it would be rather heartless not to stay and see the thing out. Especially, Mr Smith, if you would give us just an inkling of what your—little experiment—in the drawing-room—is to be?

SMITH. [*Gravely, twirling the glass in his fingers.*] I can't say

anything about it except that it isn't to take place in the drawing-room. [*He sets down the glass.*] You ladies are to go this
evening to Dolphin's room, where we shall join you presently.

> [*For the first time, Dolphin displays a reaction. In moving, at
> that moment, to the service table up* R.*, he halts, looking
> at his master's back. He then completes his first intentions.*

MRS PREEN. Why should we go there?

SMITH. [*Gently; leaning towards her.*] Because I tell you to, Mrs
Preen.

LADY WRATHIE. I go to no such room. I leave this house at once.

MRS PREEN. [*Rising.*] I also.

LADY JANE. [*Rising also.*] All of us. I want to go home.

> [*The men rise, stepping back from the chairs.*

LADY WRATHIE. [*Moving from the table.*] Joseph, come.

MRS PREEN. Willie, I am ready. I wish you a long goodbye, Mr
Smith.

> [*The rest of the ladies, having risen, move up to the door up* L.*,
> with dignity. Dolphin has reached the door in time to
> open it. The ladies stop, and some move back a pace or
> two, for a Policeman is standing just beyond the threshold.
> The ladies all turn and glare at Smith.*

SMITH. [*Without looking at them.*] The ladies will now adjourn—
to Dolphin's room.

LADY WRATHIE. I say no.

MRS CASTRO. Let us.

> [*Smith stands, as she advances to him.*

Why shouldn't the innocent ones help him?

> [*She gives him her hand with a disarming smile.*

SMITH. [*Pressing her fingers, retaining them.*] I knew you would
be on my side, Mrs Castro. [*Confidentially.*] Cold hand—
warm heart. That's the saying, isn't it?

> [*Mrs Castro shrinks back, withdrawing her hand.*

LADY WRATHIE. Those who wish to leave this man's house,
follow me.

SMITH. [*After a glance in her direction, raising his voice.*] My
brother's cigarette case was of faded green leather, and a hole
had been burned in the back of it.

> [*For some reason this takes the fight out of Lady Wrathie.
> She tosses her head and departs for Dolphin's room. The
> other ladies follow; first Mrs Preen, Lady Jane, Mrs*

>*Castro, then Miss Vaile. As Miss Vaile passes Smith he whispers a word or two to her. She is rigid for a moment and then hurries out, followed by Mrs Bland.*

VAILE. [*As these are leaving.*] What did you say to my sister?

SMITH. I only said to her that she isn't your sister.

>   [*Vaile clenches his hands at his side.*
>[*Checking Miss Isit, the last to leave.*] So you never met my brother, Miss Isit?

MISS ISIT. [*Coolly.*] Not that I know of, Mr Smith.

SMITH. I have a photograph of him that I should like to show you.

MISS ISIT. I don't care to see it.

SMITH. You are going to see it.

>   [*He whips a small photograph from his pocket and puts it before her eyes.*

MISS ISIT. [*Surprised.*] That is not——

>   [*She checks herself. Smith smiles dangerously.*

SMITH. No, that is not my brother. That is someone you have never seen. But how did you know it wasn't my brother?

>   [*Miss Isit is silent.*

I rather think you knew Dick, Miss Isit.

MISS ISIT. [*Having recovered, drops a curtsy.*] I rather think I did, Mr Sam. What then?

>   [*She goes out impudently. Dolphin closes the door. The men stare uncertainly at Smith, who with a secret smile turns away from the door. He takes up a decanter and a box of cigarettes and toddles down to the chair exactly opposite his original place. He is now with his back to the audience.*

SMITH. Draw up closer, won't you?   [*He sits.*

>   [*They all drift, very reluctantly, to the chairs nearest him on either side. The sole exception is Vaile, who is studying a picture near the door. One fancies he would go out if Smith were not looking.*

You are not leaving us, Vaile?

VAILE. [*Startled.*] I thought . . .

SMITH. [*Sharply.*] Sit down.

VAILE. Oh, quite.

>   [*He sits on the L., on the chair previously occupied by Miss Vaile. On his L. are Preen and then Jennings. Mrs Bland's chair is empty. Gourlay is in his original seat, and Sir*

*Joseph in that occupied by Mrs Preen. Vaile's original
chair is left empty.*

SMITH. You are not drinking anything, Gourlay. Captain, the
port is with you.

                    [*The wine revolves, but no one partakes.*

PREEN. [*Heavily.*] Smith, there are a few words that I think it
my duty to say. This is a very unusual situation.

SMITH. Yes. You'll have a cigarette, Preen?

          [*The cigarettes are passed round but are not accepted.*

GOURLAY. I wonder why Mrs Bland—she is the only one of
them there seems nothing against.

VAILE. A bit fishy, that.

PREEN. [*Murmuring.*] It was rather odd, my wife fainting.

CAPTAIN JENNINGS. [*Gloomily.*] I dare say the ladies are saying
the same sort of thing about us.

                    [*He lights one of his own cigarettes.*
                    [*Dolphin is offering them liqueurs.*

PREEN. [*Sulkily.*] No, thanks. [*But he takes one.*] Smith, I am
sure I speak for all of us when I say we would esteem it a
favour if you ask Dolphin to withdraw.

          [*Jennings refuses a liqueur with a shake of his head.*

SMITH. [*Accepting a liqueur.*] He has his duties.

                    [*Dolphin passes below Smith to Gourlay.*

GOURLAY. [*Pettishly.*] No thanks.

                    [*Dolphin moves on to Sir Joseph.*

He gets on my nerves. Can nothing disturb this man?

CAPTAIN JENNINGS. Evidently nothing.

SIR JOSEPH. [*Having waved Dolphin irritably away.*] Everything
seems to point to its being a woman—wouldn't you say,
Smith?

SMITH. I wouldn't say everything, Sir Joseph. Dolphin thinks
it was a man.

SIR JOSEPH. One of us here?

     [*Smith nods. The men all regard Dolphin with great distaste.
     He, as impassive as ever, is now at the sideboard, his back
     to the company.*

GOURLAY. Did he know your brother?

                              [*All listen intently.*

SMITH. He was my brother's servant out there.

VAILE. [*Rising instantly.*] What? He wasn't the fellow who . . . ?

SMITH. [*Leaning forward.*] Who what, Vaile?

PREEN. I say!

> [*He gives a significant grin to Gourlay and Sir Joseph.*

VAILE. [*Hotly.*] What do you say?

PREEN. [*Doggedly.*] Nothing. [*He looks up at him amused.*] But—
I say——

> [*Vaile looks venomously at Dolphin's back. Preen turns and looks in the same direction. The other two men are also watching Dolphin, who is busy setting liqueurs back, and arranging glasses.*

GOURLAY. Are we to understand that you have had Dolphin spying on us here?

SMITH. That was the idea. And he helped me by taking your finger-prints.

> [*Dolphin crosses back to up* R.

VAILE. [*Throwing himself back in his chair.*] How can that help?

SMITH. He sent them to Scotland Yard.

SIR JOSEPH. [*Vindictively.*] Oh, he did, did he?

> [*His napkin falls unheeded.*

PREEN. What shows finger-marks best?

SMITH. Glass, I believe.

PREEN. [*Putting down his glass.*] Now I see why the Americans went dry.

> [*Dolphin moves down the* R. *side of the table, attentive.*

SIR JOSEPH. Smith, how can you be sure that Dolphin wasn't the man himself?

> [*Smith makes no answer or sign. Dolphin imperturbably picks up Sir Joseph's napkin and returns it to him.*

PREEN. Somehow I still cling to the hope that it was a woman.

VAILE. [*Trying to keep the anxiety from his voice.*] If it is a woman, Smith, what will you do?

SMITH. [*In a cold, dry voice.*] She shall hang by the neck until she is dead. [*Almost genially.*] You won't try the Benedictine, Vaile?

VAILE. [*In a hoarse whisper.*] No, thanks.

> [*The Maid enters from up* L., *with the coffee tray, which she presents under Dolphin's superintendence. Most of the men accept. The cups are already full.*

SIR JOSEPH. [*In his lighter manner.*] Did you notice what the ladies are doing in Dolphin's room, Lucy?

[*The Maid, at Sir Joseph's elbow, gives a scared glance at
    Smith.*

MAID. [*Trembling.*] Yes, Sir Joseph, they are wondering, Sir
Joseph, which of you it was that did it.

[*She passes on to Gourlay.*

PREEN. How like women!

GOURLAY. [*Accepting coffee.*] By the way, Smith, do you know
how the poison was administered?

[*The Maid passes on to Smith.*

SMITH. [*About to take a cup.*] Yes, in coffee.

MAID. You are to take the *yellow* cup, sir.

SMITH. [*Pausing.*] Who said so?

MAID. The lady who poured out this evening, sir.

PREEN. Aha, who was she?

MAID. Lady Jane Raye, sir.

[*Smith takes the yellow cup. As the Maid passes on to above
    Jennings:*

PREEN. I don't like it.   [*Smith is about to raise his cup.*

GOURLAY. Smith, don't drink that coffee!

[*Smith withdraws his hand.*

JENNINGS. [*In wrath.*] Why shouldn't he drink it?

[*A gesture of dismissal to the Maid, who goes to above Vaile.*

GOURLAY. Well, if it was she—a desperate woman—it was given
in coffee the other time, remember. But stop, she wouldn't
be likely to do it in the same way a second time.

VAILE. [*Takes the coffee.*] I'm not so sure. Perhaps she doesn't
suspect that Smith knows how it was given the first time. We
didn't know till the ladies had left the room.

PREEN. [*Admiring him at last.*] I say, Vaile, that's good.

[*The Maid replaces the tray on the buffet and stands ready
    for further instructions. Dolphin stands above the table,
    silent and impassive.*

JENNINGS. [*During the above.*] I have no doubt she merely meant
that she had sugared it to his taste.

VAILE. [*Smiling and leaning forward.*] Sugar!

PREEN. Sugar!

GOURLAY. Couldn't we analyse it?

JENNINGS. [*Pushing his chair back; angrily.*] Smith, I insist on
your drinking that coffee.

[*Smith gives no sign or movement.*

VAILE. Lady Jane! Who would have thought it?

PREEN. Lady Jane! Who would have thought it?

JENNINGS. [*Reaching for the cup.*] Give me the yellow cup.

> [*He drains it.*
> [*The Maid presses her hand to her mouth.*

SIR JOSEPH. [*After a tense moment.*] Nobly done, in any case.
[*He leans forward to Jennings.*] Look here, Jennings—you are
among friends—it hadn't an odd taste, had it?

JENNINGS. [*Harshly.*] Not a bit.

VAILE. He wouldn't feel the effects yet.

PREEN. [*With confidence in Vaile.*] He wouldn't feel them yet.

> [*The Maid sways slightly and recovers.*

SMITH. Vaile ought to know.

PREEN. [*As before.*] Vaile knows.

SIR JOSEPH. Why ought Vaile to know, Smith?

SMITH. He used to practise as a doctor.

> [*Vaile reacts.*

SIR JOSEPH. You never mentioned that to me, Vaile.

VAILE. [*Defiantly.*] Why should I?

SMITH. Why should he? He is not allowed to practise now.

> [*Vaile shows his teeth viciously*

PREEN. A doctor—poison—ease of access——
[*His confidence in Vaile destroyed, he casts him an unpleasant
glance, rises, and wanders despondently to above the table.*

SIR JOSEPH. We are where we were again.

> [*The Maid shows signs of collapse. Dolphin is instantly at her
> side and escorts her from the room by doors up* L.C.

JENNINGS. At any rate, that fellow has gone.

> [*Gourlay gives a short laugh. All look at him.*

GOURLAY. Excuse me. I suddenly remembered that Wrathie
had called this the end of a perfect day.

SMITH. It isn't ended yet.

> [*Preen, now at the top end of the buffet, pours himself some
> brandy, swirling it thoughtfully.*

PREEN. [*As if to himself.*] I feel I am not my old bright self. [*He
sips.*] I can't believe for a moment it was my wife. [*He sips.*]
And yet—[*he sips*]—that fainting, you know. [*He sips.*] I
should go away for a bit until it blew over. [*He sips.*] I don't
think I should ever marry again.

> [*He finishes the brandy cheerfully.*

GOURLAY. There is something shocking about sitting here, suspecting each other in this way. Let us go to that room and have it out.

SMITH. I am quite ready. [*Looking around.*] Nothing more to drink, anyone? Bring your cigarette, Captain.

SIR JOSEPH. [*Hoarsely.*] Smith—Sam—before we go, can I have a word with you alone?

SMITH. [*Shaking his head slowly.*] Sorry, Joseph. And now— [*he rises*]—shall we join the ladies?

[*They all rise. As they do so, a dreadful scream is heard from the direction of Dolphin's room—a woman's scream. The men stand tense and horrified. The next moment Dolphin appears in the doorway up* L.C. *He is no longer the imperturbable butler. He is livid. He tries to speak but no words will come. He stands transfixed as the guests, led by Captain Jennings, dash past him and out. Dolphin looks at his master with mingled horror and appeal. There is no response, and Dolphin goes out blindly. Smith sits slowly. He pours and drinks a small glass of brandy deliberately. He sets down the glass and commences to rise as—*

THE CURTAIN FALLS VERY SLOWLY

COURAGE

*To The Red Gowns
of St Andrews*

Rectorial Address delivered
at St Andrews University
3rd May 1922

YOU HAVE had many rectors here in St Andrews who will continue in bloom long after the lowly ones such as I am are dead and rotten and forgotten. They are the roses in December; you remember someone said that God gave us memory so that we might have roses in December. But I do not envy the great ones. In my experience—and you may find in the end it is yours also—the people I have cared for most and who have seemed most worth caring for—my December roses—have been very simple folk. Yet I wish that for this hour I could swell into some-one of importance, so as to do you credit. I suppose you had a melting for me because I was hewn out of one of your own quarries, walked similar academic groves and have trudged the road on which you will soon set forth. I would that I could put into your hands a staff for that somewhat bloody march, for though there is much about myself that I conceal from other people, to help you I would expose every cranny of my mind.

But, alas, when the hour strikes for the Rector to answer to his call he is unable to become the undergraduate he used to be, and so the only door into you is closed. We, your elders, are much more interested in you than you are in us. We are not really important to you. I have utterly forgotten the address of the Rector of my time, and even who he was, but I recall vividly climbing up a statue to tie his colours round his neck and being hurled therefrom with contumely. We remember the important things. I cannot provide you with that staff for your journey; but perhaps I can tell you a little about it, how to use it and lose it and find it again, and cling to it more than ever. You shall cut it—so it is ordained—every one of you for himself, and its name is Courage. You must excuse me if I talk a good deal about courage to you today. There is nothing else much worth speaking about to undergraduates or graduates or white-haired men and women. It is the lovely virtue—the rib of Himself that God sent down to His children.

My special difficulty is that though you have had literary rectors here before, they were the big guns, the historians, the philosophers; you have had none, I think, who followed my more humble branch, which may be described as playing hide and seek with angels. My puppets seem more real to me than myself, and I could get on much more swingingly if I made one of them deliver this address. It is M'Connachie who has brought me to this pass. M'Connachie, I should explain, as I have undertaken to open the innermost doors, is the name I give to the unruly half of myself: the writing half. We are complement and supplement. I am the half that is dour and practical and canny, he is the fanciful half; my desire is to be the family solicitor, standing firm on my hearthrug among the harsh realities of the office furniture; while he prefers to fly around on one wing. I should not mind him doing that, but he drags me with him. I have sworn that M'Connachie shall not interfere with this address today; but there is no telling. I might have done things worth while if it had not been for M'Connachie, and my first piece of advice to you at any rate shall be sound: don't copy me. A good subject for a rectorial address would be the mess the Rector himself has made of life. I merely cast this forth as a suggestion, and leave the working of it out to my successor. I do not think it has been used yet.

My own theme is Courage, as you should use it in the great fight that seems to me to be coming between youth and their betters; by youth, meaning, of course, you, and by your betters us. I want you to take up this position: That youth have for too long left exclusively in our hands the decisions in national matters that are more vital to them than to us. Things about the next war, for instance, and why the last one ever had a beginning. I use the word fight because it must, I think, begin with a challenge; but the aim is the reverse of antagonism, it is partnership. I want you to hold that the time has arrived for youth to demand that partnership, and to demand it courageously. That to gain courage is what you come to St Andrews for, with some alarums and excursions into college life. That is what I propose, but, of course, the issue lies with M'Connachie.

Your betters had no share in the immediate cause of the war; we know what nation has that blot to wipe out; but for fifty years or so we heeded not the rumblings of the distant drum—I do not mean by lack of military preparations; and when war did come we told youth, who had to get us out of it, tall tales of what it really is and of the clover beds to which it leads. We were not meaning to deceive, most of us were as honourable and as ignorant as the youth themselves; but that does not acquit us of failings such as stupidity and jealousy, the two black spots in human nature which, more than love of money, are at the root of all evil. If you prefer to leave things as they are we shall probably fail you again. Do not be too sure that we have learned our lesson, and are not at this very moment doddering down some brimstone path.

I am far from implying that even worse things than war may not come to a State. There are circumstances in which nothing can so well become a land, as I think this land proved when the late war did break out and there was but one thing to do. There is a form of anaemia that is more rotting than even an unjust war. The end will indeed have come to our courage and to us when we are afraid in dire mischance to refer the final appeal to the arbitrament of arms. I suppose all the lusty of our race, alive and dead, join hands on that.

> And he is dead who will not fight;
> And who dies fighting has increase.

But if you must be in the struggle, the more reason you should know why, before it begins, and have a say in the decision whether it is to begin. The youth who went to the war had no such knowledge, no such say; I am sure the survivors, of whom there must be a number here today, want you to be wiser than they were, and are certainly determined to be wiser next time themselves. If you are to get that partnership, which, once gained, is to be for mutual benefit, it will be, I should say, by banding yourselves with these men, not defiantly but firmly, not for selfish ends but for your country's good. In the meantime they have one bulwark; they have a general who is befriending them as I think never, after the fighting was over, has a general befriended his men before. Perhaps the seemly thing would be for us, their betters, to elect one of these young survivors of the carnage to be our Rector. He ought now to know a few things about war that are worth hearing. If his theme were the Rector's favourite, diligence, I should be afraid of his advising a great many of us to be diligent in sitting still and doing no more harm.

Of course he would put it more suavely than that, though it is not, I think, by gentleness that you will get your rights; we are dogged ones at sticking to what we have got, and so will you be at our age. But avoid calling us ugly names; we may be stubborn and we may be blunderers, but we love you more than aught else in the world, and once you have won your partnership we shall all be welcoming you. I urge you not to use ugly names about anyone. In the war it was not the fighting men who were distinguished for abuse; as has been well said: 'Hell hath no fury like a noncombatant.' Never ascribe to an opponent motives meaner than your own. There may be students here today who have decided this session to go in for immortality, and would like to know of an easy way of accomplishing it. That is a way, but not so easy as you think. Go through life without ever ascribing to your opponents motives meaner than your own. Nothing so lowers the moral currency; give it up, and be great.

Another sure way to fame is to know what you mean. It is a solemn thought that almost no one—if he is truly eminent—knows what he means. Look at the great ones of the earth, the politicians. We do not discuss what they say, but what they may have meant when they said it. In 1922 we are all wondering, and so are they, what they meant in 1914 and afterwards. They are publishing books trying to find out; the men of action as well as the men of words. There are exceptions. It is not that our statesmen are 'sugared mouths with minds therefrae'; many of them are the best men we have got, upright and anxious, nothing cheaper than to miscall them. The explanation seems just to be that it is so difficult to know what you mean, especially when you have become a swell. No longer apparently can you deal in 'russet yeas and honest kersey noes'; gone for ever is simplicity, which is as beautiful as the divine plain face of Lamb's Miss Kelly. Doubts breed suspicions, a dangerous air. Without suspicion there might have been no war. When you are called to Downing Street to discuss what you want of your betters with the Prime Minister he won't be suspicious, not as far as you can see; but remember the atmosphere of generations you are in, and when he passes you the toast-rack say to yourselves, if you would be in the mode: 'Now, I wonder what he meant by that.'

Even without striking out in the way I suggested, you are already disturbing your betters considerably. I sometimes talk this over with M'Connachie, with whom, as you may guess, circumstances compel me to pass a good deal of my time. In our talks we agree that we, your betters, constantly find you forgetting that we are your betters. Your answer is that the war and other happenings have shown you that age is not necessarily another name for sapience; that our avoidance of frankness in life and in the arts is often, but not so often as you think, a cowardly way of shirking unpalatable truths, and that you have taken us off our pedestals because we look more natural on the ground. You who are at the rash age even accuse your elders, sometimes not without justification, of being more rash than yourselves. 'If Youth but only knew', we used to teach you to sing; but now, just because Youth has been to the war, it wants to change the next line into 'If Age had only to do'.

In so far as this attitude of yours is merely passive, sullen, negative, as it mainly is, despairing of our capacity and anticipating a future of gloom, it is no game for man or woman. It is certainly the opposite of that for which I plead. Do not stand aloof, despising, disbelieving, but come in and help—insist on coming in and helping. After all, we have shown a good deal of courage; and your part is to add a greater courage to it. There are glorious years lying ahead of you if you choose to make them glorious. God's in His heaven still. So forward, brave hearts. To what adventures I cannot tell, but I know that your God is watching to see whether you are adventurous. I know that the great partnership is only a first step, but I do not know what are to be the next and the next. The partnership is but a tool; what are you to do with it? Very little, I warn you, if you are merely thinking of yourselves; much if what is at the marrow of your thoughts is a future that even you can scarcely hope to see.

Learn as a beginning how world-shaking situations arise and how they may be countered. Doubt all your betters who would deny you that right of partnership. Begin by doubting all such in high places—except, of course, your professors. But doubt all other professors—yet not conceitedly, as some do, with their noses in the air; avoid all such physical risks. If it necessitates your pushing some of us out of our places, still push; you will find it needs shoving. But the things courage can do! The things that even incompetence can do if it works with singleness of purpose. The war has done at least one big thing: it has taken spring out of the year. And, this accomplished, our leading people are amazed to find that the other seasons are not conducting themselves as usual. The spring of the year lies buried in the fields of France and elsewhere. By the time the next eruption comes it may be you who are responsible for it and your sons who are in the lava. All, perhaps, because this year you let things slide.

We are a nice and kindly people, but it is already evident that we are stealing back into the old grooves, seeking cushions for our old bones, rather than attempting to build up a fairer future. That is what we mean when we say that the country is settling down. Make haste, or you will become like us, with only the thing we proudly call experience to add to your stock, a poor exchange for the generous feelings that time will take away. We have no intention of giving you your share. Look around and see how much share Youth has now that the war is over. You got a handsome share while it lasted.

I expect we shall beat you; unless your fortitude be doubly girded by a desire to send a message of cheer to your brothers who fell, the only message, I believe, for which they crave; they are not worrying about their Aunt Jane. They want to know if you have learned wisely from what befell them; if you have, they will be braced in the feeling that they did not die in vain. Some of them think they did. They will not take our word for it that they did not. You are their living image; they know you could not lie to them, but they distrust our flattery and our cunning faces. To us they have passed away; but are you who stepped into their heritage only yesterday, whose books are scarcely cold to their hands, you who still hear their cries being blown across the links—are you already relegating them to the shades? The gaps they have left in this university are among the most honourable of her wounds. But we are not here to acclaim them. Where they are now, hero is, I think, a very little word. They call to you to find out in time the truth about this great game, which your elders play for stakes and Youth plays for its life.

I do not know whether you are grown a little tired of that word hero, but I am sure the heroes are. That is the subject of one of our unfinished plays; M'Connachie is the one who writes the plays. If any one of you here proposes to be a playwright you can take this for your own and finish it. The scene is a school, schoolmasters present, but if you like you could make it a university, professors present. They are discussing an illuminated scroll about a student fallen in the war, which they have kindly presented to his parents; and unexpectedly the parents enter. They are an old pair, backbent, they have been stalwarts in their day but have now gone small; they are poor, but not so poor that they could not send their boy to college. They are in black, not such a rusty black either, and you may be sure she is the one who knows what to do with his hat. Their faces are gnarled, I suppose—but I do not need to describe that pair to Scottish students. They have come to thank the Senatus for their lovely scroll and to ask them to tear it up. At first they had been enamoured to read of what a scholar their son was, how noble and adored by all. But soon a fog settled over them, for this grand person was not the boy they knew. He had many a fault well known to them; he was not always so noble; as a scholar he did no more than scrape through; and he sometimes made his father rage and his mother grieve. They had liked to talk such memories as these together, and smile over them, as if they were bits of him he had left lying about the house. So thank you kindly, and would you please give them back their boy by tearing up the scroll? I see nothing else for our dramatist to do. I think he should ask an alumna of St Andrews to play the old lady [indicating Miss Ellen Terry]. The loveliest of all young actresses, the dearest of all old ones; it seems only yesterday that all the men of imagination proposed to their beloved in some such frenzied words as these: 'As I can't get Miss Terry, may I have you?'

This play might become historical as the opening of your propaganda in the proposed campaign. How to make a practical advance? The League of Nations is a very fine thing, but it cannot save you, because it will be run by us. Beware your betters bringing presents. What is wanted is something run by yourselves. You have more in common with the youth of other lands than Youth and Age can ever have with each other; even the hostile countries sent out many a son very like ours, from the same sort of homes, the same sort of universities, who had as little to do as our youth had with the origin of the great adventure. Can we doubt that many of these on both sides who have gone over and were once opponents are now friends? You ought to have a League of Youth of all countries as your beginning, ready to say to all Governments: 'We will fight each other, but only when we are sure of the necessity.' Are you equal to your job, you young men? If not, I call upon the red-gowned women to lead the way. I sound to myself as if I were advocating a rebellion, though I am really asking for a larger friendship. Perhaps I may be arrested on leaving the hall. In such a cause I should think that I had at last proved myself worthy to be your Rector.

You will have to work harder than ever, but possibly not so much at the same things; more at modern languages certainly if you are to discuss that League of Youth with the students of other nations when they come over to St Andrews for the conference. I am far from taking a side against the classics. I should as soon argue against your having tops to your heads; that way lie the best tops. Science, too, has at last come to its own in St Andrews. It is the surest means of teaching you how to know what you mean when you say. So you will have to work harder. Izaak Walton quotes the saying that doubtless the Almighty could have created a finer fruit than the strawberry, but that doubtless also He never did. Doubtless also He could have provided us with better fun than hard work, but I don't know what it is. To be born poor is probably the next best thing. The greatest glory that has ever come to me was to be swallowed up in London, not knowing a soul, with no means of subsistence, and the fun of working till the stars went out. To have known anyone would have spoilt it. I did not even quite know the language. I rang for my boots, and they thought I said a glass of water, so I drank the water and worked on. There was no food in the cupboard, so I did not need to waste time in eating. The pangs and agonies when no proof came. How courteously tolerant was I of the postman without a proof for us; how M'Connachie, on the other hand, wanted to punch his head. The magic days when our article appeared in an evening paper. The promptitude with which I counted the lines to see how much we should get for it. Then M'Connachie's superb air of dropping it into the gutter. Oh, to be a free lance of journalism again—that darling jade! Those were days. Too good to last. Let us be grave. Here comes a Rector.

But now, on reflection, a dreadful sinking assails me, that this was not really work. The artistic callings—you remember how Stevenson thumped them—are merely doing what you are clamorous to be at; it is not real work unless you would rather be doing something else. My so-called labours were just M'Connachie running away with me again. Still, I have sometimes worked; for instance, I feel that I am working at this moment. And the big guns are in the same plight as the little ones. Carlyle, the king of all rectors, had always been accepted as the archapostle of toil, and has registered his many woes. But it will not do. Despite sickness, poortith, want and all, he was grinding all his life at the one job he revelled in. An extraordinary happy man, though there is no direct proof that he thought so.

There must be many men in other callings besides the arts lauded as hard workers who are merely out for enjoyment. Our Chancellor? [indicating Lord Haig]. If our Chancellor had always a passion to be a soldier, we must reconsider him as a worker. Even our Principal? How about the light that burns in our Principal's room after decent people have gone to bed? If we could climb up and look in—I should like to do something of that kind for the last time—should we find him engaged in honest toil, or guiltily engrossed in chemistry?

You will all fall into one of those two callings, the joyous or the uncongenial; and one wishes you into the first, though our sympathy, our esteem, must go rather to the less fortunate, the braver ones who 'turn their necessity to glorious gain' after they have put away their dreams. To the others will go the easy prizes of life—success, which has become a somewhat odious onion nowadays, chiefly because we so often give the name to the wrong thing. When you reach the evening of your days you will, I think, see—with, I hope, becoming cheerfulness—that we are all failures, at least all the best of us. The greatest Scotsman that ever lived wrote himself down a failure:

> The poor inhabitant below
> Was quick to learn and wise to know,
> And keenly felt the friendly glow
>   And softer flame.
> But thoughtless follies laid him low,
>   And stained his name.

H 184

Perhaps the saddest lines in poetry, written by a man who could make things new for the gods themselves.

If you want to avoid being like Burns there are several possible ways. Thus you might copy us, as we shine forth in our published memoirs, practically without a flaw. No one so obscure nowadays but that he can have a book about him. Happy the land that can produce such subjects for the pen.

But do not put your photograph at all ages into your autobiography. That may bring you to the ground. 'My Life; and what I have done with it'; that is the sort of title, but it is the photographs that give away what you have done with it. Grim things, those portraits; if you could read the language of them you would often find it unnecessary to read the book. The face itself, of course, is still more tell-tale, for it is the record of all one's past life. There the man stands in the dock, page by page; we ought to be able to see each chapter of him melting into the next like the figures in the cinematograph. Even the youngest of you has got through some chapters already. When you go home for the next vacation some one is sure to say 'John has changed a little; I don't quite see in what way, but he has changed.' You remember they said that last vacation. Perhaps it means that you look less like your father. Think that out. I could say some nice things of your betters if I chose.

In youth you tend to look rather frequently into a mirror, not at all necessarily from vanity. You say to yourself: 'What an interesting face; I wonder what he is to be up to?' Your elders do not look into the mirror so often. We know what he has been up to. As yet there is unfortunately no science of reading other people's faces; I think a chair for this should be founded in St Andrews.

The new professor will need to be a sublime philosopher, and for obvious reasons he ought to wear spectacles before his senior class. It will be a gloriously optimistic chair, for he can tell his students the glowing truth, that what their faces are to be like presently depends mainly on themselves. Mainly, not altogether—

> I am the master of my fate,
> I am the captain of my soul.

I found the other day an old letter from Henley that told me of the circumstances in which he wrote that poem. 'I was a patient', he writes, 'in the old infirmary of Edinburgh. I had heard vaguely of Lister, and went there as a sort of forlorn hope on the chance of saving my foot. The great surgeon received me, as he did and does everybody, with the greatest kindness, and for twenty months I lay in one or other ward of the old place under his care. It was a desperate business, but he saved my foot, and here I am.' There he was, ladies and gentlemen, and what he was doing during that 'desperate business' was singing that he was master of his fate.

If you want an example of courage try Henley. Or Stevenson. I could tell you some stories about these two, but they would not be dull enough for a rectorial address. For courage, again, take Meredith, whose laugh was 'as broad as a thousand beeves at pasture'. Take, as I think, the greatest figure literature has still left to us, to be added today to the roll of St Andrews' alumni, though it must be in absence. The pomp and circumstance of war will pass, and all others now alive may fade from the scene, but I think the quiet figure of Hardy will live on.

I seem to be taking all my examples from the calling I was lately pretending to despise. I should like to read you some passages of a letter from a man of another calling, which I think will hearten you. I have the little filmy sheets here. I thought you might like to see the actual letter; it has been a long journey; it has been to the South Pole. It is a letter to me from Captain Scott of the Antarctic, and was written in the tent you know of, where it was found long afterwards with his body and those of some other very gallant gentlemen, his comrades. The writing is in pencil, still quite clear, though towards the end some of the words trail away as into the great silence that was waiting for them. It begins:

We are pegging out in a very comfortless spot. Hoping this letter may be found and sent to you, I write you a word of farewell. I want you to think well of me and my end. [After some private instructions too intimate to read, he goes on:] Goodbye—I am not at all afraid of the end, but sad to miss many a simple pleasure which I had planned for the future in our long marches. . . . We are in a desperate state—feet frozen, etc., no fuel and a long way from food, but it would do your heart good to be in our tent, to hear our songs and our cheery conversation. . . . [Later—it is here that the words become difficult—] We are very near the end. . . . We did intend to finish ourselves when things proved like this, but we have decided to die naturally without.

I think it may uplift you all to stand for a moment by that tent and listen, as he says, to their songs and cheery conversation. When I think of Scott I remember the strange Alpine story of the youth who fell down a glacier and was lost, and of how a scientific companion, one of several who accompanied him, all young, computed that the body would again appear at a certain date and place many years afterwards. When that time came round some of the survivors returned to the glacier to see if the prediction would be fulfilled; all old men now; and the body reappeared as young as on the day he left them. So Scott and his comrades emerge out of the white immensities always young.

How comely a thing is affliction borne cheerfully, which is not beyond the reach of the humblest of us. What is beauty? It is these hard-bitten men singing courage to you from their tent; it is the waves of their island home crooning of their deeds to you who are to follow them. Sometimes beauty boils over and then spirits are abroad. Ages may pass as we look or listen, for time is annihilated. There is a very old legend told to me by Nansen the explorer—I like well to be in the company of explorers—the legend of a monk who had wandered into the fields and a lark began to sing. He had never heard a lark before, and he stood there entranced until the bird and its song had become part of the heavens. Then he went back to the monastery and found there a doorkeeper whom he did not know and who did not know him. Other monks came, and they were all strangers to him. He told them he was Father Anselm, but that was no help. Finally they looked through the books of the monastery, and these revealed that there had been a Father Anselm there a hundred or more years before. Time had been blotted out while he listened to the lark.

That, I suppose, was a case of beauty boiling over, or a soul boiling over; perhaps the same thing. Then spirits walk.

They must sometimes walk St Andrews. I do not mean the

ghosts of queens or prelates, but one that keeps step, as soft as snow, with some poor student. He sometimes catches sight of it. That is why his fellows can never quite touch him, their best beloved; he half knows something of which they know nothing—the secret that is hidden in the face of the Mona Lisa. As I see him, life is so beautiful to him that its proportions are monstrous. Perhaps his childhood may have been overfull of gladness; they don't like that. If the seekers were kind he is the one for whom the flags of his college would fly one day. But the seeker I am thinking of is unfriendly, and so our student is 'the lad that will never be old'. He often gaily forgets, and thinks he has slain his foe by daring him, like him who, dreading water, was always the first to leap into it. One can see him serene, astride a Scotch cliff, singing to the sun the farewell thanks of a boy:

> Throned on a cliff serene Man saw the sun
> hold a red torch above the farthest seas,
> and the fierce island pinnacles put on
> in his defence their sombre panoplies;
> Foremost the white mists eddied, trailed and spun
> like seekers, emulous to clasp his knees,
> till all the beauty of the scene seemed one,
> led by the secret whispers of the breeze.
> The sun's torch suddenly flashed upon his face
> and died; and he sat content in subject night
> and dreamed of an old dead foe that had sought and found him;
> a beast stirred boldly in his resting-place;
> And the cold came; Man rose to his master-height,
> shivered, and turned away; but the mists were round him.

If there is any of you here so rare that the seekers have taken an ill will to him, as to the boy who wrote those lines, I ask you to be careful. Henley says in that poem we were speaking of:

> Under the bludgeonings of Chance
> My head is bloody but unbowed.

A fine mouthful, but perhaps 'My head is bloody and bowed' is better.

Let us get back to that tent with its songs and cheery conversation. Courage. I do not think it is to be got by your becoming solemn-sides before your time. You must have been warned against letting the golden hours slip by. Yes, but some of them are golden only because we let them slip. Diligence—ambition; noble words, but only if 'touched to fine issues'. Prizes may be dross, learning lumber, unless they bring you into the arena with increased understanding. Hanker not too much after worldly prosperity—that corpulent cigar; if you become a millionaire you would probably go swimming around for more like a diseased goldfish. Look to it that what you are doing is not merely toddling to a competency. Perhaps that must be your fate, but fight it and then, though you fail, you may still be among the elect of whom we have spoken. Many a brave man has had to come to it at last. But there are the complacent toddlers from the start. Favour them not, ladies, especially now that every one of you carries a possible *maréchal's* baton under her gown. 'Happy', it has been said by a distinguished man, 'is he who can leave college with an unreproaching conscience and an unsullied heart.' I don't know; he sounds to me like a sloppy, watery sort of fellow; happy, perhaps, but if there be red blood in him impossible. Be not disheartened by ideals of perfection which can be achieved only by those who run away. Nature, that 'thrifty goddess', never gave you 'the smallest scruple of her excellence' for that. Whatever bludgeonings may be gathering for you, I think one feels more poignantly at your age than ever again in life. You have not our December roses to help you; but you have June coming, whose roses do not wonder, as do ours even while they give us their fragrance—wondering most when they give us most—that we should linger on an empty scene. It may indeed be monstrous but possibly courageous.

Courage is the thing. All goes if courage goes. What says our glorious Johnson of courage: 'Unless a man has that virtue he has no security for preserving any other.' We should thank our Creator three times daily for courage instead of for our bread, which, if we work, is surely the one thing we have a right to claim of Him. This courage is a proof of our immortality, greater even than gardens 'when the eve is cool'. Pray for it. 'Who rises from prayer a better man, his prayer is answered.' Be not merely courageous, but light-hearted and gay. There is an officer who was the first of our army to land at Gallipoli. He was dropped overboard to light decoys on the shore, so as to deceive the

Turks as to where the landing was to be. He pushed a raft containing these in front of him. It was a frosty night, and he was naked and painted black. Firing from the ships was going on all around. It was a two-hours' swim in pitch darkness. He did it, crawled through the scrub to listen to the talk of the enemy, who were so near that he could have shaken hands with them, lit his decoys and swam back. He seems to look on this as a gay affair. He is a V.C. now, and you would not think to look at him that he could ever have presented such a disreputable appearance. Would you? [indicating Colonel Freyberg].

Those men of whom I have been speaking as the kind to fill the fife could all be light-hearted on occasion. I remember Scott by Highland streams trying to rouse me by maintaining that haggis is boiled bagpipes; Henley in dispute as to whether, say, Turgenev or Tolstoy could hang the other on his watch-chain; he sometimes clenched the argument by casting his crutch at you; Stevenson responded in the same gay spirit by giving that crutch to John Silver; you remember with what adequate results. You must cultivate this light-heartedness if you are to hang your betters on your watch-chains. Dr Johnson—let us have him again —does not seem to have discovered in his travels that the Scots are a light-hearted nation. Boswell took him to task for saying that the death of Garrick had eclipsed the gaiety of nations. 'Well, sir,' Johnson said, 'there may be occasions when it is permissible to,' etc. But Boswell would not let go. 'I cannot see, sir, how it could in any case have eclipsed the gaiety of nations, as England was the only nation before whom he had ever played.' Johnson was really stymied, but you would never have known it. 'Well, sir,' he said, holing out, 'I understand that Garrick once played in Scotland, and if Scotland has any gaiety to eclipse, which, sir, I deny——'

Prove Johnson wrong for once at the Students' Union and in your other societies. I must regret that there was no Students' Union at Edinburgh in my time. I hope you are fairly noisy and that members are sometimes led out. Do you keep to the old topics? King Charles's head; and Bacon wrote Shakespeare, or if he did not he missed the opportunity of his life. Don't forget to speak scornfully of the Victorian age; there will be time for meekness when you try to better it. Very soon you will be Victorian or that sort of thing yourselves; next session probably, when the freshmen come up. Afterwards, if you go in for my sort of calling, don't begin by thinking you are the last word in art; quite possibly you are not; steady yourselves by remembering that there were great men before William K. Smith. Make merry while you may. Yet light-heartedness is not for ever and a day. At its best it is the gay companion of innocence; and when innocence goes—as go it must—they soon trip off together, looking for something younger. But courage comes all the way:

> Fight on, my men, says Sir Andrew Barton,
> I am hurt, but I am not slaine;
> I'll lie me down and bleed a-while,
> And then I'll rise and fight againe.

Another piece of advice; almost my last. For reasons you may guess I must give this in a low voice. Beware of M'Connachie. When I look in a mirror now it is his face I see. I speak with his voice. I once had a voice of my own, but nowadays I hear it from far away only, a melancholy, lonely, lost little pipe. I wanted to be an explorer, but he willed otherwise. You will all have your M'Connachies luring you off the high road. Unless you are constantly on the watch, you will find that he has pushed you out of yourself and taken your place. He has rather done for me. I think in his youth he must somehow have guessed the future and been fleggit by it, flichtered from the nest like a bird, and so our eggs were left, cold. He has clung to me, less from mischief than for companionship; I half like him and his penny whistle; with all his faults he is as Scotch as peat; he whispered to me just now that you elected him, not me, as your Rector.

A final passing thought. Were an old student given an hour in which to revisit the St Andrews of his day, would he spend more than half of it at lectures? He is more likely to be heard clattering up bare stairs in search of old companions. But if you could choose your hour from all the five hundred years of this seat of learning, wandering at your will from one age to another, how would you spend it? A fascinating theme; so many notable shades at once astir that St Leonard's and St Mary's grow murky with them. Hamilton, Melville, Sharpe, Chalmers, down to Herkless, that distinguished Principal, ripe scholar and warm friend, the loss of whom I deeply deplore with you. I think if that hour were mine, and though at St Andrews he was but a passer-by, I would give a handsome part of it to a walk with Dr Johnson. I should like to have the time of day passed to me in twelve languages by the Admirable Crichton. A wave of the hand to Andrew Lang; and then for the archery butts with the gay Montrose, all a-ruffled and ringed, and in the gallant St Andrews student manner, continued as I understand to this present day, scattering largess as he rides along,

> But where is now the courtly troupe
>   That once went riding by?
> I miss the curls of Canteloupe,
>   The laugh of Lady Di.

We have still left time for a visit to a house in South Street, hard by St Leonard's. I do not mean the house you mean. I am a Knox man. But little will that avail, for M'Connachie is a Queen Mary man. So, after all, it is at her door we chap, a last futile effort to bring that woman to heel. One more house of call, a student's room, also in South Street. I have chosen my student, you see, and I have chosen well; him that sang:

> Life has not since been wholly vain,
>   And now I bear
> Of wisdom plucked from joy and pain
>   Some slender share.

> But howsoever rich the store,
>   I'd lay it down
> To feel upon my back once more
>   The old red gown.

Well, we have at last come to an end. Some of you may remember when I began this address; we are all older now. I thank you for your patience. This is my first and last public appearance, and I never could or would have made it except to a gathering of Scottish students. If I have concealed my emotions in addressing you it is only the thrawn national way that deceives everybody except Scotsmen. I have not been as dull as I could have wished to be; but looking at your glowing faces cheerfulness and hope would keep breaking through. Despite the imperfections of your

* H 184

betters we leave you a great inheritance, for which others will one day call you to account. You come of a race of men the very wind of whose name has swept to the ultimate seas. Remember—

> Heaven doth with us as we with torches do,
> Not light them for themselves. . . .

Mighty are the universities of Scotland, and they will prevail. But even in your highest exultations never forget that they are not four, but five. The greatest of them is the poor, proud homes you come out of, which said so long ago: 'There shall be education in this land.' She, not St Andrews, is the oldest university in Scotland, and all the others are her whelps.

In bidding you goodbye, my last words must be of the lovely virtue. Courage, my children, and 'greet the unseen with a cheer'. 'Fight on, my men,' said Sir Andrew Barton. Fight on—you— for the old red gown till the whistle blows.

THE COURTING OF T'NOWHEAD'S BELL

From *Auld Licht Idylls*,
1888

FOR TWO years it had been notorious in the square that Sam'l
Dickie was thinking of courting T'nowhead's Bell, and that if
little Sanders Elshioner (which is the Thrums pronunciation of
Alexander Alexander) went in for her he might prove a formidable rival. Sam'l was a weaver in the Tenements, and Sanders
a coal-carter whose trade mark was a bell on his horse's neck
that told when coals were coming. Being something of a public
man, Sanders had not perhaps so high a social position as Sam'l,
but he had succeeded his father on the coal-cart, while the
weaver had already tried several trades. It had always been against
Sam'l, too, that once when the kirk was vacant he had advised
the selection of the third minister who preached for it on the
ground that it came expensive to pay a large number of candi-
dates. The scandal of the thing was hushed up, out of respect
for his father, who was a God-fearing man, but Sam'l was
known by it in Lang Tammas's circle. The coal-carter was called
Little Sanders to distinguish him from his father, who was not
much more than half his size. He had grown up with the name,
and its inapplicability now came home to nobody. Sam'l's
mother had been more far-seeing than Sanders's. Her man had
been called Sammy all his life because it was the name he got as
a boy, so when their eldest son was born she spoke of him as
Sam'l while still in his cradle. The neighbours imitated her, and
thus the young man had a better start in life than had been
granted to Sammy, his father.

It was Saturday evening—the night in the week when Auld
Licht young men fell in love. Sam'l Dickie, wearing a blue
glengarry bonnet with a red ball on the top, came to the door
of a one-storey house in the Tenements and stood there wriggling, for he was in a suit of tweed for the first time that week,
and did not feel at one with them. When his feeling of being a
stranger to himself wore off he looked up and down the road,
which straggles between houses and gardens, and then, picking
his way over the puddles, crossed to his father's hen-house and
sat down on it. He was now on his way to the square.

Eppie Fargus was sitting on an adjoining dike knitting stockings, and Sam'l looked at her for a time.

'Is't yersel, Eppie?' he said at last.

'It's a' that,' said Eppie.

'Hoo's a' wi' ye?' asked Sam'l.

'We're juist aff an' on,' replied Eppie cautiously.

There was not much more to say, but as Sam'l sidled off the hen-house he murmured politely: 'Ay, ay.' In another minute he would have been fairly started, but Eppie resumed the conversation.

'Sam'l,' she said, with a twinkle in her eye, 'ye can tell Lisbeth Fargus I'll likely be drappin' in on her aboot Mununday or Teisday.'

Lisbeth was sister to Eppie, and wife of Tammas McQuhatty, better known as T'nowhead, which was the name of his farm. She was thus Bell's mistress.

Sam'l leant against the hen-house as if all his desire to depart had gone.

'Hoo d'ye kin I'll be at the T'nowhead the nicht?' he asked, grinning in anticipation.

'Ou, I'se warrant ye'll be after Bell,' said Eppie.

'Am no sae sure o' that,' said Sam'l, trying to leer. He was enjoying himself now.

'Am no sure o' that,' he repeated, for Eppie seemed lost in stitches.

'Sam'l?'

'Ay.'

'Ye'll be speirin' her sune noo, I dinna doot?'

This took Sam'l, who had only been courting Bell for a year or two, a little aback.

'Hoo d'ye mean, Eppie?' he asked.

'Maybe ye'll do't the nicht.'

'Na, there's nae hurry,' said Sam'l.

'Weel, we're a' coontin' on't, Sam'l.'

'Gae wa wi' ye.'

'What for no?'

'Gae wa wi' ye,' said Sam'l again.

'Bell's gei an' fond o' ye, Sam'l.'

'Ay,' said Sam'l.

'But am dootin' ye're a fell billy wi' the lasses.'

'Ay, oh, I d'na kin, moderate, moderate,' said Sam'l in high delight.

'I saw ye', said Eppie, speaking with a wire in her mouth, 'gae'in on terr'ble wi' Mysy Haggart at the pump last Saturday.'

'We was juist amoosin' oorsels,' said Sam'l.

'It'll be nae amoosement to Mysy', said Eppie, 'gin ye brak her heart.'

'Losh, Eppie,' said Sam'l, 'I didna think o' that.'

'Ye maun kin weel, Sam'l, 'at there's mony a lass wid jump at ye.'

'Ou, weel,' said Sam'l, implying that a man must take these things as they come.

'For ye're a dainty chield to look at, Sam'l.'

'Do ye think so, Eppie? Ay, ay; oh, I d'na kin am onything by the ordinar.'

'Ye mayna be,' said Eppie, 'but lasses doesna do to be ower partikler.'

Sam'l resented this, and prepared to depart again.

'Ye'll no tell Bell that?' he asked anxiously.

'Tell her what?'

'Aboot me an' Mysy.'

'We'll see hoo ye behave yersel, Sam'l.'

'No 'at I care, Eppie; ye can tell her gin ye like. I widna think twice o' telling her mysel.'

'The Lord forgie ye for leein', Sam'l,' said Eppie, as he disappeared down Tammy Tosh's close. Here he came upon Henders Webster.

'Ye're late, Sam'l,' said Henders.

'What for?'

'Ou, I was thinkin' ye wid be gaen the length o' T'nowhead the nicht, an' I saw Sanders Elshioner makkin's wy there an oor syne.'

'Did ye?' cried Sam'l, adding craftily, 'but it's naething to me.'

'Tod, lad,' said Henders, 'gin ye dinna buckle to, Sanders'll be carryin' her off.'

Sam'l flung back his head and passed on.

'Sam'l!' cried Henders after him.

'Ay,' said Sam'l, wheeling round.

'Gie Bell a kiss frae me.'

The full force of this joke struck neither all at once. Sam'l began to smile at it as he turned down the school-wynd, and it came upon Henders while he was in his garden feeding his ferret. Then he slapped his legs gleefully, and explained the conceit to Will'um Byars, who went into the house and thought it over.

There were twelve or twenty little groups of men in the square, which was lit by a flare of oil suspended over a cadger's cart. Now and again a staid young woman passed through the square with a basket on her arm, and if she had lingered long enough to give them time, some of the idlers would have addressed her. As it was, they gazed after her, and then grinned to each other.

'Ay, Sam'l,' said two or three young men, as Sam'l joined them beneath the town clock.

'Ay, Davit,' replied Sam'l.

This group was composed of some of the sharpest wits in Thrums, and it was not to be expected that they would let this opportunity pass. Perhaps when Sam'l joined them he knew what was in store for him.

'Was ye lookin' for T'nowhead's Bell, Sam'l?' asked one.

'Or mebbe ye was wantin' the minister?' suggested another, the same who had walked out twice with Christy Duff and not married her after all.

Sam'l could not think of a good reply at the moment, so he laughed good-naturedly.

'Ondoobtedly she's a snod bit crittur,' said Davit archly.

'An' michty clever wi' her fingers,' added Jamie Deuchars.

'Man, I've thocht o' makkin' up to Bell mysel,' said Pete Ogle. 'Wid there be ony chance, think ye, Sam'l?'

'I'm thinkin' she widna hae ye for her first, Pete,' replied Sam'l, in one of those happy flashes that come to some men, 'but there's nae sayin' but what she micht tak ye to finish up wi'.'

The unexpectedness of this sally startled everyone. Though Sam'l did not set up for a wit, however, like Davit, it was notorious that he could say a cutting thing once in a way.

'Did ye ever see Bell reddin' up?' asked Pete, recovering from his overthrow. He was a man who bore no malice.

'It's a sicht,' said Sam'l solemnly.

'Hoo will that be?' asked Jamie Deuchars.

'It's weel worth ye while', said Pete, 'to ging atower to the T'nowhead an' see. Ye'll mind the closed-in beds i' the kitchen?

Ay, weel, they're a fell spoilt crew, T'nowhead's litlins, an' no that aisy to manage. Th' ither lasses Lisbeth's hae'n had a michty trouble wi' them. When they war i' the middle o' their reddin up the bairns wid come tumlin' about the floor, but, sal, I assure ye, Bell didna fash lang wi' them. Did she, Sam'l?'

'She did not,' said Sam'l, dropping into a fine mode of speech to add emphasis to his remark.

'I'll tell ye what she did,' said Pete to the others. 'She juist lifted up the litlins, twa at a time, an' flung them into the coffin-beds. Syne she snibbit the doors on them, an' keepit them there till the floor was dry.'

'Ay, man, did she so?' said Davit admiringly.

'I've seen her do't mysel,' said Sam'l.

'There's no a lassie maks better bannocks this side o' Fetter Lums,' continued Pete.

'Her mither tocht her that,' said Sam'l; 'she was a gran' han' at the bakin', Kitty Ogilvy.'

'I've heard say', remarked Jamie, putting it this way so as not to tie himself down to anything, ''at Bell's scones is equal to Mag Lunan's.'

'So they are,' said Sam'l, almost fiercely.

'I kin she's a neat han' at singein' a hen,' said Pete.

'An' wi't a'', said Davit, 'she's a snod, canty bit stocky in her Sabbath claes.'

'If onything, thick in the waist,' suggested Jamie.

'I dinna see that,' said Sam'l.

'I d'na care for her hair either,' continued Jamie, who was very nice in his tastes; 'something mair yallowchy wid be an improvement.'

'A'body kins', growled Sam'l, ''at black hair's the bonniest.'

The others chuckled.

'Puir Sam'l!' Pete said.

Sam'l not being certain whether this should be received with a smile or a frown, opened his mouth wide as a kind of compromise. This was position one with him for thinking things over.

Few Auld Lichts, as I have said, went the length of choosing a helpmate for themselves. One day a young man's friends would see him mending the washing-tub of a maiden's mother. They kept the joke until Saturday night, and then he learned from them what he had been after. It dazed him for a time, but in a year or so he grew accustomed to the idea, and they were then married. With a little help he fell in love just like other people.

Sam'l was going the way of the others, but he found it difficult to come to the point. He only went courting once a week, and he could never take up the running at the place where he left off the Saturday before. Thus he had not, so far, made great headway. His method of making up to Bell had been to drop in at T'nowhead on Saturday nights and talk with the farmer about the rinderpest.

The farm kitchen was Bell's testimonial. Its chairs, tables and stools were scoured by her to the whiteness of Rob Angus's sawmill boards, and the muslin blind on the window was starched like a child's pinafore. Bell was brave, too, as well as energetic. Once Thrums had been overrun with thieves. It is now thought that there may have been only one, but he had the wicked cleverness of a gang. Such was his repute that there were weavers who spoke of locking their doors when they went from home. He was not very skilful, however, being generally caught, and when they said they knew he was a robber he gave them their things back and went away. If they had given him time there is no doubt that he would have gone off with his plunder. One night he went to T'nowhead, and Bell, who slept in the kitchen, was wakened by the noise. She knew who it would be, so she rose and dressed herself, and went to look for him with a candle. The thief had not known what to do when he got in, and as it was very lonely he was glad to see Bell. She told him he ought to be ashamed of himself, and would not let him out by the door until he had taken off his boots so as not to soil the carpet.

On this Saturday evening Sam'l stood his ground in the square, until by and by he found himself alone. There were other groups there still, but his circle had melted away. They went separately, and no one said good night. Each took himself off slowly, backing out of the group until he was fairly started.

Sam'l looked about him, and then, seeing that the others had gone, walked round the townhouse into the darkness of the brae that leads down and then up to the farm of T'nowhead.

To get into the good graces of Lisbeth Fargus you had to know her ways and humour them. Sam'l, who was a student of women, knew this, and so, instead of pushing the door open and walking in, he went through the rather ridiculous ceremony of knocking. Sanders Elshioner was also aware of this weakness of Lisbeth's, but, though he often made up his mind to knock, the absurdity of the thing prevented his doing so when he reached the door. T'nowhead himself had never got used to his wife's refined notions, and when anyone knocked he always started to his feet, thinking there must be something wrong.

Lisbeth came to the door, her expansive figure blocking the way in.

'Sam'l,' she said.

'Lisbeth,' said Sam'l.

He shook hands with the farmer's wife, knowing that she liked it, but only said: 'Ay, Bell,' to his sweetheart, 'Ay, T'now-head,' to McQuhatty, and 'It's yersel, Sanders,' to his rival.

They were all sitting round the fire, T'nowhead, with his feet on the ribs, wondering why he felt so warm, and Bell darned a stocking, while Lisbeth kept an eye on a goblet full of potatoes.

'Sit into the fire, Sam'l,' said the farmer, not, however, making way for him.

'Na, na,' said Sam'l, 'I'm to bide nae time.' Then he sat into the fire. His face was turned away from Bell, and when she spoke he answered her without looking round. Sam'l felt a little anxious. Sanders Elshioner, who had one leg shorter than the other, but looked well when sitting, seemed suspiciously at home. He asked Bell questions out of his own head, which was beyond Sam'l, and once he said something to her in such a low voice that the others could not catch it. T'nowhead asked curiously what it was, and Sanders explained that he had only said: 'Ay, Bell, the morn's the Sabbath.' There was nothing startling in this, but Sam'l did not like it. He began to wonder if he was too late, and had he seen his opportunity would have told Bell of a nasty rumour that Sanders intended to go over to the Free Church if they would make him kirk-officer.

Sam'l had the goodwill of T'nowhead's wife, who liked a polite man. Sanders did his best, but from want of practice he constantly made mistakes. Tonight, for instance, he wore his hat in the house because he did not like to put up his hand and take it off. T'nowhead had not taken his off either, but that was because he meant to go out by and by and lock the byre door.

It was impossible to say which of her lovers Bell preferred. The proper course with an Auld Licht lassie was to prefer the man who proposed to her.

'Ye'll bide a wee, an' hae something to eat?' Lisbeth asked Sam'l, with her eyes on the goblet.

'No, I thank ye,' said Sam'l, with true genteelity.

'Ye'll better?'

'I dinna think it.'

Hoots aye; what's to hender ye?'

'Weel, since ye're sae pressin', I'll bide.'

No one asked Sanders to stay. Bell could not, for she was but the servant, and T'nowhead knew that the kick his wife had given him meant that he was not to do so either. Sanders whistled to show that he was not uncomfortable.

'Ay, then, I'll be stappin' ower the brae,' he said at last.

He did not go, however. There was sufficient pride in him to get him off his chair, but only slowly, for he had to get accustomed to the notion of going. At intervals of two or three minutes he remarked that he must now be going. In the same circumstances Sam'l would have acted similarly. For a Thrums man it is one of the hardest things in life to get away from anywhere.

At last Lisbeth saw that something must be done. The potatoes were burning, and T'nowhead had an invitation on his tongue.

'Yes, I'll hae to be movin',' said Sanders hopelessly, for the fifth time.

'Guid nicht to ye, then, Sanders,' said Lisbeth. 'Gie the door a fling-to, ahent ye.'

Sanders, with a mighty effort, pulled himself together. He looked boldly at Bell, and then took off his hat carefully. Sam'l saw with misgivings that there was something in it which was not a handkerchief. It was a paper bag glittering with gold braid, and contained such an assortment of sweets as lads bought for their lasses on the Muckle Friday.

'Hae, Bell,' said Sanders, handing the bag to Bell in an off-hand way as if it were but a trifle. Nevertheless he was a little excited, for he went off without saying good night.

No one spoke. Bell's face was crimson. T'nowhead fidgeted on his chair, and Lisbeth looked at Sam'l. The weaver was strangely calm and collected, though he would have liked to know whether this was a proposal.

'Sit in by to the table, Sam'l,' said Lisbeth, trying to look as if things were as they had been before.

She put a saucerful of butter, salt and pepper near the fire to melt, for melted butter is the shoeing-horn that helps over a meal of potatoes. Sam'l, however, saw what the hour required, and jumping up, he seized his bonnet.

'Hing the tatties higher up the joist, Lisbeth,' he said with dignity; 'I'se be back in ten meenits.'

He hurried out of the house, leaving the others looking at each other.

'What do ye think?' asked Lisbeth.

'I d'na kin,' faltered Bell.

'Thae tatties is lang o' comin' to the boil,' said T'nowhead.

In some circles a lover who behaved like Sam'l would have been suspected of intent upon his rival's life, but neither Bell nor Lisbeth did the weaver that injustice. In a case of this kind it does not much matter what T'nowhead thought.

The ten minutes had barely passed when Sam'l was back in the farm kitchen. He was too flurried to knock this time, and, indeed, Lisbeth did not expect it of him.

'Bell, hae!' he cried, handing his sweetheart a tinsel bag twice the size of Sanders's gift.

'Losh preserve's!' exclaimed Lisbeth; 'I'se warrant there's a shillin's worth.'

'There's a' that, Lisbeth—an' mair,' said Sam'l firmly.

'I thank ye, Sam'l,' said Bell, feeling an unwonted elation as she gazed at the two paper bags in her lap.

'Ye're ower extravegint, Sam'l,' Lisbeth said.

'Not at all,' said Sam'l; 'not at all. But I widna advise ye to eat thae ither anes, Bell—they're second quality.'

Bell drew back a step from Sam'l.

'How do ye kin?' asked the farmer shortly, for he liked Sanders.

'I spiered i' the shop,' said Sam'l.

The goblet was placed on a broken plate on the table with the saucer beside it, and Sam'l, like the others, helped himself. What he did was to take potatoes from the pot with his fingers, peel off their coats, and then dip them into the butter. Lisbeth would have liked to provide knives and forks, but she knew that beyond a certain point T'nowhead was master in his own house. As for

Sam'l, he felt victory in his hands, and began to think that he had gone too far.

In the meantime Sanders, little witting that Sam'l had trumped his trick, was sauntering along the kirk-wynd with his hat on the side of his head. Fortunately he did not meet the minister.

The courting of T'nowhead's Bell reached its crisis one Sabbath about a month after the events above recorded. The minister was in great force that day, but it is no part of mine to tell how he bore himself. I was there, and am not likely to forget the scene. It was a fateful Sabbath for T'nowhead's Bell and her swains, and destined to be remembered for the painful scandal which they perpetrated in their passion.

Bell was not in the kirk. There being an infant of six months in the house it was a question of either Lisbeth or the lassie's staying at home with him, and though Lisbeth was unselfish in a general way she could not resist the delight of going to church. She had nine children besides the baby, and being but a woman, it was the pride of her life to march them into the T'nowhead pew, so well watched that they dared not misbehave, and so tightly packed that they could not fall. The congregation looked at that pew, the mothers enviously, when they sang the lines:

> 'Jerusalem like a city is
> Compactly built together.'

The first half of the service had been gone through on this particular Sunday without anything remarkable happening. It was at the end of the psalm which preceded the sermon that Sanders Elshioner, who sat near the door, lowered his head until it was no higher than the pews, and in that attitude, looking almost like a four-footed animal, slipped out of the church. In their eagerness to be at the sermon many of the congregation did not notice him, and those who did put the matter by in their minds for future investigation. Sam'l, however, could not take it so coolly. From his seat in the gallery he saw Sanders disappear, and his mind misgave him. With the true lover's instinct he understood it all. Sanders had been struck by the fine turn-out in the T'nowhead pew. Bell was alone at the farm. What an opportunity to work one's way up to a proposal. T'nowhead was so overrun with children that such a chance seldom occurred, except on a Sabbath. Sanders, doubtless, was off to propose, and he, Sam'l, was left behind.

The suspense was terrible. Sam'l and Sanders had both known all along that Bell would take the first of the two who asked her. Even those who thought her proud admitted that she was modest. Bitterly the weaver repented having waited so long. Now it was too late. In ten minutes Sanders would at be T'nowhead; in an hour all would be over. Sam'l rose to his feet in a daze. His mother pulled him down by the coat-tail, and his father shook him, thinking he was walking in his sleep. He tottered past them, however, hurried up the aisle, which was so narrow that Dan'l Ross could only reach his seat by walking sideways, and was gone before the minister could do more than stop in the middle of a whirl and gape in horror after him.

A number of the congregation felt that day the advantage of sitting in the laft. What was a mystery to those downstairs was revealed to them. From the gallery windows they had a fine open view to the south; and as Sam'l took the common, which was a short cut through a steep ascent, to T'nowhead, he was never out of their line of vision. Sanders was not to be seen, but they guessed rightly the reason why. Thinking he had ample time, he had gone round by the main road to save his boots— perhaps a little scared by what was coming. Sam'l's design was to forestall him by taking the shorter path over the burn and up the commonty.

It was a race for a wife, and several onlookers in the gallery braved the minister's displeasure to see who won. Those who favoured Sam'l's suit exultingly saw him leap the stream, while the friends of Sanders fixed their eyes on the top of the common where it ran into the road. Sanders must come into sight there, and the one who reached this point first would get Bell.

As Auld Lichts do not walk abroad on the Sabbath, Sanders would probably not be delayed. The chances were in his favour. Had it been any other day in the week Sam'l might have run. So some of the congregation in the gallery were thinking, when suddenly they saw him bend low and then take to his heels. He had caught sight of Sanders's head bobbing over the hedge that separated the road from the common, and feared that Sanders might see him. The congregation who could crane their necks sufficiently saw a black object, which they guessed to be the carter's hat, crawling along the hedge-top. For a moment it was motionless, and then it shot ahead. The rivals had seen each other. It was now a hot race. Sam'l, dissembling no longer, clattered up the Common, becoming smaller and smaller to the onlookers as he neared the top. More than one person in the gallery almost rose to their feet in their excitement. Sam'l had it. No, Sanders was in front. Then the two figures disappeared from view. They seemed to run into each other at the top of the brae, and no one could say who was first. The congregation looked at one another. Some of them perspired. But the minister held on his course.

Sam'l had just been in time to cut Sanders out. It was the weaver's saving that Sanders saw this when his rival turned the corner; for Sam'l was sadly blown. Sanders took in the situation and gave in at once. The last hundred yards of the distance he covered at his leisure, and when he arrived at his destination he did not go in. It was a fine afternoon for the time of year, and he went round to have a look at the pig, about which T'nowhead was a little sinfully puffed up.

'Ay,' said Sanders, digging his fingers critically into the grunting animal; 'quite so.'

'Grumph,' said the pig, getting reluctantly to his feet.

'Ou ay; yes,' said Sanders thoughtfully.

Then he sat down on the edge of the sty, and looked long and silently at an empty bucket. But whether his thoughts were of T'nowhead's Bell, whom he had lost for ever, or of the food the farmer fed his pig on, is not known.

'Lord preserve's! Are ye no at the kirk?' cried Bell, nearly dropping the baby as Sam'l broke into the room.

'Bell!' cried Sam'l.

Then T'nowhead's Bell knew that her hour had come.

'Sam'l,' she faltered.

'Will ye hae's, Bell?' demanded Sam'l, glaring at her sheepishly.

'Ay,' answered Bell.

Sam'l fell into a chair.

'Bring's a drink o' water, Bell,' he said.

But Bell thought the occasion required milk, and there was none in the kitchen. She went out to the byre, still with the baby in her arms, and saw Sanders Elshioner sitting gloomily on the pigsty.

'Weel, Bell,' said Sanders.

'I thocht ye'd been at the kirk, Sanders,' said Bell.

Then there was a silence between them.

'Has Sam'l spiered ye, Bell?' asked Sanders stolidly.

'Ay,' said Bell again, and this time there was a tear in her eye. Sanders was little better than an 'orra man', and Sam'l was a weaver, and yet—— But it was too late now. Sanders gave the pig a vicious poke with a stick and, when it had ceased to grunt, Bell was back in the kitchen. She had forgotten about the milk, however, and Sam'l only got water after all.

In after days, when the story of Bell's wooing was told, there were some who held that the circumstances would have almost justified the lassie in giving Sam'l the go-by. But these perhaps forgot that her other lover was in the same predicament as the accepted one—that of the two, indeed, he was the more to blame, for he set off to T'nowhead on the Sabbath of his own accord, while Sam'l only ran after him. And then there is no one to say for certain whether Bell heard of her suitors' delinquencies until Lisbeth's return from the kirk. Sam'l could never remember whether he told her, and Bell was not sure whether, if he did, she took it in. Sanders was greatly in demand for weeks after to tell what he knew of the affair, but though he was twice asked to tea to the manse among the trees, and subjected thereafter to ministerial cross-examinations, this is all he told. He remained at the pigsty until Sam'l left the farm, when he joined him at the top of the brae, and they went home together.

'It's yersel, Sanders,' said Sma'l.

'It is so, Sam'l,' said Sanders.

'Very cauld,' said Sam'l.

'Blawy,' assented Sanders.

After a pause:

'Sam'l,' said Sanders.

'Ay.'

'I'm hearin' yer to be mairit.'

'Ay.'

'Weel, Sam'l, she's a snod bit lassie.'

'Thank ye,' said Sam'l.

'I had ance a kin' o' notion o' Bell mysel,' continued Sanders.

'Ye had?'

'Yes, Sam'l; but I thocht better o't.'

'Hoo d'ye mean?' asked Sam'l a little anxiously.

'Weel, Sam'l, mairitch is a terrible responsibeelity.'

'It is so,' said Sam'l, wincing.

'An' no the thing to tak up withoot conseederation.'

'But it's a blessed and honourable state, Sanders; ye've heard the minister on 't.'

'They say', continued the relentless Sanders, ''at the minister doesna get on sair wi' the wife himsel.'

'So they do,' cried Sam'l, with a sinking at the heart.

'I've been telt', Sanders went on, ''at gin ye can get the upper han' o' the wife for a while at first, there's the mair chance o' a harmonious exeestence.'

'Bell's no the lassie', said Sam'l appealingly, 'to thwart her man.'

Sanders smiled.

'D'ye think she is, Sanders?'

'Weel, Sam'l, I d'na want to fluster ye, but she's been ower lang wi' Lisbeth Fargus no to hae learnt her ways. An a'body kins what a life T'nowhead has wi' her.'

'Guid sake, Sanders, hoo did ye no speak o' this afore?'

'I thocht ye kent o't, Sam'l.'

They had now reached the square, and the U.P. kirk was coming out. The Auld Licht kirk would be half an hour yet.

'But, Sanders,' said Sam'l, brightening up, 'ye was on yer wy to spier her yersel.'

'I was, Sam'l,' said Sanders, 'and I canna but be thankfu ye was ower quick for's.'

'Gin't hadna been you,' said Sam'l, 'I wid never hae thocht o't.'

'I'm sayin' naething agin Bell,' pursued the other, 'but, man Sam'l, a body should be mair deleeberate in a thing o' the kind.'

'It was michty hurried,' said Sam'l woefully.

'It's a serious thing to spier a lassie,' said Sanders.

'It's an awfu' thing,' said Sam'l.

'But we'll hope for the best,' added Sanders in a hopeless voice.

They were close to the Tenements now, and Sam'l looked as as if he were on his way to be hanged.

'Sam'l?'

'Ay, Sanders.'

'Did ye—and ye kiss her, Sam'l?'

'Na.'

'Hoo?'

'There's was varra little time, Sanders.'

'Half an 'oor,' said Sanders.

'Was there? Man Sanders, to tell ye the truth, I never thoct o't.'

Then the soul of Sanders Elshioner was filled with contempt for Sam'l Dickie.

The scandal blew over. At first it was expected that the minister would interfere to prevent the union, but beyond intimating from the pulpit that the souls of Sabbath-breakers were beyond praying for, and then praying for Sam'l and Sanders at great length, with a word thrown in for Bell, he let things take their course. Some said it was because he was always frightened lest his young men should intermarry with other denominations, but Sanders explained it differently to Sam'l.

'I hav'na a word to say agin the minister,' he said; 'they're gran' prayers, but Sam'l, he's a mairit man himsel.'

'He's a' the better for that, Sanders, isna he?'

'Do ye no see', asked Sanders compassionately, ''at he's tryin' to mak the best o't?'

'Oh, Sanders, man!' said Sam'l.

'Cheer up, Sam'l,' said Sanders, 'it'll sune be ower.'

Their having been rival suitors had not interfered with their friendship. On the contrary, while they had hitherto been mere acquaintances, they became inseparable as the wedding day drew near. It was noticed that they had much to say to each other, and that when they could not get a room to themselves they wandered about together in the churchyard. When Sam'l had anything to tell Bell he sent Sanders to tell it, and Sanders did as he was bid. There was nothing that he would not have done for Sam'l.

The more obliging Sanders was, however, the sadder Sam'l grew. He never laughed now on Saturdays, and sometimes his loom was silent half the day. Sam'l felt that Sanders's was the kindness of a friend for a dying man.

It was to be a penny wedding, and Lisbeth Fargus said it was delicacy that made Sam'l superintend the fitting-up of the barn by deputy. Once he came to see it in person, but he looked so ill that Sanders had to see him home. This was on the Thursday afternoon, and the wedding was fixed for Friday.

'Sanders, Sanders,' said Sam'l, in a voice strangely unlike his own, 'it'll a' be ower by this time the morn.'

'It will,' said Sanders.

'If I had only kent her langer,' continued Sam'l.

'It wid hae been safer,' said Sanders.

'Did ye see the yellow floor in Bell's bonnet?' asked the accepted swain.

'Ay,' said Sanders reluctantly.

'I'm dootin'—I'm sair dootin' she's but a flichty, licht-hearted crittur after a'.'

'I had ay my suspeecions o't,' said Sanders.

'Ye hae kent her langer than me,' said Sam'l.

'Yes,' said Sanders, 'but there's nae gettin' at the heart o' women. Man, Sam'l, they're desperate cunnin'.'

'I'm dootin't; I'm sair dootin't.'

'It'll be a warnin' to ye, Sam'l, no to be in sic a hurry i' the future,' said Sanders.

Sam'l groaned.

'Ye'll be gaein up to the manse to arrange wi' the minister the morn's mornin',' continued Sanders in a subdued voice.

Sam'l looked wistfully at his friend.

'I canna do't, Sanders,' he said, 'I canna do't.'

'Ye maun,' said Sanders.

'It's aisy to speak,' retorted Sam'l bitterly.

'We have a' oor troubles, Sam'l,' said Sanders soothingly, 'an' every man maun bear his ain burdens. Johnny Davie's wife's dead, an' he's no repinin'.'

'Ay,' said Sam'l, 'but a death's no a mairitch. We hae haen deaths in our family too.'

'It may a' be for the best,' added Sanders, 'an' there wid be a michty talk i' the hale countryside gin ye didna ging to the minister like a man.'

'I maun hae langer to think o't,' said Sam'l

'Bell's mairitch is the morn,' said Sanders decisively.

Sam'l glanced up with a wild look in his eyes.

'Sanders,' he cried.

'Sam'l?'

'Ye hae been a guid friend to me, Sanders, in this sair affliction.'

'Nothing ava,' said Sanders; 'dount mention'd.'

'But, Sanders, ye canna deny but what your rinnin oot o' the
kirk that awfu' day was at the bottom o'd a'.'

'It was so,' said Sanders bravely.

'An' ye used to be fond o' Bell, Sanders.'

'I dinna deny 't.'

'Sanders, laddie,' said Sam'l, bending forward and speaking
in a wheedling voice, 'I aye thocht it was you she likeit.'

'I had some sic idea mysel,' said Sanders.

'Sanders, I canna think to pairt twa fowk sae weel suited to
ane anither as you an' Bell.'

'Canna ye, Sam'l?'

'She wid mak ye a guid wife, Sanders. I hae studied her weel,
and she's a thrifty, douce, clever lassie. Sanders, there's no the
like o' her. Mony a time, Sanders, I hae said to mysel, There's
a lass ony man micht be prood to tak. A'body says the same,
Sanders. There's nae risk ava, man: nane to speak o'. Tak her,
laddie, tak her, Sanders; it's a grand chance, Sanders. She's
yours for the spierin. I'll gie her up, Sanders.'

'Will ye, though?' said Sanders.

'What d'ye think?' asked Sam'l.

'If ye wid rayther,' said Sanders politely.

'There's my han' on 't,' said Sam'l. 'Bless ye, Sanders; ye've
been a true frien' to me.'

Then they shook hands for the first time in their lives; and
soon afterwards Sanders struck up the brae to T'nowhead.

Next morning Sanders Elshioner, who had been very busy
the night before, put on his Sabbath clothes and strolled up to
the manse.

'But—but where is Sam'l?' asked the minister; 'I must see
himself.'

'It's a new arrangement,' said Sanders.

'What do you mean, Sanders?'

'Bell's to marry me,' explained Sanders.

'But—but what does Sam'l say?'

'He's willin',' said Sanders.

'And Bell?'

'She's willin' too. She prefers 't.'

'It is unusual,' said the minister.

'It's a' richt, said Sanders.

'Well, you know best,' said the minister.

'You see the hoose was taen, at ony rate,' continued Sanders. 'An I'll juist ging in til't instead o' Sam'l.'

'Quite so.'

'An' I cudna think to disappoint the lassie.'

'Your sentiments do you credit, Sanders,' said the minister; 'but I hope you do not enter upon the blessed state of matrimony without full consideration of its responsibilities. It is a serious business, marriage.'

'It's a' that,' said Sanders, 'but I'm willin' to stan' the risk.'

So, as soon as it could be done, Sanders Elshioner took to wife T'nowhead's Bell, and I remember seeing Sam'l Dickie trying to dance at the penny wedding.

Years afterwards it was said in Thrums that Sam'l had treated Bell badly, but he was never sure about it himself.

'It was a near thing—a michty near thing,' he admitted in the square.

'They say', some other weaver would remark, ''at it was you Bell liked best.'

'I d'na kin,' Sam'l would reply, 'but there's nae doot the lassie was fell fond o' me. Ou, a mere passin' fancy's ye micht say.'

FAREWELL, MISS JULIE LOGAN

First published, December 1931

I. The English

THIS IS Dec. 1, 186–; I think it prudent to go no nearer to the date, in case what I am writing should take an ill turn or fall into curious hands. I need not be so guarded about the weather. It is a night of sudden blasts that half an hour ago threw my window at me. They went skirling from room to room, like officers of the law seeking to seize and deliver to justice the venturesome Scots minister who is sitting here ready to impeach all wraiths and warlocks. There was another blast the now. I believe I could rope the winds of the manse to my bidding tonight, and by running from door to door, opening and shutting, become the conductor of a gey sinister orchestra.

I am trying to make a start at the Diary the English have challenged me to write. There is no call to begin tonight, for as yet not a flake has fallen in this my first winter in the glen; and the Diary is to be a record of my life here during the weeks ('tis said it may be months) in which the glen is 'locked', meaning it may be so happit in snow that no one who is in can get out of it, and no one who is out can get in. Then, according to the stories that crawl like mists among our hills, where the English must have picked them up, come forms called the 'Strangers'. You 'go queer' yourself without knowing it and walk and talk with these doolies, thinking they are of your world till maybe they have mischieved you.

It is all, of course, superstitious havers, bred of folk who are used to the travail of out of doors, and take ill with having to squat by the saut-bucket; but I have promised with a smile to keep my eyes and ears intent for tergiversations among my flock, and to record them for the benefit of the English when they come back next August.

My name is the Rev. Adam Yestreen; and to be candid I care not for the Adam with its unfortunate associations. I am twenty-six years of age and, though long in the legs, look maybe younger than is seemly in my sacred calling, being clean-shaven without any need to use an implement; indeed I may say I have desisted for two years back.

I took a fair degree at St Andrews, but my Intellectuals suffered from an addiction to putting away my books and playing on the fiddle. When I got my call to this place my proper course was to have got rid of the fiddle before I made my entry into the glen, which I did walking with affected humility behind three cart-loads of funiture all my own, and well aware, though I looked down, that I was being keeked at from every window, of which there are about two to the mile.

When the English discovered how ashamed I was of my old backsliding with the fiddle, they had the effrontery to prig with me to give them a tune, but I hope it is unnecessary for me to say that they had to retire discomfited. I have never once performed on the instrument here, though I may have taken it out of its case nows and nans to fondle the strings.

What I miss, when my unstable mind is on the things of this world, is less my own poor cajoling with the gut than not hearing the tunes from better hands; the more homely Scottish lilts, I mean, for of course the old reprehensible songs that kow-tow to the Stewarts find no asylum with me.

Though but half a Highlander, I have the Gaelic sufficiently to be able to preach in it once every Sabbath, as enjoined; but the attendances are small, as, except for stravaigers, there are not so many pure Hielandmen nowadays in the glen.

My manse and kirk are isolated on one side of the burn, and the English call them cold as paddocks, but methinks a noble look falls on them when the sabbath bell is ringing. My predecessor, Mr Carluke, tore down the Jargonelle tree, which used to cling to my gable-end, because he considered that, when in flourish (or as the English say, in blossom, a word with no gallantry intilt), it gave the manse the appearance of a light woman. The marks are still scarted on the wall. Round the manse, within a neat paling that encloses my demesne, there are grossart bushes, rizers and rasps, a gean, bee-skeps and the like, that in former hands were called the yard, but I call it the garden, and have made other improvements.

The gean is my only tree, but close by is a small wood of fir and birch with a path through it that since long before my time has been called the Thinking Path because so many ministers have walked up and down it before the diets of worship with their hands behind their backs. I try to emulate them, but they were deeper men than I am, and many a time I forget to think, though such had been my intention. In other days a squirrel frequented this wood, and as you might say adopted one minister after another, taking nuts from their hands, though scorning all overtures from the laity; but I have never seen it, and my detractors, of whom there are a flow (though I think I am well likit as a whole), say that it deserted the wood as a protest when it heard that I preached in a gown.

There is a deal of character about the manse, particularly, of course, in the study, which is also my living-room. It and my dining-room are the only two rooms in the glen (except at the Grand House) without a bed in them, and I mention this, not with complacence to show how I live nowadays, but as evidence that we are a thrifty people, though on Sabbath well put on. Some are also well plenished within; and to have their porridge with porter instead of milk is not an uncommon occurrence.

The finest of my gear, all the chairs in horsehair, belong to the dining-room, which, however, is best fitted for stately occasions, and you would know it is seldom used by the way the fire smokes. I cannot say that I am at ease in it, while, on the other hand, I never enter my study up the stair without feeling we are sib; to which one might say it responds.

Never have I a greater drawing to my study than when the lamp is lit and the glow from the fire plays on my red curtains and the blue camstane and my clouty rug. It is an open fireplace without a grate, and I used to be shamed of its wood and peat scattering such a mess of ashes till the English told me that piles of ashes are a great adornment, since when I have conflict with my bit maid, because she wants to carry them away daily, not having the wit to know that they are an acquisition.

Most of my wall space and especially two presses are sternly lined with mighty books, such as have made some of my congregation thankful that they have never learned to read. Yet it is a room that says to anyone of spirit: 'Come in by and take a chair, and not only a chair but the best chair,' which is the high-backed grandy, agreeably riven in the seat. I seldom occupy it myself, except at a by-time on a Sabbath afternoon when the two diets have exhausted me a wee, but Dr John sinks into it as naturally as if he had bought it at the roup. This was the auction of such plenishing as Mr Carluke did not take away with him, and in the inventory there was mentioned as part of the study furniture, 'servant's chair', which puzzled some of the bidders, but I saw through it at once. It meant, not to his glorification, that a kitchen chair was kept here for the servant to sit on, and this meant that he held both morning and evening family exercise in the study, which meant again that he breakfasted and supped there; for he wouldna have two fires. It made me smile in a tolerant way, for one would have thought, on the night I spent with him, that the dining-room was his common resort.

On the other side of the burn, but so close that I can keep a vigilant eye on them, are the Five Houses in a Row, which the English say, incorrectly but with no evil design, contain all the congregation I can depend upon in a tack of wild weather. On the contrair, there is a hantle of small farms in the glen, forbye shepherds' shielings and bothies, and an occasional roadside bigging of clay and divot in which may be man or beast; truly, when I chap I am sometimes doubtful which will come to the door.

The English, who make play with many old words that even our Highlandmen have forgotten, call the Five Houses the 'clachan'. They are one-storey houses, whitewashed and thacked, and every one of them (to the astonishment of the English) has a hallan to itself. We may be poor, say the Scottish, but we will not open into a room. The doors face the glen road, on which grows a coarse bent grass in lines as straight as potato drills, and carriage-folk who do not keep the ruts are shaken most terrible. One of the English told me that his machine sometimes threw him so high in the air that when he was up there he saw small lochs hitherto unknown to man, and stopped his beast and fished them. The English, however, who have many virtues, though not of a very solid kind, are great exaggerators.

The carriage-folk, except when she lets what is familiarly called the Grand House to the English, consist of Mistress Lindinnock alone, who is called (but never to her face) the Old Lady. She had two spirited ponies, but not so spirited as herself. She goes to Edinburgh while the Grand House is let, and, excepting myself (on account of my office), she is the chief person in the glen. She has been a fine friend to me, but I have sometimes to admonish her for a little coarseness in her language, which may escape from her even when she is most genteel. I grieve to say that this lady of many commendable parts plays cards, and I once saw her at it. Her adversary was a travelling watchmaker, one of those who traverse the whole land carrying a wooden box of watches on his back, with a dozen more ticking in his many waistcoat pockets. They were playing for high sums too, the Old Lady sitting inside one of her windows and the man outside it on his box. I think this is done to preserve the difference in rank; but when I called her before me for it she said the object was to make all right for her future, as the players being on different sides of the window took away the curse.

She is also at times overly sly for one so old and little, and I am now referring to my gown. Soon after my settlement the ladies of the congregation presented me with a gown, and she as the most well to pass was the monetary strength of the movement; but though I was proud to wear my gown (without vainglory), we had members who argued that it had a touch of Rome. One may say that the congregation was divided anent it, and some Sabbaths I was sore bested whether to put it on or not. Whiles the decision was even taken out of my hands, for the gown would disappear at the back-end of the week and be returned to its nail on the Monday morning, the work undoubtedly of the no-gown party. On those occasions, of course, I made shift without it, and feeling ran so high that I could not but be conscious as I ascended the pulpit that they were titting at one another's sleeves.

They invented the phrase 'a gown Sabbath'. I took to hiding it, but whoever were the miscreants (and well I knew they were in their pews in front of me, looking as if they had never heard the word gown), they usually found my hoddy place. I mind once sitting on it a long Saturday night when I was labouring at my sermon, the which incident got about among my people. The Old Lady was very sympathetic and pressed me to lay the trouble before the Session, which in fairness to her as the outstanding subscriber I ettled to do, until (could anyone believe it?) I discovered that she was the miscreant herself. I sorted her for it.

She is back again now, for the English, of course, have departed long since, and will not be seen again in the glen till next year's shooting time comes round. On the day they left they crossed over to remind me that they were looking forward to the Diary, and when I protested that I did not even know how to begin they said in their audacious way: 'You could begin by writing about us.' I have taken them at their word, though they little understand that I may have been making a quiet study of them while they thought that I was the divert.

As I say, I have found them to be very pleasant persons, so long as you make allowances for them that one could not be expected to make for his own people. The bright array of their kilts is a pretty bit of colour to us, the trousered people of the glen. They have a happy knack of skimming life that has a sort of attraction for deeper but undoubtedly slower natures.

The way they riot with their pockets is beyond words; I am credibly informed by Posty that they even have worms sent to them by post in tins.

They are easy to exploit for gain, as Posty was quick to see, and many a glass of —— has he, to my grief (for I am a totaler), got from them by referring to himself as 'she'. I have written that word with a dash because, now I cast back, I believe I have never heard it spoken by the glen folk. One might say that it is thus, ——, pronounced by them. They invite you to partake, and you are dull in the uptake if you don't understand of what you are being asked to partake.

They make a complete sentence by saying of a friend: 'He is one who on a market day,' and leaving the rest to the listener's common sense.

Similarly they say: 'He never unless he is in company,' or 'He just at a time because he is lonely like.'

Now the English in this matter as in many others are different, and they give the thing its name and boldly say, with pride in knowing the word, Usquebaugh. In this I hold that they come out of the murky affair with greater honesty but more shamelessly than we do.

They were hospitable to me, and had me up at the Grand House once, giving me the most attractive lady to take in on my arm to dinner, and putting the most popular man on the other side of her to make up for me. They are so well-meaning that it would have vexed them to know I noticed this, and of course I gave it the go-by; but there are few things that escape my observation. On the Sabbath there were always some of them in the kirk, where they were very kindly to the plate but lazy at turning up the chapters. When they had new arrivals these were always brought to see the shepherd's dogs in the pews; in fact, I have decided that the one thing the English know for certain about Scottish religion is that there are shepherds' dogs in the pews.

The English, how quick they are compared to a cautious Scot like myself. He may be far deeper in the fundamentals when there is time to take soundings; but they are so ready.

That time I dined with them the talk might be on subjects I was better versed in than any of them, but they would away to another topic before I could steady myself and give utterance. My most pitiful posture was when I was unable not only to say a thing worth while but to say anything at all, however superficial. Is man ever more lonely than in company when all language forsakes him and he would be thankful if he could cry out 'Agamemnon?' At that dinner I sometimes wished I could have had a dictionary on my knees so as to get hold of any word whatever.

The man on the other side of the lady I was in charge of made a flattering remark to her about her looking very pretty tonight (they stick at nothing), and said to me across her did I not agree with him. It may just have been a considerateness in him to bring the dum into the talk, a meritorious quality they have; but to be approached in such a direct manner about a lady's looks before her face threw me off my balance, and all I could reply was that I had not given the subject sufficient consideration to be able to make a definite statement about it. She stooped quickly at that, like one looking for her feet, but on reflection I had a suspicion she was anxious not to let me see her making a mouth, at which they are great adepts; and she will never know now that I can say a neat thing myself if they will give me time.

The thoughtlessness of them is something grievous, but their manners make me wae for my own.

When they said goodbye to me at the Five Houses their departure was like a flight of birds. As the poet says, they seemed to take away the sun in their pockets.

At the manse I had shown them my study, this room I am now sitting in (with the wind still on the rampage), and especially I drew their attention to what I have called the finest plenishing thereof, the two presses containing theological and classical tomes of great girth, somewhat warped in the binding. My friends cried out at this being all the reading I had to carry me through the time when the glen may be locked, and they sniffed (but in a polite way) at the closeness of my cosy room, not understanding, as any Presbyterian would have done, that what they mistook for mustiness was the noble smell of learning.

The ladies said that what I needed to madden me pleasantly was not a Diary but a wife. They were at the Five Houses by this time, getting into their machines, and I countered them with 'Who would have me?' I was not putting them to the question, but all the ladies cried out, 'I will,' and made pretence to want to leap from their carriages. I can see now they were just getting after me.

Such are this strange race, the English, whose light-heartedness, as in this extraordinary scene, can rise to a pitch called by the French abandon. I dare say they had forgotten all about me before they were out of the glen, and will never have another thought of the Diary; indeed, now as I look at my shelves of massive volumes, which were not of my collecting, I wish I had not agreed to call it a Diary, for that is a word of ill omen in this manse.

II. SOMEONE WHO WAS WITH HIM

Dec. 3.—I have read the above more than once and then hid it away from Christily, because it is written on sermon paper.

Christily is a most faithful young woman with a face as red and lush as a rasp, who knows her carritches both ways, and has such a reverence for ministers that she looks upon me more as an edifice than a mortal. She has an almost equal pride in herself for being a minister's servant, and walks into the kirk in her cheeping lastic sides with an official genteelity that some consider offensive. She has also a provoking way of discussing me in my presence as if I was not there, telling visitors the most intimate things about me, such as the food I like but it does not like me, the while she stands in what is meant to be a respectful attitude, neither inside nor outside the door.

My visitors are likely to be few for some time to come; neighbours from the Five Houses whiles, and I hope Mistress Lindinnock and Dr John from Branders.

The smith at the Five Houses is my chief elder, and as his bairns are innumerable, the family in their two pews are a heartsome sight. A more cautious man in argument I have never known. About as far as he will go is, 'I agree with you to a certain extent,' or 'My answer to that is Yes and No.' Posty has a story that he made the second of these answers at his marriage when asked if he took this woman.

Posty is also at the Five Houses, and is the kind that bears ill will to none, even if they catch him cheating at the dambrod, which he does with the elbow. He has the cheery face that so often goes with roguery and being good at orra jobs, but though I don't lippen to him in matters of import, I like to fall in with him more than with some better men. I sometimes play at the teetotum with the smith's bairns, when there is a prize of cracknuts, and undoubtedly on such occasions Posty's pranks add to the festive scene. He will walk miles, too, to tell any ill news.

His most valued possession is a velocipede, which has so often come to bits when he was on it that near every man in the glen has been at the repairing of it, including myself, or at least has contributed twine or iron girds. He brings the letters from Branders on this machine, and as it often runs away with him, we all, dogs, hens and humans, loup the dyke when we see him bearing down on us. He carries telegrams too, but there are so few of these, now the English have gone, that when we see him waving one we ask, 'Who is dead?'

My great friend is Dr John, who is sometimes in the glen to succour us, though he lives at Branders, where he sits under Mr Watery, with whom I sometimes niffer pulpits.

Branders is an overgrown place of five hundred inhabitants, and stands high near a loch, out of which two streams run in opposite directions, like parties to a family feud that can no longer be settled with the claymore. In a spate as many new burns come brawling into this loch as there are hairs on a woman's head, and then are gone before they can be counted. Branders is not in the glen but just at the head of it, and, according to Dr John, it stopped there because it said to itself:

'Those who go farther will fare worse.' It is jimply six miles from my manse in summer weather, but seventeen from the nearest railway station and electric telegraph. Dr John says that whether Branders is the beginning or end of desolation depends on your looking up or down the road.

A gnarled, perjink little figure of about fifty is Dr John, grandly bearded, but for a man of larger size. His blue eyes are hod away in holes, sunken into them, I suppose, because he has looked so long on snow. He wears a plaid in all weathers and sometimes even in the house, for, as he says, before he has time to wap it off and find it again somebody on a cart-horse will be clattering at his door to hurry him to my glen. I have seen him, too, sitting behind on that clattering horse. Repute says that for humane ends he will get through when the glen is locked to all others, though his sole recompense may be a ham at the killing, or a kebbock or a keg of that drink I have spelt ——. Though I touch it not, I cannot deny that he partakes as if it were water, and is celebrated (and even condoled with) for never being the worse of it. He always takes it hot, which he calls never mixing his drinks, and I don't know a neater hand at squeezing down the sugar with the ladle.

If he is in the glen he sometimes puts up his shalt at the Five Houses and stays the night with me, when we have long cracks, the kettle-lid plopping while he smokes his pipe, grunting, which is the Scottish way of bringing out the flavour. Last night was such an occasion, and up here in the study as we sat into the fire we got on to the stories about 'Strangers', of which he says humorously he has heard many clutters though he has never had the luck to encounter the carls themselves. He maintains that the origin of all the clavers and cleeking of nowadays was that lamentable affair of the '45, which, among its misdeeds, for long gave an ill name to the tartan.

The glen had been a great hiding-place of 'pretty men' of the period, and among its fearsome crags and waur cleughs, if ancient tales be true, those ill-gettit gentlemen had lurked for months and some of them for years.

It is said that forbears of folk still in the glen used to see them from below searching for roots atween the rocks, and so distraught with hunger that they went on searching openly while they were being shot at by the redcoats, who would not face the speel. When the glen was in a sink of snow, and pursuit for a time at an end, they sometimes lay at the Grand House (which was loyal to their dark cause), and held secret carouse there.

They were talked of with an intake of the breath by the glen folk, who liked best to be of no party unless they were of both, would not betray them to an enemy that hunted them with bloodhounds, yet would hold no intercourse with them willingly, and looked the other way if they came upon one of the gaunt red-shanks unexpectedly, as sometimes happened, carrying braxy mutton or venison to his lurking-place, or a salmon that the otters had left by the burn after taking one nip from its neck.

Those glen folk were too mouse to call the fugitives Jacobites. 'The Strangers,' they said.

In one case they said 'Someone Who Was With Him', as if that was as far as it was canny to go. The Him was the Stranger who is believed by the simple to have been the Chevalier himself. He is said to have lain in the glen for a time in July month, fevered and so hard pressed that no friends dared go nigh him with nourishment lest it led to his capture. I have not seen his hoddy place, but the doctor tells me it is still there and is no more than a lair beneath what we call a bield, a shelter for sheep. Very like it began by being a tod's hole, and was torn bigger with dirks. If it ever existed, the lair has been long filled up with stones, which are all that remain to mark the royal residence.

Sheep again shelter in the bield, but there were none there in the time of the Prince, if it was he, nor, as I say the story goes, could food be passed to him. In his extremity he was saved by the mysterious Someone Who Was With Him.

Of course the legend has it that she was young and fair and of high degree, and that she loved much.

She fed him with the unwilling help of the eagles. The Eagles Rock, which is not far from the bield, is a mighty mass said by the ghillies of today to be unscalable by man because of what is called the Logan stone. No eagles build there now; they have fallen to the guns of their modern enemies, the keepers, who swear that one pair of eagles will carry a hundred grouse or more to their nest to feed their young.

At that time there was an eagle's nest on the top of the rock. The climb is a perilous one, but now and again hardy folk get up as far as the Logan stone, where they turn back. There are

Logan stones, I am told, throughout the world, and they are rocking stones. It is said they may be seen rocking in the wind, and yet hold on for centuries. Such a monster hangs out from our Eagles Rock, and you cannot reach the top save by climbing over it, nor can you get on to it without leaping. Twice men of the glen have leapt and it threw them off. Natheless, the story is that this Someone Who Was With Him got through the searchers in the dark, reached the top of the rock by way of the Logan stone, and after sometimes fighting the parent eagles for possession, brought down young grouse for her lord.

By all kind accounts she was a maiden, and in our glen she is remembered by the white heather, which, never seen here till then, is said, nonsensically, to be the marks of her pretty naked feet.

The white heather brought her little luck. In a hurried and maybe bloody flitting she was left behind. Nothing more is recorded of her except that when her lord and master embarked for France he enjoined his Highlanders 'to feed her and honour her as she had fed and honoured him'. They were faithful though misguided, and I dare say they would have done it if they could. Some think that she is in the bield in the hole beneath the stones, still waiting. They say, maybe there was a promise.

Such was the doctor's tale as we sat over the fire. 'A wayward woman,' was how he summed her up, with a shake of the head.

III. THE SPECTRUM

Dec. 3 (Contd).—'I am thinking,' Dr John was saying when I caught up with him again, for my mind had been left behind with this woman, and I was wondering if she was 'wayward', and what was wrong with it, for I liked the word. 'I am thinking that all the clash about folk of nowadays meeting "Strangers" when the glen is locked comes out of that troubled past. In a white winter, as you have jaloused yourself, there is ower little darg for a hardy race, and they hark back by the hearth-stone to the forgotten, ay, and the forbidden. But I assure you,

Mr Yestreen, despite the whispers, the very name of the '45
is now buried in its own stour. Even Posty, though he is so gleg
with the pipes, gets by himself if you press him about what his
old ballants mean. Neither good luck nor mischief, so far as
I can discover, comes to the havrels of nowadays who think
they have talked or walked with a Stranger; unless indeed,
as some say, it was one of them who mairtered poor Mr H.;
and I understand he, being a learned man, always called it a
Spectrum.'

This set us talking of him of whom I may have already let
out that he once kept a Diary in this manse. It was so far
back as to be just hearsay even to Dr John, and belongs to
the days when there were no seats in my kirk and all stood on
their shanks. Though I say we talked about him we really said
very little, unless an occasional furtive glance be speech. All
in these parts become furtive when a word, falling as meaning-
less you would say as a cinder from the fire, brings a sough
of the old man back to mind.

Mr H. was a distant predecessor of mine, and a scholar such
as the manse is not likely to house again. It was he who collected the library of noble erudition that is in the presses of
this room, many of the volumes bound by his own hands that
may have dawted them as he bound. His Diary was written
on the fly-leaves of a number of them.

I believe he thought in Latin and Greek quicker than in
his own tongue, for his hurried notes are often in those languages and the more deliberate ones in ours. I am in a dunce's
cap with the Greek, but I can plod along with a Latin dictionary, and his entries in the Latin have made me so uneasy that
I have torn out the pages and burned them. Mr Carluke, whom
I succeeded, had to confine himself, having no Latin, to the
English bits, and he treated some of them similarly, for as
he said to me they were about things that will not do at all.

They appear suddenly amidst matter grandly set forth, as if
a rat had got at the pages. Minute examination has made me
question their being in the same handwrite, though an imitation.
This tampering, if such it was, had got by Carluke's attention.
'You mean', Dr John said to me when I had let him study these
bits of Diary (which he peered into with a magnifier the size
of a thimble that he carries in his waistcoat pocket and is near

as much dreaded by malingerers as he is himself), 'that it is the handwrite of the Spectrum?' If Dr John has a failing it is that he hankers too much to tie one down to a statement, and of course I would not accept this interpretation, for I do not believe in Spectrums.

It is not known even by the credulous when, in Mr H.'s distorted fancy, the Spectrum first came chapping softly at the manse door, and afterwards blattering on it, in a wicked desire to drive the lawful possessor out of the house and take his place. But it was while the glen was locked. Sometimes one of the twain was inside the house and sometimes the other. Sounds were heard, they say, coming from the study, of voices in conflict and blows struck. The dwellers of that time in the Five Houses, of whom two carlines are still alive, maintained that they had seen Mr H. sitting on his dike at night, because the other was in possession. By this time no servant would bide in the manse after gloaming; and yet, though Mr H. was now the one chapping at the door, they said they could see a light being carried in the house from room to room, and hear something padding on the floors. He did not walk, they said, he padded.

'When they found the minister, according to the stories,' Dr John said, 'his face was in an awful mess.'

What had caused that, I asked, and he said shortly that he supposed Spectrums had teeth.

It was eerie to reflect that to those two carlines, as we call ancient women, my study must still be more his than mine, and that they would not be taken aback if they came into it at that moment and found the old man in the grandy chair.

'The wayward woman was a better visitor to the glen than this other at any rate,' I ventured, and the answer he made I would as soon he had kept to himself. 'According to some of the ranters,' he said, with a sort of leer at me, 'they are the same person.'

We tried to get on to more comfortable subjects, but it was as if the scholar's story would not leave the room. 'I feel as if there were three of us here tonight,' I said to the doctor.

'Ay,' said he, 'and a fourth keeking in at the window.'

As usual, the old-wife gossip in which we had been luxuriating (for what more was it?) was interrupted by Christily coming in to announce that our sederunt was at an end. She did this, not in words, but by carrying away the kettle. This garr'd us to our beds, fuming at her as being one of those women, than whom there are a few more exasperating, who think all men should do their bidding. I had to be up betimes this morning to see him take the gate.

IV. THE LOCKING OF THE GLEN

Dec. 19.—In this white wastrie of a world the dreariest moment is when custom makes you wind up your watch. Were it not for the Sabbath I would get lost in my dates. Not a word has gone into my Diary for a fortnight bypast. Now would be the time for it if there were anything to chronicle; but nothing happens, unless one counts as an event that I brought my hens into the manse on discovering that their toes were frozen to the perch (I had to bring the perch too). My two sheep are also in by, and yesterday my garden slithered off to the burn with me on it like a passenger. I have sat down at an antrin time to the Diary to try to fill up with an account such as this of the locking of the glen, and the result has been rather disquieting to me, as I will maybe tell farther on and maybe not.

The glen road, on which our intercourse with ourselves as well as with the world so largely depends, was among the first to disappear under the blankets. White hillocks of the shape of eggs have arisen here and there, and are dangerous too, for they wobble as though some great beast beneath were trying to turn round. The mountains are so bellied out that they have ceased to be landmarks. The farm-towns look to me to be smored. I pull down my blinds so that I may rest my eyes on my blues and reds indoors. Though the Five Houses are barely a hundred yards away I have to pick out signs of life with my spy-glass.

I am practically cut off from my kind. Even the few trees are bearing white ropes, thick as my wrists, instead of branches, and the only thing that is a bonny black is the burn, once a mere driblet but now deep, with a lash around at corners, and un-chancy to risk. At times of ordinary wet they cross here to the kirk in two easy jumps on boulders placed there for the purpose, and called the brig, but the boulders are now like sunk boats, and of the sprinkling of members who reached the kirk on the 9th, one used a vaulting-pole and lost it.

Last Sabbath I did not open the kirk but got down to the burn and preached to a handful standing on the other side. My heart melted for the smith's bairns, every one of whom was there, and I have cried a notice across the burn that next Sabbath the bell will ring as a solemn reminder, but the service will be in the smiddy, whether I find that man's pole or not.

Two or three times Posty, without his velocipede, has penetrated to Branders and delivered my letters and a newspaper to me by casting them over the burn tied to stones. There is no word of Dr John. For nearly a week, except for an occasional shout, I have heard no voice but Christily's. I sit up here o' nights trying to get meanings out of Mr H.'s Diary, and not so much finding them in the written books as thinking I hear them padding up the stair as a wayward woman might do. In the long days I go out and shule, and get dunted by slides from the roof.

Of an evening Posty struts up and down in front of the Five Houses, playing on his pipes. I can see him like a pendulum passing the glints of light. I can hear him from the manse, but still better from the burn-side, if I slue down to listen in the dark. On one of those nights I got a dirl in the breast of me. It was when I went back to the manse after hearing him finish that Border boast, 'My name it is little Jock Elliot'. The glen was deserted by all other sound now, but as I birzed open the manse door (for the snow had got into the staples) I heard my fiddle playing 'My name it is little Jock Elliot'. For a moment I thought that Christily was at it, but then I knew she must be bedded, and she has no ear, and it was grander playing than Posty's though he is a kittle hand. I suppose I did not stand still in my darkened hallan for more than half a minute, and when I struck a light to get at a candle the music stopped. There is no denying that the stories about the Spectrum flitted through me, and it needed a shove from myself to take me up the stair. Of course there was nobody. I had come back with the tune in my ears, or it was caused by some vibration in the air. I found my fiddle in the locked press just as I had left it, except that it must have been leaning against the door, for it fell into my arms as I opened the press, and I had the queer notion that it clung to me. I could not compose myself till I had gone through my manse with the candle, and even after that I let the instrument sleep with me.

More reasonable fancies came to me in the morning, as that it might be hard on a fiddle never to be let do the one thing it can do; also that maybe, like the performers, they have a swelling to cry out to rivals: 'I can do better than that.' Any allure I may have felt, to take advantage of this mere fancy and put the neck-rest beneath my chin again, I suppressed; but I let Posty know he could have the loan of my instrument on condition that he got it across the burn dry. By the smith's connivance this was accomplished in a cart. It is now my fiddle Posty plays instead of his pipes, which are not in much better condition than his velocipede and are repaired in a similar manner. I extracted just one promise from him, that he would abstain from the baneful Jacobite lilts he was so fond of; but he sometimes forgets or excuses himself across the burn by saying: 'She likes that kind best, and she is ill to control once she's off.' It is pretty to hear him in the gloaming, letting the songs loose like pigeons.

To write this account of the glen when it is locked has been an effort, for the reason that I have done it twice already and in the morning it was not there. I sat down by lamplight on both occasions to write it and thought I had completed my task, but the next morning I found just a few broken lines on other-wise blank pages. Some of them were repeated again and again like a cry, such as 'God help me', as if I were a bird caught in a trap. I am not in any way disturbed of mind or body, at any rate in the morning. Yet this was what I had written. I am none so sure but what it may prove to be all I have written again.

I will now go and say good night to the Old Lady, for though it is barely half nine on the clock, we keep early hours in the wilderness. This is a moment I owe to her ingenuity. The Grand House, which has of course a statelier name of its own, is a steep climb from here and is at present inaccessible, the approach having thrown in its lot with the fields, but it is visible, and at half nine o'clock she shoots her blind up twice, and I reply with mine. Hers, I am thankful to say, is red, or the lamp behind it has a red shade, and this shooting of the blinds is our way of saying good night to each other. When she shoots hers three times it means something personal about my gown, and I make

no answer. There is a warmth, however, in saying good night
to a living being when the glen is so still that I am thinking you
could hear a whit-rit on the move. Sometimes I stand by my
window long after hers is dumb, and I have felt that night was
waiting, as it must have done once, for the first day. It is the
stillness that is so terrible. If only something would crack the
stillness.

V. THE STRANGER

Dec. 21.—For the first time since the glen was locked Dr
John 'threw in', as we say, this morning.

He came straight to the study, where he found us at family
exercise. I did not look up from my knees, but Christily
whispered to me: 'Be short,' which I dare say made me in consequence a little longer. Yet I knew she would not have taken
such a liberty unless there was something untoward with the
man, and though I found when I rose that he was on his knees
with us, I saw that he had gone to sleep on them. His face was
so peaked that I sent Christily hurriedly for the bottle of brandy
which has lain in the manse uncorked since I came here six
months ago, and as soon as he had partaken she hauled off his
boots and ran him on to the stair-head to wring and scrape him,
for he was getting on to the carpet.

I saw he ettled to be rid of her before communicating something by-ordinar to me, and he took the best way to effect this
by saying in a sentence that he had got through to Joanna
Minch and it was a girl and both were doing well; whereupon
Christily was off to cry the tidings across the burn.

He was nodding in the grandy with fatigue, so that it looked
as if only by sudden jerks could he keep his head on, but he
brought out the words: 'There is more in it than I told Christily.
I have been to the shieling, but I did not get through in time.
There were two lives saved in that bit house in the small hours;
but don't be congratulating me, for I had naught to do with it.'

Having said this, he fell head foremost into sleep, and I had
ill rousing him, which I was sweer to do, but he had made it
plain that he wanted to say more.

'It's such a camsterie tale', he told me, 'as might banish sleep in any man; but I am dog-tired and unless you keep pulling my beard with all the strength that is in you I'll be dovering again.'

I may say here that I had to do as he instructed me several times. We must have looked a strange pair, the doctor yawning and going off in the middle of sentences while I tugged fiercely at the beard.

I will put his bewildering tale together as best I can. He had forced his way last evening to the farm of the Whammle, where a herd was lying with two broken legs. While he was there Fargie Routh, the husband of Joanna, had tracked him down to say that she was terrible near her reckoning. The doctor started off with him rather anxious, for Fargie was 'through-ither', and it was Joanna's first. Dr John had floundered into worse drifts, but a stour of snow was plastering his face and he lost Fargie at the sleugh crossing. He tumbled and rumbled down in a way at which he is a master-hand, and reached the shieling hours before the husband, who is a decent stock but very unusual in the legs. The distance is a short mile when the track is above-ground. Dr John was relieved to smell smoke, for he feared to find he was on a sleeveless errand, and that the woman would be found frozen.

I told him I knew the house, which is a lonesome one-roomed cot of double stone and divot, with but a hole window. I asked if he had found Joanna alone, but he had taken the opportunity of my making a remark to fall asleep again.

I got his eyes open in the manner recommended by him, and he said with one of his little leers at me: 'She was not quite alone; but maybe you are one of those who do not count an infant till it be christened.'

'If there is any haste for that——' I cried, looking for my boots.

'There is none,' he said.

'But who had been with her? Was she in such a bad condition that she could give you no information about that?'

'She was in fine condition and she could and she did,' he said. 'I was with her till Fargie, who had gone back to the Whammle, brought down the gude-wife, and I have no doubt Joanna is now giving the particulars to them. They are such uncommon particulars', he went on, taking a chew at them, 'that I can fancy even the proud infant sitting up to listen.'

Then who was it that had acted in his place, I inquired, not daring to be more prolix lest he should again be overtaken.

That, he said, was what he was asking me.

'Dr John——'

'Be assured', said he, 'that I am too dung ower with tire to be trifling with you; but this will become more your affair than mine. It is not to me they will look to be told who she was, but to their minister.'

'I hope I shall not fail them,' I said loftily. Nevertheless I dreed what was coming, and I insisted on his keeping awake 'or I would lay a hot iron on the beard'.

He said he had found a kettle on a bright fire and Joanna in her bed with the child, who was fittingly swaddled in her best brot. He would not let her talk until he had satisfied himself that everything necessary had been done, and then (for the curiosity was mounting to his brain) he said with pretended casualness: 'I see you have been having a nice cup of tea.'

'And merry she was at the making of it,' replied Joanna, turning merry herself.

'I forget', said he, 'if you mentioned who she was?'

'Of course it was one of the Strangers,' she said.

'Of course it would be one of those curiosities,' said he, 'but I never chanced to fall in with ane; what was she like?'

'Oh,' said Joanna, 'she was like the little gentleman that sits under his tail'—meaning a squirrel.

'I thought she would be something like that,' he said; 'but had you no fear of her?'

'Never,' said Joanna, 'till after the bairn was born, and then for just a short time, when she capered about mad-like with glee, holding it high in the air, and dressing and undressing it in the brot, so as to have another peep at it, and very proud of what she had done for me and it till a queer change came over her and I had a sinking that she was going to bite it. I nippit it from her.'

'To bite them is not my usual procedure at a birth,' the doctor had said, 'but we all have our different ways.'

Joanna gave him a fuller story of the night than, as he said, would be of any profit to a sumph of a bachelor like Adam Yestreen, but he told me some of its events.

The door had blown open soon after Fargie's departure, leaving naught but reek to heat her, and the bole closed, and when the fire went down she would have been glad to cry back the reek. She thought the cold candle of her life was at the flicker. The Stranger relit the fire, but there was no way she could conceive of heating that body on the box-bed. Then the thought came to her.

'She strippit herself naked,' Joanna said, 'and made me keep my feet on her, as if she was one of them pig bottles for toasting the feet of the gentry; and when my feet were warm, she lay close to me, first on one side and then on the other. She was as warm as a browning bannock when she began, but by the time the heat of her had passed into me I'se uphaud she was cold as a trout.'

As to the actual birth, though this was Joanna's first child, she knew more about the business than did her visitor, who seems to have been in a dither of importance over the novelty of the occasion. She was sometimes very daring and sometimes at such a loss that in Joanna's words, 'she could just pet me and kiss me and draw droll faces at me with the intent to help me through, and when she got me through she went skeer with triumph, crying out as she strutted up and down that we were the three wonders of the world'.

The whole affair, Dr John decided, must have been strange enough 'to put the wits of any medical onlooker in a bucket', and if he let his mind rest on it he would forget how to sleep as well as how to practise surgery; so in the name of Charity would I leave him in the land of Nod for an hour while I thought out some simple explanation for my glen folk.

He got his hour, though sorely did I grudge it, for I was in a bucket myself.

When he woke refreshed I was by his side to say at once, as if there had not been a moment's interruption: 'Of course she was some neighbour.'

There was a glint in his blue eyes now, but he said decisively: 'There is no way out by that road, my man; Joanna is acquaint with every neighbour in the glen.'

'An outside woman of flesh and blood', I prigged with him, 'must have contrived to force the glen; as, after all, you did yourself.'

That, he maintained, was even less possible than the other.

I was stout for there being some natural explanation, and he reminded me unnecessarily that there was the one Joanna gave. At this I told him sternly to get behind me.

I could not forbear asking him if he had any witting of such stories being common to other lonely glens, and he shook his head, which made me the more desperate.

He saw in what a stramash I was, and, dropping his banter, came kindly to my relief. 'Do you really think', he said, in his helpful, confident way, 'that I have any more belief in warlocks and "Strangers" than you have yourself? I'll tell you my conclusion, which my sleep makes clearer. It is that Joanna did the whole thing by herself, as many a woman has done before her. She must at some time, though, have been in a trance, which are things I cannot pretend to fathom, and have thought a woman was about her who was not there. It cows to think of a practical kimmer like Joanna having, even in her hour of genius, such an imagination; that bit about nearly biting the bairn is worthy of Mr H.'s Spectrum.'

'None of that,' I cried. 'She no doubt got that out of the old minister's story.'

'Ay,' he granted, 'let's say that accounts for it. I admit it is the one thing that has been worrying me. But at any rate it is of no importance, as we are both agreed that Joanna was by her lonesome. She had no joyous visitor, no. Heigh-ho, Mr Yestreen, it's almost a pity to have to let such a pleasantly wayward woman go down the wind.'

It was far from a pity to me. I was so thankful to him for getting rid of her that I pressed his hand repeatedly. I was done with wayward women.

VI. Superstition and its Antidote

Dec. 26.—I got as far as the shieling two days behind Joanna's story and held a kirstening, this being the first at which I have ever officiated.

The usual course is to have it in the kirk toward the end of a

service, but in urgent cases it may be on the day of birth. There
was maybe no reason for precipitancy in this case, the child
being lusty, but in the peculiar circumstances I considered it my
duty to make her safe. When I took her in my arms, by far the
youngest I had ever meddled with, I was suddenly aware of my
youthful presumption. I should have been warned beforehand
about the beauty of their finger nails.

Yet I dared not let on that I was the most ignorant in the
room, for I was the minister, and therefore to be looked up to.
Also Joanna swore to her visit from the Stranger, with side-looks
at me as if she had given birth to a quandary as well as to a
litlun; and the lave of the party present were already familiar
with her story and were all agog.

So, knowing how ill it fares with a minister's usefulness if he
does not keep upside with his flock, I was bolder than I felt,
and told them in a short exposition that there had been no
'Stranger' in the affair; otherwise some of them would certainly
have seen her.

They all nodded their agreement and thanked me for making
it so clear, but I knew in my bones that they did not accept one
word of my redding up, though they regarded it as very proper
for a minister, especially one who was new to the glen.

This way they have, of heartily accepting what you tell them
and then going their own gate, is disheartening to me, and at one
time I thought of making any dirdum about Strangers a subject
of stern discipline from the pulpit. Fear did not enter into my
reluctance, for I knew they would esteem me the more the
harder I got at them, but I drew back from the ease of superi-
ority toward men and women whose simple lives have been so
often more grimly fought than my own. It relieves me, therefore,
to have decided that I may get through their chinks more
creditably in another manner.

The amelioration in the weather, which probably will not
last, is what put the idea into my head. Some of us have been
able to step about a little these last days. A curran herd, weary
of bothy life, have made so bold as to find out where the glen
road is. Of course they cannot shule down to it, but they have
staked some of the worst bits, and several carts have passed
along as if the proximity to it gave them courage. I saw from the
manse the Old Lady's carriage trying for Branders. The smith's

klink-klink from the smiddy, which is the most murie sound in a countryside next to a saw-mill, shows that he had had at least one to shod. Posty had ridden on his velocipede the length of the Five Houses and back, with the result that you can hardly see his face for the brown paper.

It is true that there is no possibility of opening the kirk on Sabbath, for though we have thrown planks across the burn, with a taut rope to hand on by, the place is too mortal cold for sitting in through a service. There is, however, the smiddy, which can be used for other purposes besides preaching.

All our large social events take place in the smiddy, and the grandest consist of Penny Weddings, when you are expected, if convenient, to bring, say, a hen or a small piece of plenishing to the happy pair. The actual marriage, of course, takes place in the bride's home, and not, in the queer English way, in the kirk. We have had no weddings since I came, but twice last month we had Friendlies which we consider the next best thing.

Our Friendlies are always in two parts, the first part being devoted to a lecture by the minister or some other person of culture, who is usually another minister. This lecture is invariably of a bright, entertaining character, and some are greater adepts at unbending in this way than others, the best being Mr Watery of Branders, whose smile is of such expansion that you might say it spreads over the company like honey. Laughter and the clapping of hands in moderation are not only permissible during the lectures but encouraged.

The second part of a Friendly is mostly musical with songs, and is provided by local talent, in which Posty takes too great a lead. There is an understanding that I remain for the first song or so, whether I am lecturing or in the Chair. This is to give a tone to the second part, and then I slip away, sometimes wishing I could bide to enjoy the mirth, but I know my presence casts a shadow on their ease. The time in which Friendlies would be most prized is when the glen is locked, but the difficulty for all except the Five Houses lies in getting to the smiddy.

Nevertheless we are to attempt a Friendly on Thursday, though Mr Watery, who was to be the lecturer with a magic lantern, which of course is a great addition, has cried off on account of nervousness lest the weather should change before he gets home again. I have undertaken to fill his place to the best of my more limited ability, as indeed it is.

I am doing so the more readily because of this idea that came to me, which promises to be a felicitous one. It is to lecture to them on Superstition, with some sly and yet shattering references to a recent so-called event in the glen, all to be done with a light touch, yet of course with a moral, which is that a sense of humour is the best antidote to credulity. There are few of the smaller subjects to which I have given greater thought than to Humour, its ramifications and idiosyncrasies, and I have a hope that I may not do so badly at this. I wish Mr Watery could be present, for I think I can say that I know more about Humour than he does, though he is easier at it.

VII. MISS JULIE LOGAN

Dec. 28.—Hours have passed since I finished my lecture. I know not how many times I have sat down to write about her, and then taken to wandering the study floor instead. My mind goes back in search of every crumb of her, and I am thinking I could pick her up better on my fiddle than in written words.

My eyes never fell on her till I got to my peroration. This is no reflection on my sight, for all the company in the smiddy, and there were more than thirty, had to sit in darkness so that they could better watch my face between the two candles. She was with Mistress Lindinnock, who presented me to her, and they came over to the manse while the shelties were being yoked. I held her hand to guide her across the planks. She is the Old Lady's grand-niece, and her name is Miss Julie Logan. I am glad of her Christian name, for it has always been my favourite.

In the past few years, up to this night, my lot had thrown me mostly among my seniors, and a glow that once I knew seemed to be just a memory warning me that ministers must be done quickly with the clutches of youth.

I am no hand at describing the garb of beauty, and the nearest I can get to her, after much communing, is that she is a long stalk of loveliness. She carried a muff of fur, and at times would raise it to her face as if she knew no better than to think it was a scent-bottle, or peep over it like a sitting bird in the bole of a tree.

The upper part of her attire was black and the rest green.

There was a diverting mutch on her head which, for some reason I cannot as yet determine, you could have got on smiling terms with though you had met it hanging on a knob.

She is from Edinburgh, and it was to get her that I saw the Grand House carriage fighting its way to Branders yesterday.

I have only seen her for twenty minutes. There is such a beloved huskiness in her voice that she should be made to say everything twice. She glides up a manse stair with what I take to be the lithesomeness of a panther. I like her well when she is haughty, and even better when she is melting, and best of all when she is the two together, which she often is.

I was all throughither when she sat down on the one of my chairs that I have hitherto held to be of the least account. She looked as meek at that moment as if a dove was brooding in her face.

It is not beauty of person that I heed but internal beauty, which in her is as plain to read as if she wore it outside.

What I would last part with is the way her face sparkles, not just her eyes but her whole face. This comes and goes, and when it has gone there is left the sweet homeliness that is woman's surest promise to man. Fine I knew for ever that I needed none but her.

Fain would I have made observations to her that put a minister in a favourable light. I am thinking that the Old Lady spoke at times, for she is a masterpiece at conversation, but all I remember of her is that she soon fell asleep in the grandy chair, which is a sudden way she has. This disregard of her company has sometimes annoyed me at kirk meetings (where we have to pause till she wakes up), but not on this occasion.

In my lecture I had spoken about humour which is profound and humour which is shallow, such as pulling away your chair. Miss Julie Logan said to me in the manse that she was only interested in the profound kind, with its ramifications and idiosyncrasies. She said she found it a hard kind to detect, and wished she could be so instructed as to recognize profound humour, whether written or spoken.

When she said this there was something so pleading in her shining eyes that, instead of replying in a capable manner, I offered to explain the thing with a bit of paper and a pencil.

I drew a note of exclamation, and showed her how they were put into books, at the end of sentences, to indicate that the remark was of a humorous character. She got the loan of the pencil and practised making notes of exclamation under my instruction.

She said she questioned whether profound humour would not still baffle her in the spoken word, and I agreed that here it was more difficult, but told her that if you watched the speaker's face narrowly you could generally tell by a glint in it; and if there was no glint his was the mistake and not yours.

She asked me to say something humorous to her, the while she would watch for the glint, which I did, and she saw it.

She said she feared it would be a long time before she could do my glint, and asked me to watch her face while she practised it; and I was very willing.

She said she would like to have my opinion on the statement of an Englishman about the bagpipes, namely that they sound best if you are far away from them, and the farther away the better. Other people present had laughed at that, and could I tell her why?

I said that no doubt what they laughed at was at the man's forgetting that if you were too far away from the pipes you would not hear them at all.

Even in those moments I was not such a gowk as to be unaware that I was making a deplorable exhibition of myself. Whatever she seemed to want me to say I just had to say it, for the power had gone from me to show her that I was not mentally deficient. However, when it came to this about the pipes I broke up and laid my face on the table, and she raised my head, and was woebegone when she saw the ruin she had made.

'Have I hurt you?' she asked, and I could just nod. 'Why did you let me?' she said with every bit of her, and I answered darkly: 'I cannot help saying or doing whatever Miss Julie Logan wants.'

The wet glittered on her eyes in a sort of contest as you can sometimes hear them do on the strings.

I said: 'It is bitter mortifying to me to be seen in such

disadvantageous circumstances by Miss Julie Logan at the very time of all others when I should have liked to be better than my best.'

I stroked her muff and, somehow, the action made me say: 'This is a very unhomely manse,' though I had never thought that before.

She held out her hand to me, with the palm upwards like one begging for forgiveness, and I have been wondering ever since what she meant me precisely to do with it. I pressed it on my heart, and I filled at long last with what becomes a man in his hour and I said: 'I love you, Miss Julie Logan,' and she said as soft as a snowflake: 'Yes, I know.' Then Christily came in with the blackberry wine on a server, and when Miss Julie Logan drank it I could see her throat flushing as it went down, which they say also happened with Mary Stewart. Then the Old Lady woke up and said that the ponies must be yoked by this time, so I took the ladies across to the carriage, Christily going in front with the lamp. I could hear Miss Julie Logan talking sweetly to her, though it was the Old Lady who was on my arm.

It is now on the chap of midnight, and since I wrote the above I have been down to my kirk and unlocked the door and lit a candle and stood looking for a long time at the manse pew. It is in a modest position on the right of the pulpit, disdaining to call attention to itself. For my part, I could never walk down the aisle of any kirk without being as conscious of which was the manse pew as of which was the pulpit. I do not look, I just feel it.

Usually there is only Christily in my pew, and she sits at the far end. Not all manse pews have a door, but mine has, and I would sit next it if I were out of the pulpit, which can only be if another minister is officiating for me. When a minister is a married man, as all ministers ought to be, it is the lawful right of his wife to sit next the door, with a long empty space between her and the servant, unless they be blessed with children. I stood by my manse pew picturing Miss Julie Logan sitting next the door. She is a tall lady, and I wondered whether the seat was too low for her; and such is my condition that, if I had brought nails and a hammer with me, I would have raised it there and then.

VIII. CHRISTILY GOES QUEER

Dec. 30.—In the midst of my exaltation come disquieting symptoms in Christily. I think, now I look back, that she has been unsettled these past few days and that occasionally she has glanced covertly at me as if she feared I suspected her of something. Whether this was so or not, she is in a bad state now, and I am very ravelled in my mind about her.

It showed itself this morning when I made a remark to her about Miss Julie Logan. I knew it would be more befitting not to bring that name into everyday conversation, but something within me hankered to hear how it sounded on other lips. Nothing could have been more carefully casual than the way I introduced the subject, and yet the dryness came into my mouth that makes it so desirable for a public speaker to have a glass of water handy.

'And so', I said, 'there is a young lady at the Grand House now, Christily.'

'Is there?' said she, like one cheering up for a gossip.

'Did you not know', I inquired, 'that it is there Miss Julie Logan is staying?'

'What Miss Julie Logan?' she asked.

'The young lady', I said patiently, 'whom Mistress Lindinnock brought to the manse the night before last.'

'I saw no young lady,' she said; 'there was just the two of you came in, you and Mistress Lindinnock.'

'Is this temper, Christily,' I demanded, 'or what is it? You helped Miss Julie Logan to a glass of blackberry wine; also you carried the lantern when I escorted them back to the carriage, and you were in front conversing with her.'

Her eyes stood out as in some sudden affliction, and, when I stepped towards her, asking if she was ill, she cried 'God help me!' and rushed out of the study.

What did it portend? Had I unwittingly opened the door to some secret the poor soul had been keeping from me? I was very riven and I followed on her heels to the kitchen, but she had locked the door and no answer could I get when I spoke through the keyhole to her. This was very disturbing from such an excellent woman, and I went on my knees, with the door between us, and called in a loud voice to the malevolent one to come out of her. I could hear her wailing sore.

In much perturbation I got across to the Five Houses on the chance of finding Dr John, as Posty's wife is down with a complaint that beats the skill of her neighbours; the silly tod has found out that she is four years older than she thought, and though until that moment in robust health she at once took to her bed.

Fortunately I got the doctor, and on our way across I told him of what had happened. I was relieved to find that he did not take the matter with my seriousness; indeed he was more interested in Miss Julie Logan, of whom he had not heard till now, than in Christily's case, which he foretold would turn out to be tantrums brought on by my writing so many love-letters. It seems, though news to me, that Christily is responsible for tattle about my sitting for hours writing love-letters, these being what she has made of my Diary. However meddlesome this is, it took a load from my mind, and I was feeling comfortable when he went off to the kitchen, grinning, and declaring that he would shake her like a doctor's bottle.

He was gone for a long time, and it was a very different Dr John who came back. I have seen him worry his way through some rasping ordeals, but never showing the least emotion. Now, however, he was in such a throb that at sight of him I cried out: 'Is it as bad as that?'

'It's bad,' he said. 'Man, it is so bad and so unexpected that for the first time in my practice I cannot even pretend to know how to act; let me be for a minute.' He paced the floor, digging his gnarled fists into his eyes, a way he had when in pursuit of a problem, as if the blackness thus created helped him to see better.

'There is one of two things that must be done,' he said, 'and I have got to choose, but the responsibility is very terrible.'

I waited, thinking he was to take me into his confidence, but, instead, he just fell to staring in a kind of wonderment at me. I began to assure him that every help I could give would be forthcoming, and at that he gave a jarring laugh. I was offended, but he was at once contrite and asked for my advice.

'We could ask the young lady to come down with Mistress Lindinnock and show herself,' I suggested.

'No, we could not,' he said, so sharply that I got stiff again. He put the matter right, though when he told me of the two courses he had to decide between, for, after all, what I had proposed was one of them; namely to confront the poor sufferer with the two ladies, which he called the kill or cure step. The second course was to go canny for a few days in the hope that the hallucination might pass of itself. She might even wake up on the morrow without it, which at the worst would be a more gentle awakening than the other.

He asked me, not like a consultant but as one who needed a stronger man to lean on, which line of action I would prefer to be taken if I was in Christily's place, and on consideration I admitted that the first one seemed to carry the more grievous shock.

After some discussion we decided to give the softer plan a short trial. I said there could be no harm in it at any rate.

He said, still very worried, indeed he was shaking, that there might be great harm in it, but that he would risk it.

We agreed that, as on all subjects save the one she was as right as I was, it would be best for me in our daily intercourse to be just my usual, but not to talk to her as if I knew she was possessed by an evil spirit.

As the doctor was anxious she should be kept from brooding I also agreed to a proposal from him that her brother, Laurie, who is at present at a loose end in Branders, should pay a visit to the manse for a few days, ostensibly to brighten her, but really of course to watch her on the quiet.

This gives small promise for the time being of a comfortable manse; but what is running in my head even now is that to-morrow afternoon I go, be the weather what it likes, to the Grand House to see Miss Julie Logan again. It will be the last day of the year, but Laurie should be here by then, and Christily will be safe in his care.

Today I am keeping an observant eye on her myself. She has brought up my meals in her old exemplary way and we have exchanged a few cautious words about household affairs, but her face is sore begrutten, and if I try to be specially kind to her she knows the reason and there is more than a threatening of a breakdown.

Poor woman, it is like to be a sad New Year's Eve to her, and a heavy one too for Dr John, who left the manse, very broken. As I let him out I said: 'It is as if the Spectrum had come back to this house.'

'Wheesht, man,' he said.

IX. THE END OF A SONG

Dec. 31.—I will try to put down the events of this terrible night with clearness and precision.

It was in the early afternoon, the snow shimmering like mica, which is sheep's-silver, that I set out for the Grand House, buttoned very thick. Despite the darkness that encompassed Christily I was in an awful and sublime state of happiness.

This may have got into my very appearance and made it unusual, for I met some of the smith's bairns, who generally run to me, but they hinted back, and when I asked what fleyed them one said: 'Your face has come so queer.' I could have danced to them in the snow from sheer joy. I am not sure but what I did dance, though I never learned it.

Some of the windows in the Five Houses already showed a glime of light, not that it was needed yet, but my folk were practising precautions against my seeing them presently, for it is always a night of solemn gallanting. These precautions largely consisted in hanging heavy cloths, such as human habiliments, behind the blinds, so as to deaden the light to me should I be watching from the manse. There was no music as yet, and I was wondering where Posty and my fiddle were, when I fell in with them on the way. Though he has forgotten who the broken men were about whom he likes to play, I notice that one little bit from his forbears, as I take it, still clings to him; he walks up and down, while he is playing the fiddle, as if it were the pipes. On this occasion, however, I expect he was on the march for seasonable largess at the Grand House, which I am sure he always receives with complete surprise.

A thing commonly said about the Grand House is that it should be called the Grand Houses, there being in a manner two of them: though the one is but a reflection of the other in a round of water close by.

This lochy is only a kitten in size but deep; and I know not whether its unusual reflective properties are accidental, or, as some say, were a device of olden times to confuse the enemy when in liquor. At any rate one cannot easily tell in certain lights, unless you are particular about things being upside down, which is the house and which the reflection.

There is an unacceptable tale of the lord of the glen having been tracked to the house after Culloden, and of the redcoats being lured by a faithful retainer into the water, where they tried doors and windows till they drowned, the lord and his faithful retainer keeking over the edge at them and crying 'Bo.'

The house is of many periods, but its wonder is the banqueting hall, or rather a window therein.

They never banquet now in the hall, not even the English, and indeed it is nigh empty of gear except for tapestries on the walls, which the ignorant take to be carpets damaged in the '45. The great bowed window is said by travelled persons to stand alone among windows, for it is twenty-eight feet in height and more than half as wide. All who come to look at it count its little lozens, as we call the panes, which are to the number of two hundred and sixteen. These panes are made of some rare glass that has a tint of yellow in it, so that, whatever the weather is, to anyone inside the hall it looks to be a sunny day. In the glen this glass is not thought much of and they say it should be renewed. The house is a bit old and weary, and I dare say these lozens are the only part of it that would shame renewal.

It was not here but in a bien little chamber where however indiscriminately you sit down you sit soft, that Mistress Lindinnock received me. She was tatting (but that cannot be the right word) at a new tapestry, or mending an old one, which was so voluminous that she rose out of it as from the snow. She is such a little old person that when she stands up you may think she has sat down; nevertheless she is so gleg at coming to the boil that contradictious men have stepped back hurriedly from the loof of her hand, and yet not been quick enough. She has always, as I have said, been a fine friend to me till this unhappy day.

She was the same woman though unusual quiet while we were talking of the ravel Christily was in, which I did not have to stress, as I found Dr John had obligingly gone straight to her with the story from the manse yesterday. I could not help inquiring, with all the look of its being an extra question, how he had taken to Miss Julia Logan.

Sharp I got the dreadful answer: 'He had no opportunity, for I had already packed the woman back to Edinburgh.'

I was to have worse blows than this tonight, though at the moment I could not have credited it; so I will only say that when I rallied I asked with cold politeness when the young lady was coming back.

Mistress Lindinnock, I could see, was eyeing me closely to find out how I stood the news, but she replied at once, like one prepared for war: 'Never, I hope; I don't like your Miss Julie Logan, my good sir.'

I will not say that even in that stern moment I got no gliff of pleasure out of hearing her called my Miss Julie Logan. Also it gave me an opportunity to reply with the thunderbolt: 'That is what I want her to be.'

She stamped her foot at me, but I never weakened. 'I demand her address,' I said. She refused it, and I replied loftily that it mattered not as I was confident she would write to me.

She raised her arms at that, like one appealing to a Higher Power, and said: 'If she writes to you I give the thing up.' Once she swung me round with a rage I could not construe and said on her tiptoes: 'I could tell you things about her any one of which would make you drop her in the burn, though you were standing in the middle of it with the jade in your arms.'

I replied in my stateliest, which has froze many, that I would stand defiant in the middle of the ocean with Miss Julie Logan on those terms; and I meant it too, though I am no swimmer.

I dare say I was a rather dignified spectacle towering there, very erect, with my arms folded: at any rate she shuddered like one cowed who had never been cowed before; or else she became cunning, for she prigged with me to do as she, my old friend, wanted, saying endearing things about how much she had liked me in the days when I was sensible, and that if I were not such a calf I would see she was now fonder of me in my imbecility. Her words were not all, as will be seen, fittingly chosen, nor did I like the pity with which she glowered at me, for she was the one in need of it.

Yet I had a melting for her at moments; especially as I was going away with but a scantling of courtesy. When she said that it would be the first time I had left her house (and she might have added any house in the glen) without calling for a benison on it, I stood rebuked. As we went on our knees she whispered rather tremulously: 'Pray, dear minister, for all who may be in trouble this night, and even danger,' and I did so, and it made the tangled woman greet.

Of course I presumed she meant Christily, but as I was shaking hands with her my mind took a shrewd turn and I said almost threateningly: 'You were not referring, were you, to Miss Julie Logan?' It spoilt the comparative friendliness of our parting, for she flared up again and said: ''Deed no; she is the only one that is in no need of those words tonight.'

Unfortunate being, she little knew, nor did I, the impiety of that remark.

When I got outside I was like one with no gate to go. The tae half of me was warring with the other half. I sat down very melancholic by the little round of water I have spoken of. The night was forlorn, with the merest rim of the moon in sight, and no reflection on the water beyond some misty stars. I don't know why I sat there. It was not to keep vigil; I am sure I had no suspicion that Miss Julie Logan was still in the house.

I may have been there a considerable time before I saw or heard anything. What I heard came first: distant music. It may just have been Posty playing far away the most reprehensible but the loveliest of all the Jacobite cries, 'Will you no come back again?' Soon after he finished, if it was mortal man who played, all was as still again as if the death-cart my folk tell about was nearing the glen to cart away the old year.

Candles to a great number, and very sly, were beginning to get lit in the water. I spied on them interestedly. The full moon was now out of the clouds, and it was one of those nights when she wanders. The big window nearly filled the pond, and through it I saw a throng of people in the hall. So long as my eyes were fixed on the water of course it was only their reflections I saw. I saw them on their heads as in an inverted mirror, and they looked just as agreeable as the other way; maybe Nature herself does things with a disordered mind in the last gasp of the year.

They were in the Highland dress of lang syne. I never saw them all at once, because if they came nearer they were lost in the weeds and if they went back they had a neat way of going through the walls. The older ladies were in fine headdresses and others in their ringlets; they were more richly attired than the men, and yet the men made the finer show. I could see the trews and an occasional flashing silver button or a gleam of steel; but near all colour had been washed out of them, as if they had been ower long among the caves and the eagles.

There was plenty of food on a table that sometimes came forward, and they drank toasts thereat. I could not always put a meaning to what they did, but I saw them dancing and conversing, and though they were perhaps poor and desperate, they all, the gentlemen as much as the ladies, seemed to me to be of the great. They did rochly things as if they had forgotten the pretty ways, and next minute there would be a flourish in their manners that would have beat the pipes.

There was no music, though, and when this came to me I minded that I was not getting a sound across the water from the hall itself, though owing to the quietness of the night I heard in the open as infinitely small a thing as the letting-go of a twig. The company were as quiet as their reflections. This made me look across the pond at the window itself, which so far I had been jouking lest the company there should take tent of me. I had a mistrust they were up to ploys that were not for a minister to see, and would mischief me if they catched me spying. But that stealthy stillness garr'd me look up and I took a step or two to see better. They were all on the move, but at once stopped, hands on dirk, and I opined they suspected a watcher. I doukit, and after that, except for a wink now and again, I looked at nothing but the reflections. I knew I was in danger, but this did not greatly fash me so long as I was not catched.

I had never lost a feeling that there was an air of expectancy about them. I saw them backing against the walls to leave more space in the middle, and all eyes turned to the door, as if awaiting a great person. I suppose the tune was still swimming in my head, for I thought I knew who was coming in, he who was fed from the eagle's nest, and I had a sinking that it would be my duty to seize him and hand him over.

But it was a woman, it was Miss Julie Logan. She was not

finely attired like the other ladies, but so poorly that her garments were in tatters. She would have made a braver show if each of the ladies had torn off an oddment and made a frock for her between them.

It was not, however, as one of little account that they treated her or she treated them. She was the one presence in the hall to them. They approached her only when she signed to them that she could do with it, and as if overpowered by the distinction that was befalling them. The men made profound obeisance, and the ladies sank in that lovely way to the floor. On some she smiled and let them salute her hand, and others she looked at in a way I did not see, but they backed from her as if she had put the fear of Death into them. She gave the back of her hand to Mistress Lindinnock, and I never saw an old woman look so gratified.

With a few she took a step or two in the dance, mayhap to make others glower, and soon something was taking place that I could not at first fathom.

It was clear she was about to leave them; for a ceremony similar in most respects to that with which she had been received was repeated and the doors thrown open for her passing. But then they all gathered in the far end of the hall, or sank through it, with their backs to her, which was baffling to me; for up to that moment you could see how carefully they gave her their faces. Yet they did it of set purpose, or possibly at her command, for she was watching them more haughtily than ever.

As soon as she was sure that every face was to the wall a complete change came over her. She hastened—she almost ran in her eagerness—to a corner of the window and lifted from the floor a good-sized basket that I dare say they had placed there for her. She lifted it like one who knew for certain it would be there. She filled it with viands from the table, picking and choosing them with affectionate interest.

I thought that, being in some way I had to grope for, the one they held highest, she was too proud to let them know how hungry she was, though that very knowledge was what had made them place the basket so handily and look the other way while she filled it.

I thought that, reckless of correct behaviour, as all on that side were, they were Strangers, come trailing back into the present day under a command to honour and feed one who had long ago been left behind.

While she had been lording it so imperiously in the hall, she was belike thinking more about the basket than that she was the last sough of a song.

A moment after she was gone from the hall, with a withering look for any peeping face, I heard the first sound that had reached me from the house since I took to looking in the water. It was the closing of the front door. I hurried forward, and was in time to meet Miss Julie Logan, no longer a reflection, coming down the steps with the basket.

She cried: 'Carry the basket, Adam,' and I carried it, but first I put my topcoat on her, and she slipped my hand into one of the pockets along with her own.

I think it was snowing again, or a tempest or something of the kind, but we were not heeding.

She took me to a small ruin of a bield for sheltering sheep in, and in a corner of it where was a pile of stones, maybe to mark some old grave, we sat down on them and opened the basket. She was very hungry, and I myself was also slow to desist from eating. For drinking we ate the snow, against which I have warned my Sabbath-school scholars. The basket was so crammed with food of an engaging nature that when we paused, replete, there was still near a basketful left. Never in my life was I so merry as sitting on those stones, and she was also very droll. She had a way of shining her face close into mine and showing her pretty teeth like a child. It was the gaiety of her, but I did not quite like it. When we wandered on I wanted to bring the basket, but she said that was the place to leave it.

We said the kind of things a man and woman never say till they know each other through and through. It was all about ourselves, and love was one of the words I did not scruple to handle.

We were not bothering about far-back times or Mistress Lindinnock; but when we came to the burn it minded me of what the Old Lady had said I would do in a certain hap. Miss Julie Logan demanded of me to repeat to her the exact words, which I did, with one exception, namely: 'I could tell you things about her any one of which would make you drop her in the burn, though you were standing in the middle of it with the jade in your arms.' I omitted the word jade, so as not to lessen the Old Lady.

Miss Julie Logan was in a dance of delight and handed me back my coat, crying: 'Adam, let us try it!'

I said there was danger in it, and she said: 'I like danger fine,' and she coaxed me, saying: 'When you have got me there I'll tell you what the Old Lady meant, and then, if you don't drop me, belike I will be yours, Adam.' I lifted her in my arms, and in the exultation of my man's strength she was like one without weight. I carried her into the burn. It was deep and sucking. She rubbed her head on my shoulder in a way that would make a man think she liked to be where she was. She peeped up at me, and hod. I am thinking now she was wae for both of us, though she was glittering too.

She said: 'Kiss me first, Adam, in case you have to drop me.' I kissed her. 'Hold me closer,' she said, 'lest by some dread undoing you should let me slip.' I held her closer. 'Adam dear,' she said, 'it is this, I am a Papist.' At that awful word I dropped her in the burn. That she is still there I do not doubt, though I suppose she will have been carried farther down.

I have written this clear statement in the study, to be shown by Laurie to Dr John and by him to the Branders constabulary. I have put down everything exactly as it happened, and I swear to its accuracy.

I have refused to go to my bed this night, and I know that Laurie is sitting on a chair outside my door. I have told him none of the facts, but I can see that the man already suspects me.

I can remember nothing after I heard the splash, but he says he found me running up and down the water-side, and that he had to take a high hand with me to get me home. I would not change out of my wet things for all his blustering, but Christily, her face swollen with misery, came bursting in and tore them off me and put me into something dry. This is the last service she will ever render to me.

X. A Quarter of a Century

It is a quarter of a century since I stopped writing this Diary and put the thing out of my sight.

Circumstances made me want to look through it again; and there it was in the garret, between the same two boards of waxcloth where I had kept it hidden from Christily in the days of my windy youth. I had forgotten that it was written on sermon paper, and such dereliction from propriety disturbs my conscience now even more than the vapours set down in it about the Roman woman.

Of course I am aware now that she never existed. I have been aware all these twenty-five years that I was the one who went queer, and not the self-sacrificing Christily, that it was to watch me that the man Laurie was brought to the manse, and that the story the Old Lady told me was invented for her by Dr John. My two good friends had to work their way through thorns to clear my disordered mind, but they managed it by the time the glen road had come up again like a spring flower.

I was long pithless and bedded with fevers, for which the doctor blamed the burn, and in that quiet time I got rid of all my delusions; though once in the middle of my rally I escaped everybody and made for the sheep bield to decide for certain that the basket was not still there. I was perfectly sane, and yet I did that. The result of my escapade was to retard my recovery for another month.

I left the glen for good early in August, just before the return of the English, with whom, though I liked them well, I had no desire to have further discourse about Diaries or what may seem to happen when that glen is locked. I have had two charges since I gave up my first, and for eighteen years I have been minister in this flourishing place in a mining district. Two years after my call I married a lady of the neighbourhood and it has been a blessed union, for my Mima is one in a thousand and the children grow in grace. I tell Mima everything except about the Roman, that being a passage in my life that never took place, nor have I sufficient intellect to be able to speak about it without doing so as if it were real.

I am thankful to say that the Roman is to me as if she never

had been (and of course she never was, that just being a slip
of the pen). A Scottish minister has few topcoats in his life, and
when any old clothes will suffice I sometimes wear the one that
is in the Diary. Many a night in this part where the rain turns
black as it alights, I have been out in the old topcoat without
remembering how pretty she looked in it; and this is natural,
for she never was in it.

I have only once revisited my first charge, and it was a month
ago. I stayed a night at Branders with Dr John, who has got a
partner now. My old friend's hold on life has become little more
than a bat's to a shutter, but he will still be at it, and some day
I suppose he will be found among his own hills stiff and content.

I walked down the glen through the heather, a solitary, unless
it may be said that in a sense the young Adam I had been walked
with me. The English were on the hills, but they were not my
English.

I lay for two nights in the old manse, and preached twice.
They were not great sermons, but are held by some to be my
two best, and I keep them for visits. The lad that once I was
thought himself a gifted preacher, but the man he became knows
better. That is nothing to boast of, for there is naught that
houks the spirit from you so much as knowing better.

Mr Gallacher, who is the new minister, the second in succes-
sion to me, was preaching at Branders, and his wife, a genteel
thick lady, sat in my old pew, nearest the door. It gave me, may
I be forgiven, a sort of scunner of her. Gallacher was very civil,
but he is not the kind of man, I think, that the Old Lady would
have waved good night to with her window-blind. She of course
has been away with it this many a year.

There is a new postman, who, 'tis said, has trudged a distance
equal to round the world since the days of my Posty. Christily
is married on a provision merchant in Ireland, and once a year
sends me a present of eggs, with a letter inquiring very guardedly
about my health. Joanna Minch and the lass have gone to some
other glen. The only faces I could give a name to in the Five
Houses are the smith and two of his sons. The once lusty man
is now an old carl sitting on his dike, having reached that terrible
time for a Scotsman of knowing that he will never be allowed by
his well-intentioned offspring to do another's day work for ever
and ever. Sometimes, to give him an hour's pride, they let him

wheel a barrow. He will have to die gradual on a fine bed of straw, but he would rather be gotten with his hammer in his hands.

There have been great changes at the manse, inside and out. One hardly knows the study now, for there is a sofa fornent the fireplace. It has a grate. They burn coal. I had sold the grandy to Mr Gallacher, and one could see by the look of it that it had never missed me. There is an erection containing a foreign plant on the identical spot where the Roman sat; but she never sat there.

Outside, the chief change in the manse is that Mr Gallacher has lifted the hen-house to the gable-end, which I consider a great mistake. He has also cut down my gean tree.

The glen has not been what can be called locked for the last eight years, and Mr Gallacher knows very little about the old superstitions that plagued young Adam. He had heard something nonsensical about a red-shanked man on a horse whose hoofs made no marks, a poor affair though unaccountable. Mr Gallacher was very sound about the hallucinations all being clavers unworthy of investigation, and on that point at least we were in agreement. I asked him, just to keep the conversation going, if any Stranger woman had been seen, but he had heard of none, nor could he, for there never was one.

Of course I could not go for a walk on the Sabbath day; but as I was leaving for Branders on the Monday I got up betimes to have a last wander in the glen. I did not specially want to do this, and I prefer to put it that the fillip came from the Adam I had been. The sun soon got very masterly, though there was a nip in the air at first, and I made the mistake of wearing the old topcoat.

I sat for a time among the heather by the pond, where the reflection from the Grand House is still to be seen, but it is somewhat spoilt by a small windmill having been erected close by to provide the breeze in which, 'tis said, the trout rise best. I am told that this was Posty's last contrivance to make things easy for the English. I thought with little respect of the Jacobites and the '45, and a dog that may have been of old descent drove me away.

I went on to the bield, but nothing is left of it now except the pile of stones. I stood looking for a long time at the place where we had left the basket.

I went to Joanna's shieling, though I knew she was gone, and I found it gone too. I just went because I was sure that Joanna's visitor had been my visitor, though we were both in a dwam when we thought we saw her. I liked to mind the Roman's bonny act in making a pig of herself to heat the cold body of Joanna. I wished she had been given a chance to do this. She would have done it if she could.

I went to the Eagles Rock, and it looked the more sinister because there was a scarf of rime hiding the Logan stone. When the rime drifted I thought I could see the stone shogging.

I left my visit to the burn-side to the end. There is now a swinging bridge for the convenience of church-goers in the back-end of the year; but though little more than a wimple of water was running and sometimes coming to a standstill, I found the exact bend in the burn where I dropped her, if she had been there to drop. I stood, unruffled, keeping an iron grip on myself, my mind so rid of the old fash that I marvelled at my calm. It was not so, however, with my topcoat, which I found becoming clammy-cold, as if recalling another time by the burn and feeling we were again too near for safety. You might have said it tugged at me to come away, but that of course was just a vagary of my mind.

The young Adam in me must have had the upper hand, for looking back, I see it was to him rather than to me it happened. He thought he had catched into his arms something padding by, whose husky voice said 'Adam' lovingly, the while her glamorous face snuggled into his neck, the way a fiddle does. Next moment he gave a cry because he thought he was running with blood; and even I had a sinking till I tried my throat with my handkerchief. Whatever had been there was gone now; and I hurried away myself, for I was as shaken as if it had been the Spectrum.

I bided the night at Branders with Dr John, to whom all my story was so familiar except just one happening that I had always sworn never to reveal even to him.

We sat long over his pipe talking about what he called the old dead-and-done affair. We were very intimate that night, the one of us an ancient and the other getting on.

'Let us be thankful', the doctor said, 'that it can all be so easily construed, for the long and the short of it is that you were just away in your mind. Any other construing of it would be too uncomfortable to go to our beds on even now.'

I said, taking a higher line: 'It is not even allowable'; and yet we discussed the possibility of its having had any backing to it for, I suppose, the last time. This would have meant that the glen, instead of its minister, does sometimes go queer in the terrible stillness of the time when it is locked. 'We should have to think', the doctor said, with the kettle in his hand, 'that it all depended on the stillness of the glen. If it got to be stiller than themselves it woke them up, and they were at their old ploys again.'

'I am not seeing', I said, 'how even that could bring me into it.'

'Nor am I,' he agreed, pouring out cosily, 'but let us say that in such incredible circumstances you might by some untoward accident have got involved while the rest of us escaped.'

The word accident is not a friend of mine, and so, or for some other reason, I said: 'I would rather think she had picked me out.' He smiled at that, not grasping that I was speaking for young Adam.

'Maybe', he said to make me laugh, but failing, 'it was her echo that was back in the glen, and by some mischance you got into the echo.'

Then he grew graver, and said he would have none of those superstitions; the affair could only be construed naturally so long as we accepted the experiences I once thought I had gone through as having been nothing but the fancies of a crazy man.

'All of them?' I could not help saying.

'Every one,' said he, clapping me confidently on the shoulder; 'do you not see, man, that if any one of them was arguable it would be less easy to dispose of the lave?'

'That day during my illness', I said, 'when I was but three parts convinced by your construing, and slipped away from you all to the bield to make certain that the basket was not there——'

'Precisely,' said he, 'that would be a case in point. What strange ravels might we have got entangled in if you had found that basket!'

My many years' old resolution to keep the thing dark from all, even from him, broke down, and I spoke out the truth. 'Dr John,' I told him, 'I did find the basket that day.'

For long he threepit with me that I was away in my mind again, but he had to listen to me while I let out the tale, which has ceased to perturb me, though I have a sort of a shiver at writing it down. I found the basket with its provender in the bield where we had left it, and at that the peace which had been coming to me threatened to go, and my soul was affrichted. I prayed long, and I took the basket down to the burn and coupit its sodden gear therein, and itself I tore to bits and scattered. It was far waur to me at that time to think that she had been than that she was just a figment of the brain.

I told all this to Dr John, and at first he was for spurning it, nor can I say for certain that he believes it now. I leave it at that, but fine I know it would be like forsaking the callant that once I was to cast doubt on what lies folded up in his breast.

I am back now, secure and serene, in my mining town which, in many ways, with its enterprise and modern improvements, including gas and carts to carry away any fluff of snow that falls, is far superior to my first charge. I have a wider sphere of usefulness and a grand family life. As I become duller in the uptake, time will no doubt efface every memory of Miss Julie of the Logan; and of mornings I may be waking up without the thought that I have dropped her in the burn. Of course it is harder on young Adam. I have a greater drawing to the foolish youth that once I was than I have pretended. When I am gone it may be that he will away back to that glen.